WADING IN WATER

WADING IN WATER

Spirituality and the Arts

ROBERT P. VANDE KAPPELLE

WIPF & STOCK · Eugene, Oregon

Wipf & Stock
An Imprint of Wipf and Stock Publishers
199 W. 8th Ave., Suite 3
Eugene, OR 97401

www.wipfandstock.com

PAPERBACK ISBN: 978–1-6667–9127–3
HARDCOVER ISBN: 978–1-6667–9125–9
EBOOK ISBN: 978–1-6667–9126–6

OCTOBER 29, 2021 1:50 PM

Contents

PREFACE

HUMAN EXISTENCE IS FILLED WITH mental and emotional tension, much of it caused by conflict and polarity. In fact, one cannot live without conflict, and the secret of life is learning to embrace and somehow reconcile one's polarities. To do so successfully requires spirituality. Without spirituality, human beings find themselves trapped in cycles of boredom, irritation, and discontent. By spirituality, I don't mean religion, though they are related.

In the past, people of faith rarely distinguished between being religious and being spiritual. Actually, they rarely used the terms "spiritual" or "spirituality," collapsing them under the broader category of religion. What we call spirituality today they might have called "piety," analogous to "being religious." Today, the terms "spiritual" and "spirituality" are in vogue, as opposed to the term" religious," which, like "piety," is often used negatively or pejoratively as a synonym for "religiosity."

While we can define religion or theology with some degree of meaning and specificity, the word "spirituality" is often used traditionally with little or no clear meaning, or in a broad and vague manner. In antiquity, the word was not used, and when first introduced in the English-speaking world, it referred to the clergy, specifically to the ecclesiastical vocation, as distinct from secular or temporal vocations. From this sixteenth-century usage, the term came to describe spiritual as distinct from material things, including spirits, ghosts, or souls.

The meaning of a religious way of life, notably one's piety or acts of religious devotion, came still later, although its use in Ignatius Loyola's *Spiritual Exercises* referred to the practice of piety and more specifically, techniques of devotion. When first used in the French-speaking world, the term "spirituality" was a term of reproach, associated with mystical or ascetic devotion such as used by pietists and related sects and movements not in the religious mainstream. In this respect, spirituality represented an excess of striving after the purely immaterial.

By the nineteenth century, the term was no longer one of reproach but simply a description of prayerful piety, with a view toward the practice of ascetics and mystics. At times spirituality came to be associated with the "inner" or "interior life" of humans in general. In the first half of the twentieth century, the terms spirituality and spiritual theology were applied to ascetic and mystical theology, as opposed to dogmatic and moral theology.

In nineteenth- and twentieth-century Protestant liberalism, with the advance of biblical criticism and widespread skepticism on matters of faith, pious people focused on religious practice (*lex orandi*) over against the vicissitudes of historical belief (*lex credenti*), and "spirituality" expressed what was sought. In the late twentieth century, the word "spirituality" found wide usage yet went undefined, having a vague association with living holistically, contemplatively, fully, and harmoniously with nature, others, and all of life. This latter perspective, that all life has a spiritual aspect, is associated widely with spirituality, and the term has become disengaged from theology in general or religion in particular.

Such lack of specificity, however, makes the concept so universal as to lack value. For our purposes, I reconnect the term with its root meaning, that is, with Spirit, or as the ancient Hebrews did, with the "wind" or "breath" of God. To be spiritual is to breathe deeply and harmoniously with Reality (Infinity). Spirituality, then, is a hopeful, creative, life-filled path, a Spirit-filled way of living. In using the term "path," Taking a path is a different way of living from driving down a highway. Unlike highways, paths seem more personal. Unlike a highway, paths are not goal-oriented, for spirituality implies choice, uncertainty, and risk-taking. To quote Matthew Fox, one of today's leading spiritual teachers, spirituality is

> the way itself, and every moment on the way is a holy moment; a sacred seeing takes place there. All who embark on a spiritual path need to be willing to learn and to let go; to know that none of us has all the answers, and yet that none of us is apart from deity . . . What is common to all paths that are spiritual is, of course, the Spirit—breath, life, energy. That is why all true paths are essentially one path—because there is only one Spirit, one breath, one life, one energy in the universe. It belongs to none of us and all of us. We all share it. Spirituality does not make us otherworldly; it renders us more fully alive. The path that spirituality takes is a path away from the superficial into the depths; away from the

"outer person" into the "inner person"; away from the privatized and individualistic into the deeply communitarian.[1]

Spirituality, traditionally defined by Christians as "life in the Spirit," encompasses the journey of life from a distinct perspective. Spirituality is the journey of life "from God, to God, and with God." As a result, it is also a journey toward self. In other words, the process of coming to know or to experience God is also the process of knowing oneself. Through this process, one comes to differentiate between one's temporary or false self, which we call the ego, and one's permanent or True Self, that part of us made in the image of God and made for ongoing or everlasting relationship with God. In the end, we discover that we know God by being known, much like one loves by being loved.

Thinking comprehensively, then, spirituality involves what is, what can be, and what ought to be. When activity, rationality, and morality are infused with creativity and imagination, meaning that when body, mind, and soul are inspirited or harmonious with Spirit (that is, inspired, infused and energized by Spirit), spirituality is authentic, healthy, and vital.

The central defining characteristic of spirituality is an individual's sense of connection to a greater whole. At its heart, spirituality involves an emotional experience of awe and reverence. Such experience is highly desired, fervently sought, endlessly disagreed upon, and thoroughly fascinating. Why did our ancestors have such a wonderful idea of God? Because they lived in an awesome world. They wondered at the magnificence of whatever it was that brought the world into being. This led to a sense of adoration. This adoration, this gratitude, we call religion. Now, as the outer world is diminished, our inner world is drying up. The task of spirituality is to help us regain our sense of awe and reverence, beginning with a profound commitment to nature and continuing with an equal commitment to the whole of humanity and every living creature. If we do not love what is visible around us, how can we love God, whom we cannot see? (1 John 4:19–20).

According to the historian Charles A. Beard, one of the lessons of history can be summed by the proverb, "The bee fertilizes the flower it robs." This is particularly true of monotheism and paganism, as seen in the religious and cultural borrowings of Israel from the Canaanites, the Jews from Hellenism, Christianity from Judaism, Romans from Greeks, Europeans from the Celts, and so on. In the early centuries of the Common Era, many

---

1. Fox, *Creation Spirituality*, 12.

educated Christians, together with Hellenized Jews, engaged philosophically with their pagan counterparts, intellectualizing and mythologizing their belief systems to make them more accessible, attractive, and compatible with their cultural and philosophical traditions. The same process took place in the Christianizing of Europe, Christians engaging with pagan neighbors to unify culture.

While Judaism and Christianity claims their spirituality derives from divine inspiration, such claims are not unique, for not only have other religions made similar claims, but this understanding is also central to Greco-Roman sensibility, whether in its Homeric, Pythagorean, Stoic, Platonic, Aristotelian, Hermetic, or Neoplatonic recensions. Greco-Roman sensibility, derived from paganism, in turn influenced Jewish, Christian, Muslim, even Hindu and Buddhist spirituality. Underlying Greco-Roman civilization, its cosmology, anthropology, epistemology, and theology, is its intuitive and unifying approach to reality, an approach evident in its mythology.

A fascinating aspect of Greek mythology for spirituality is its conception of the Muses, who, together with the three Graces, incarnated grace and beauty, bringing inspiration, joy, and fulfillment to human life. The Muses, goddesses by birth and nature, were nine in number, daughters of Zeus and Mnemosyne, a Titan whose name means "memory." Companions of Apollo, the god of Truth, the Muses danced and sang at parties held by gods and human heroes. When the gods were happy, humans were happy. For the Greeks, the Muses inspired poetry, music, and dance. Later, other spiritual activities were added to their care: Clio was Muse of history, Urania of astronomy, Melpomene of tragedy, Thalia of comedy, Terpsichore of dance, Calliope of epic poetry, Erato of love poetry, Polyhymnia of song, and Euterpe of lyric poetry.

OVERVIEW

As you may have surmised, the title, *Wading in Water*, is taken from the lyrics of the well-known spiritual "Wade in the Water," associated with Harriet Tubman and the Underground Railroad. In that song and in the entire African-American movement toward emancipation, the road to freedom can be seen both as "walking on water" and as "wading in water." At times, crossing the river to the Promised Land requires supernatural grace, and other times human effort. The lyrics to the spiritual tell us that "God's gonna trouble the Waters," a reference to the biblical exodus and the experience of enslavement, with images of turbulence and change as well as of assurance that things will work out when God is involved.

Having received praise for *Walking on Water*, my study on Mindfulness, Mystery, Metaphor, and Myth, and heeding requests for additional material on creative spirituality, I write *Wading in Water* as companion to my earlier volume. In this project, I collaborate with my former student and longtime friend, Jess Dale Costa, a lawyer and an independent writer, a "Renaissance man" by interest and insight, equally competent and knowledgeable in literature, history, technology, spirituality, and the arts. While the final product is mine, Jess's input and brilliance are particularly evident in chapters 6–9 and 12, where his researching role has provided guidance and inspiration.

Wading in Water charts a second-half-of-life vision, distinguishing between binary (dualistic) models for living, based on reductionist principles, and ternary and quaternary models that embrace conflict, polarities, newness, and change, utilizing creativity and imagination to produce results that are integrative and holistic. Whereas *Walking* comprises reflections on my 2019 summer-long residence at Chautauqua Institution in Chautauqua, New York, *Wading* reflects on the larger Chautauqua mission, building spiritual community by integrating religion with education, recreation, and the arts. While *Wading* may be seen as a text on spirituality, its uniqueness is its connection of spirituality with the arts. Expanding on topics covered in *Walking*, *Wading* explores the association between spirituality and the creative arts through the disciplines of poetry, literary allegory, film, theatre, drama, and dance. *Wading* is not a comprehensive study, for it does not cover all of the arts, nor is it exhaustive or in-depth. My intent is suggestive, for the purpose is to promote the enrichment of life through beauty, creativity, diversity, risk-taking, newness, serendipity, and synchronicity, joint features of spirituality and the arts.

If, as the world's religions teach, God is everywhere, then humans cannot not be in God's presence. As the psalmist indicates, even if we go up to the heavens or underneath the earth, or if we go to the most remote parts of the earth or enter the deepest darkness of the unknown, God's presence is deeper still (Ps 139:7–12). The realms described by the psalmist as marginal, remote, or inaccessible are precisely the realms explored by artists. Yet, as artists know, these are not the only realms of gold, for the infinite Mystery of God also dwells in the concrete, the specific, and the ordinary. We cannot know something spiritually by saying it is "not this or not that";

we can only know it by meeting it in its precise and irreplaceable uniqueness—in its aliveness. This book's emphasis on spirituality and the arts, or, if you prefer, on finding God in the arts, seeks to do just that. The principle here is this: "go deep in any one place and you will meet the infinite aliveness that is God, for God is everywhere!"

Part I

EMBODIED SPIRITUALITY

Chapter 1

Our Evolving Story

WHEN SCIENTISTS DESCRIBE THE UNIVERSE today, sooner or later they tell a story, for they understand the universe differently than did Isaac Newton and his eighteenth-century successors. Newton understood the universe to be static: space is infinite; time marches onward; and in the three dimensions of space, the solid matter making up the stars and planets of our galaxy ceaselessly follows the law of universal gravitation. Newton and his contemporaries believed that the universe was created, and that God was responsible for setting it in motion.

How differently scientists understand the universe today! Scientists now know that we live in an *unfinished* universe, with a beginning and probably an end, though that end is not yet in sight. It is now a fact that we live in an expanding universe, that space is filled with a background radiation left over from the Big Bang, and that galaxies and stars are still coming into existence and passing away. Some 13.7 billion years ago, all the matter and energy that we now are able to discern or confidently theorize was compressed into a "singularity" of zero size and infinite density, governed by laws of physics not yet understood. From this singularity, space-time erupted into existence in a cosmic fireball.

Around two hundred million years after the Big Bang, the first stars ignited, thus beginning galaxies of one hundred billion stars or more. Most stars in the galaxies were formed during the first five billion years of the universe's history, though these stellar and galactic processes continue today. Many of the first stars were massive, consuming their fuel rapidly and within a few million years exploding as giant supernovae. These explosions created the heavier elements, from carbon on up, and from the enormous dust clouds created by these explosions, aided by gravity, successive generations of stars appeared. Eventually, thanks to these stellar explosions, all of the elements in our universe were created. Planetary systems began to form around stars; our own sun, a third-generation star, formed about 5 billion years ago, and our earth became a planet by about 4.6 billion years ago. Upon it began another universe story, the story of life.

All during the billions of years of our universe's existence, the galaxies and their clusters continued to be carried by the expanding space, and at the present, no end of the process is in sight. Looking out into space, we see a visible universe that is about 28 billion light-years across; looking back in time, we see the remnants of its earliest moments 13.7 billion years ago. Far from static, our universe is characterized on the cosmic level by the emergence of new stars and galaxies with their own life cycles. And on our planet, over its immense age, new forms of living things have continually emerged and lived out their own life cycles. There is no sign that these evolutionary processes are reaching a conclusion. Hence, Jesuit paleontologist Pierre Teilhard de Chardin (1881–1955) often said that the "cosmos is not a fixed body of things, but a *genesis*—a still unfolding drama . . . The world is still coming into being."[1]

As Michael Dowd indicates in *Thank God for Evolution*, evolution is not only applicable to scientific or institutional change, but is essential for spiritual growth. In Romans, Paul assumes what we today call biological or cosmic evolution, particularly when he asserts, "We know that the whole creation has been groaning in labor pains until now" (8:22).

For people educated liberally in college, that is, exposed to philosophy, literature, the arts, and the social and natural sciences, it seems odd that there should be resistance to evolution or evolutionary thinking anymore in Christian theology or spirituality. Because of evolution's centrality to progress and change, Christians should have been first in line to recognize and cooperate with this dynamic notion of God, instead of siding with static and antiquated notions of truth and reality. A static conception of reality makes everything else static too, including notions of spirituality, history, science, medicine, sociology, and religion.

A superficial examination of the Christian doctrine of the Trinity reveals a God who is not only relational, but also an indwelling Holy Spirit

1. Haught, *Deeper Than Darwin*, 162.

who both moves us and moves with us. Sadly, even doctrines such as incarnation and resurrection have traditionally been understood as static, one-time anomalies concerning Jesus, rather than as promises and models for us as well.

Resistance to spiritual growth and change reflects a limited inner experience of God. Anyone who has practiced contemplative prayer knows that God is never static within us. Only when we hold God at a distance can we think of God as inert, static, and unchanging. Those who pay attention to the inner life or who read history books surely recognize that life and love are cumulative, growing, and going somewhere that is forever new and forever beyond human comprehension. Resistance to change might well be driven by fear and lack of control, as if humans could ever control, define, or conceptualize God. As the New Testament writers and early Christian theologians recognized, a dynamic understanding and unfolding of God and truth is inevitable and continuous, halted only by canonical, creedal, and institutional attempts at finality. In retrospect, the early church's attempts to encapsulate religious truth in authoritative and unchanging formulas appear to many liberally educated individuals like theological counterparts of Amish attempts to freeze society in seventeenth-century lifestyles.

For those who have studied early church history and the development of biblical theology, a dynamic understanding of God and truth are not only obvious but exciting, particularly when we remember that the most appropriate language available to religion is metaphor. In this respect, God is always explained and understood in terms humans can experience visibly and directly. As philosopher of religion John Hick notes, all God language is limited to personal and impersonal imagery, to personifications of the divine that cannot apply, even analogically, to "The Real *an sich*," namely, to God's essential nature and identity. However, since human beings cannot worship or achieve union with the Ultimate, but only with one or another of its personal or impersonal personifications, that is, to what the various religious traditions describe as God or the Ultimate, they are unable to relate to God or the Ultimate as it is in itself (*an sich*).

Thereby, in relating to the one divine reality that lies at the heart of all religions, people of faith must be willing to set aside cherished practices such as evangelism and doctrines such as salvation, heaven, hell, Jesus Christ as the sole mediator to God, and the authority of scripture. If all humans are made in the divine image (see Gen 1:26), namely, in the image of the God who is love, then Christians, together with monotheists of all faiths, must participate in the divine dynamic of giving and receiving, of infinite outpouring and receiving. If, as Teilhard de Chardin wrote, "love is the physical structure of the universe," then creation, like love, is not only impelled by an unfolding inner dynamism, but also moving in a positive direction, drawn by a divine goal.

In the past, Christianity confined its "good news" to an elect minority, failing to understand that the gospel is not only good news for a select group of individuals, but good news for the social and cosmic realms as well. Foundational hope demands foundational belief in a world that is forever unfolding to something better. This is the virtue of hope. It is almost impossible for the gospel to bring protracted healing to people if the entire cosmic arc is not also a trajectory toward the goal.

If we look at nature, signs of newness and renewal are manifold, springing up like wildflowers after rain. Love is a force of renewal that cannot be contained. Today, as we look at society, we see new forces gathering from every direction: people who have lived rutted lives are coming alive; people who have been silent are speaking out; people who have been spectators are getting involved. This is the sign of hope for which we have been waiting. The tipping point of faith is the threshold of spiritual energy, where what we believe becomes what we do.

Sometimes, in our troubled world, we forget that love is all around us. We imagine the worst of other people and withdraw into our own skepticism. But simply look around, and you will see the signs of love over and over: young mothers with children, couples laughing together, people of different races standing in solidarity with victims of discrimination and abuse. The more we look, the more we see. Love is everywhere, around us and within. Signs of love abound, reminding us of God's essential nature. Notice how love beckons. How will we reply?

Commenting on humanity's moral and spiritual development, integral theorist Ken Wilber offers four major strategies for transformative living:

1. *Cleaning Up*, basing our morality, not on superficial and time-bound "purity codes," on external rules that leave us unchanged within, but on mature morality that keeps us focused on God's grace and love.

2. *Growing Up*, focusing on the process of psychological and emotional maturity that leads to personal and cultural transformation.

3. *Waking Up*, practicing spiritual experiences that affirm union, dependence, and cooperation with God and others for the betterment of nature and society.

4. *Showing Up*, engaging holistically (bodily, mentally, emotionally, and spiritually) in efforts for social, economic, and ecological justice and peace, thereby participating more fully in God's creative intention for our lives (see Eph 2:10).

Early in the history of Christianity, an interpretive principle arose to help Christians reconcile supernatural and natural revelation, namely, the concept of the Two Books, the Book of Nature and the Book of Scripture. This influential notion was articulated by Tertullian (c. 160–c. 230), an early Christian theologian whom Galileo cited approvingly in his 1615 treatise on the use of biblical quotations in matters of science. Galileo agreed with Tertullian that both nature and scripture proceed alike from the creative Word of God. Therefore, when properly read and interpreted, the truths revealed at each level cannot contradict one another. Sir Francis Bacon (1561–1626), who promoted the scientific method of induction, agreed with Galileo that if one establishes by assured empirical and logical processes the truth of something in nature that appears to be in conflict with a biblical passage, then the problem is not with what the biblical text *says* but with the *interpretation* placed upon its words.

The notion of God's "Two Books" became a commonplace in Christian thought and is still cited by those writing about the relationship between religion and science. Even the great nineteenth-century champion of inerrancy, Charles Hodge, agreed with Galileo and Bacon, but he put the matter bluntly. He insisted "in common with the whole Church, that this infallible Bible must be interpreted by science," a proposition he considered "all but self-evident." Throughout history, those who promoted the "Two Books" concept were concerned to defend the integrity of both the study of nature and the study of scripture, but when the language of the latter seemed to contradict the former, they encouraged readers of scripture to invoke another important element in their interpretive framework, the principle of accommodation. Accommodation is the notion that the biblical writers describe phenomena of nature in a way that is understandable and accessible to ordinary and unlearned people.

Because the universe has a history, the metaphor of the Book of Nature is still relevant. But nature's book and the story of nature it tells are unfinished; the story is still being written. When they tell the story, scientists can take it only to the present moment. People might speculate about its future on the basis of what science has learned about its past, with some confidence that the processes by which nature has unfolded over time are likely to continue. Nevertheless, the future remains open, whatever one might speculate.

Today's naturalists view with astonishment the extent and range of life in all of its incredible diversity. As evolutionary biologists point out, more than two million existing species of plants and animals have been named and described: many more remain to be discovered, at least ten million according to most estimates. The two million include approximately 250,000 species of living plants, 100,000 species of fungi, and 1.5 million species of animals and microorganisms, each occupying its own peculiar ecological setting or niche. The fossil evidence from earth's long history indicates that many more, perhaps 90 percent of all species ever alive, are now extinct. No less astonishing is the incredible variety of species and their habitats. Living species range in size from the giant sequoias of California to bacteria less than one-thousandth of a millimeter in length. The range of life's habitats is equally staggering, for species are found in every nook and cranny on earth, from the peaks of the Himalayas to the deepest ocean vents, in the coldest ice masses in Antarctica and the hottest springs in Yellowstone Park. While thousands of species of microbial life do good or ill in our intestines, mites too small for the naked eye clean our eyelashes.[2] There is hardly a niche on earth where life does not dwell.

How do we account for all of this incredible diversity? Scientists claim it is the outcome of evolutionary processes. All living things are interrelated, all descending over time from one or a few common ancestors. Charles Darwin called this process "descent with modification," a phrase still accurately describing what scientists today technically call macroevolution.

To speak knowledgeably of evolution, particularly of human evolution, is to recognize change—and our adaptation to it—as integral to life. Evolution requires awareness and trust in the process of life. In this regard, evolution challenges us to lean into life's changing patterns, to embrace an emerging future with creativity, sharing our gifts with others for the sake of the whole. To conceive of life as static and unchanging, to resist newness,

---

2. The Human Microbiome Project, a recent effort involving hundreds of scientists and dozens of universities, has counted over 10,000 microbial species in humans, weighing a total of 6 or more pounds in a 150-pound person.

as if life has always been a certain way and should forever remain that way, is to ignore evolution. Such thinking is both arrogant and erroneous. To attempt to stop history's ongoing momentum—whether by clinging to the past or by longing for "the good old days"—is to be ignorant of history. If we learn nothing else from history, it should be this: stability is an illusion; only impermanence is permanent.

The Buddha intuitively grasped the notion of evolution by advocating detachment, not necessarily meaning giving up the things of this world, but rather accepting and being consciously aware that nothing is permanent. So, too, Francis of Assisi taught the principle of dispossession, by which he meant not living without things, but living without possessing or controlling things. If evolution is the language of growth and change, then an evolving faith is one that accepts and even embraces change.

While the word "change" normally refers to new beginnings, real transformation happens more often when something secure or traditional falls apart or stops working. For example, what happens when we notice a crack in a wall or in the driveway? Our first instinct might be to ignore it or to patch it. This might work for a while, but over time, ignoring a problem can get us into deep trouble. Eventually a professional examines the area and reveals the bad news: there is deep damage here, and if you don't fix it, before long the entire structure can become compromised. If we ignore the expert's advice, it will only get worse. If we wait too long, the damage may be irreparable.

The same is true in our lives. If we ignore the cracks that appear, they will undoubtedly get worse. Another possibility—and this is the spiritual option—is to acknowledge the cracking or breaking as the bearer of truth and even as a gift. Perhaps the unraveling is the nudging of the Holy Spirit, calling us to think creatively or embrace new possibilities. However, sometimes the cracks have to get worse before we see them for what they are: an obsession, a disease, anger, guilt, or stress.

In a sense, discontent and a sense of malaise—whether in our individual lives or in society as a whole—can be the work of God. Persons that have been humbled by disruption may become less arrogant or presumptuous. They may have fewer illusions about their own power and importance or even become curious and open to change. The same can happen with churches, groups, and organizations. They may suffer decline or experience dissension and discord. They may shut the doors and close down operations, or they may open to newness and change. The latter are people and groups God can work with, for they have become Christlike, kingdom people.

QUESTIONS FOR DISCUSSION AND REFLECTION

1. Do you view the cosmos as divinely created or as a naturally ending process based on chance? Can one be a creationist and an evolutionist simultaneously? Explain your answer.

2. Throughout history, people have been resistant to change. In your estimation, why is this so? Do you agree with Teilhard de Chardin that our world is still evolving? If so, what role should religious faith have? Should it have a conserving or progressive bias? Explain your answer.

3. If traditional Christianity is built upon unchanging dogma and creeds, do you agree with John Hick that its theology is essentially an ideology rather than a living faith? Explain your answer.

4. Religious traditions seem caught in a tug of war between two opposing points of emphasis—between what makes them distinctive, and what they hold in common with other religions. If you were forced to choose between these ideals, to which would you grant your primary allegiance? Explain your answer.

5. In light of Ken Wilber's four strategies for transformative living, which of his approaches best represents your current point of emphasis? Which one best represents your aspirational strategy? Explain your answer.

6. Explain and assess the merits of the concept of the Two Books.

7. Regarding the interpretation of scripture, explain and assess the principle of accommodation.

8. Explain and assess the merits of the statement, "only impermanence is permanent."

9. Are there any "cracks" in your life you have been ignoring? If so, what truth do they reveal about your life, and what lessons can they provide?

10. In your estimation, what is the primary insight gained from this chapter? Explain your answer.

Chapter 2

OUR INCARNATIONAL STORY

DESPITE THE SIGNIFICANCE TO CHRISTIANITY of the doctrine of resurrection, a belief that marks both the climax of the Jesus story and made possible the birth of the church, resurrection is not Christianity's most significant teaching. More determinative to the Christian perspective, more decisive to its message, is incarnation. Christianity's true and unique storyline has always been incarnation.

While most Christians today think of incarnation in singular terms, as a reference to the birth of Jesus, in its fullest meaning, this doctrine teaches Christians to view all reality—the spiritual and the natural, the immaterial and the physical—as one. These have always been one, ever since the Big Bang took place some 13.7 billion years ago.

Incarnation did not just happen when Jesus was born, although that is when we became aware of the human incarnation of God (the Christ) in Jesus. It seemingly took until two thousand years ago for humanity to be ready for what the Jewish philosopher Martin Buber (1878–1965) called an I-Thou relationship with God. However, matter and spirit had been one since "the beginning," when God first became manifested as creation.

What was personified in the body of Jesus was a manifestation of this universal truth: matter is, and has always been, this hiding place for Spirit, forever offering itself to be discovered anew. Perhaps this is what Jesus meant when he said, "I am the door" (John 10:7). This is what medieval Franciscan scholar John Duns Scotus (1266–1308) meant when he said that Christ was not Plan B; God did not plan to remain absent until Adam and

Eve ate from the Tree of Knowledge, or until the coming of Jesus for our salvation. Rather, Christ was Plan A from the beginning, the first idea in the mind of God, as it were (John 1:1–4). In the beginning, God, the formless, eternal, and timeless One essentially said, "I am going to manifest who I am in what humans will call physicality, materiality, or the universe."

If this is true, it means that everything we have ever seen with our physical eyes is the mystery of incarnation. The Christian word for that is "the Christ," which comes from the Jewish word Messiah or Anointed One, a reference to the One who would come to reveal what God is doing, everywhere and all the time. For Christians, "the Christ" became manifested in Jesus of Nazareth, a view biblical scholars call "the scandal of particularity."

In this respect, Christians come to see the mystery of incarnation in one concrete moment. Therein is its strength. However, that is not the whole truth of incarnation. What most Christians miss when they fall in love with the vulnerable newborn babe at Christmas is that what is true in one particular place is true universally, meaning that what is true for the particular ends up being true everywhere.

Christians must move beyond a merely sentimental understanding of Christmas, with its particularist application of Jesus' birth and death as the sole means of salvation, to an adult and communal appreciation of the message of the incarnation of God in Christ. Redemption (salvation) is a necessary part of incarnation, already present in Jesus' birth, because in that birth God was telling humanity that it is good to be human, for God is on the side of humanity, fully like us, yet fully unlike us.

The celebration of Christmas is not merely a sentimental remembrance of the birth of a child. It is much more a celebration of the rebirth of history. According to the apostle Paul, creation is forever pregnant with new birth, always waiting for the participation of humanity with God in its renewal (Rom 8:20–23). To focus solely on the birth of a baby at Christmas is to be content with "infant Christianity."

INDIVIDUAL EMBODIMENT

In incarnation, God clearly wants friends and partners to image divine diversity. God, it seems, want mature religion and a thoughtful, free response from human beings. In incarnation, God beckons us to partnership, and as it happens, we eventually become the God that we love.

As noted in *Walking on Water*, when ordinary people become Christians, that is, "little Christ's," they embody or enact in their lives the "third incarnation" of God, or the "Second Coming" of Christ.[3] Let me explain what I mean. The first incarnation is the moment described in Genesis 1 as "the first day," when God became the Universal Christ, joining in unity with the physical universe and becoming the light inside of everything. This is described in Genesis 1:3–4 by the statement, "Then God said, 'Let there be light'; and there was light . . . and God separated the light from the darkness." This teaching is affirmed in the prologue of John's Gospel, by the relationship between God and Christ (the Word/Logos): "In the beginning was the Word, and the Word was with God, and the Word was God . . . in him was life, and the life was the light of all people. The light shines in the darkness, and the darkness did not overcome it" (John 1:1, 4–5). The first incarnation—what we might call the Universal Christ—is the divine presence pervading creation since the beginning. What scientists call the Big Bang is the scientific name for that event, and "Christ" is its theological name. From this perspective, wherever the material and the spiritual coincide, we have the Christ.

The second incarnation of God and the "first coming" of Christ represent what Christians believe about the historical incarnation we call Jesus. Let us be clear: Christ is not Jesus' last name. The word Christ is a title, meaning Anointed One. When Christians speak of Jesus Christ, they include the entire sweep of the meaning of the Christ, which includes all the divine activity since the beginning of time (see Rom 1:20; Heb 1:3; Col 3:11). Of this activity, Jesus is the visible map, the one who brings this eternal message home personally.

The third incarnation of God (the "Second Coming of Christ") occurs whenever true discipleship occurs, when Jesus Christ is born in us. Paul affirmed this truth when he declared, "It is no longer I who live, but it is Christ who lives in me" (Gal 2:20). Exhorting believers to adopt the mind of Jesus (Phil 2:5), he also confirmed that Christians incarnate Christ, since they possess "the mind of Christ" (1 Cor 2:16). When individuals become Jesus people—incarnations of Christ—they exchange one mindset for another, their "monkey mind" (the obsessive, noisy chattering we observe during silent meditation) for the mind of Christ.

---

3. For a discussion of the three incarnations of God, see Vande Kappelle, *Walking on Water*, 103–4. The concept of three incarnations, exemplified in what Richard Rohr calls an incarnational worldview, is articulated in his book *Universal Christ*, 12–21.

Speaking humanistically, grace rarely means getting what we want, for God is not a permissive parent, but speaking spiritually, grace means always getting what we want, for our desires become the desires of Christ. This is likely what Paul meant when he called believers God's new creation: "If anyone is in Christ, there is a new creation: everything old has passed away; see, everything has become new" (2 Cor 5:17). For Paul, when the minds of believers are transformed into the mind of Christ, their bodies become temples, dwelling places of God's Spirit (1 Cor 3:16–17; see Rom 12:1–2).

The Christ we await at Christmas includes our own rebirth as well as the rebirth of history and creation, what the author of the book of Revelation calls "a new heaven and a new earth" (Rev 21:1). This is the cosmic Christ Christians invoke when they say, "Come, Lord Jesus" (Rev 22:20). This understanding of incarnation makes our entire lives, and the history and life of the entire cosmos, one huge "advent." "The Christ" includes the whole sweep of creation and history joined with him, as well as each of us. This togetherness is the Universal or Cosmic Christ. To use biblical imagery, the followers of this Jesus are members of the "body of Christ," even though they are not the historical Jesus. So Christians rightly believe in "Jesus Christ," and both words are essential. We all come from union, and all longing is a movement back toward union. As the medieval theologian Augustine reflected about God in his *Confessions*, "You shed your fragrance about me; I drew breath and now I gasp for your sweet perfume. I tasted you and now I hunger and thirst for you. You touched me, and I am inflamed with love of your peace" (Book 10. 27).

Each of us, in our own way, knows what Augustine meant. There are, however, the dangers of excess and misdirection. In spirituality, as in sexuality, eating, consuming, drug use, and other addictive experiences of life, there lies the tendency to focus on ecstasies and thrills, where our senses, urges, and desires remain unsatisfied, creating urges that, while intoxicating and profound, are fleeting. These experiences are essential, however, for they are seeds of the fullness that beckons. They can set us on the path of spirituality, but they are not the Journey, and certainly not the goal of transformation, mystical union, or enlightenment. They can provide glimpses of the destination, but they are not final. Indeed, those who dwell in what the Danish philosopher Søren Kierkegaard called the sensual or aesthetic phase of life still occupy the cellar of their dwelling. They may think that they have arrived, but in reality, they have hardly set out. Those who become addicted to simply seeking more thrills or more ecstasies will never reach their spiritual destination.

When we taste the Mystery, we long to drink deeply, to be possessed by it, to surrender to it. This is mirrored powerfully in the images of spiritual communion, where, as Augustine noted, we become what we eat; as the psalmist write, "taste and see that the Lord is good" (Ps 34:8). The heart of all yearning is to become that for which we taste and hunger, not partially or temporarily but fully and permanently. At the heart of all ecstasy is the longing for wholeness, for union with our eternal Lover.

There is a reason why the Song of Songs was included in the biblical canon, for it remains a testament to human longing and its fulfillment in divine love." Let him kiss me with the kisses of his mouth." So opens this book of the Bible, also called the Song of Solomon. "Love is as strong as death," the writer proclaims, "passion fierce as the grave" (8:6).

Incarnation overcomes the gap between God and everything visible and concrete. It is the synthesis of matter and spirit. Without incarnation, God remains separate from us and from creation. Because of incarnation, God is with us but also in us and in everything else God has made. We all have the divine DNA; everything bears the divine fingerprint. That, of course, is the mystery of embodiment.

The belief that God is different from us, beyond us and somehow "other," is the basic dualism tearing humans apart from themselves, from nature, and from the divine. Our view of God as separate and distant harms our relationship to life, including our bodies, our food, and our possessions. This loss is foundational to why we live anxious and fragmented lives. Jesus came to put life together for us and in us. This is God's world, Jesus affirmed; the natural and the physical can be trusted and enjoyed. This world, including our bodies, is the dwelling place and the setting for God's presence and revelation. To be human—to have a body, a mind, and emotions; to have appetites such as hunger, longing, and sexuality—is good. Notice, for example, the meaning of the word "sex." This term comes from the Latin word *sectare* (to cut or rend), the root implying that reality is cut or divided into two. Having split reality into matter and spirit, maleness and femaleness, head and heart, body and soul, human life becomes a search for union with our other half.

To understand Christianity, we must understand incarnation. Jesus was not simply "Word of God"; Jesus was flesh, born, like all of us, of "water and Spirit" (John 3:5). When we buy into sacred/secular dualism, we lack trust in God, questioning the value of our humanity and that of others as well. When we view God as separate from ourselves, we view ourselves as separate from others and from nature. For Christians, Jesus becomes the great synthesis, the icon and embodiment of the mystery of life. As we read in Colossians 2:9–10, "In (Christ) the whole fullness of deity [of Reality] dwells bodily," and in him we, too, find our fullness. Because traditional Christians are not very much at home in this world or even in their bodies, Jesus shows us that it is our human and "this-world" experience that we can and must trust.

Understanding the fuller meaning of incarnation, believers come to view reality anew, not as a perfect world gone bad, but as a place for revelation and divine encounter. While most believers look for transcendence, higher states of consciousness, or moral perfectionism, Jesus bids us live lavishly and enjoy life fully here and now. To return to the Garden, we must overcome duality in nature, recognizing that all is one Ultimate Reality. The guardian of the Garden, drawing a sword "to guard the way to the tree of life" (Gen 3:24), is none other than human ignorance and fear. Clinging to individualism, to ego identity, is what keeps us out of the Garden of goodness and blessing. That is the meaning of crucifixion and resurrection. They bid us to let go of our individuality, our separation, our exile, and gain eternity, which is in us and in all things.

Jesus hanging on the Tree is like the Buddha seated under the Tree. To be a follower of Jesus is to awaken to the fact that we are what we seek. What Buddhism declares openly (you are the Buddha already), Christianity hints at (you are the Christ, only you don't know it). As the eighteenth-century German poet Novalis declared, "The seat of the soul is where the inner and the outer worlds meet." The outer world is what we get in theology, literature, music, drama, dance, and song; the inner world is our response. As Irish novelist James Joyce affirmed, "Any object [or text, story, or song] properly regarded can be the gateway to the gods [the divine]."

Because we have lost the great mythic universe, we find ourselves in a post-Christian era dominated by rationalism, with its desire to understand and control. Mythic language is nature-based and mystery-filled, always pointing inward and upward. As Richard Rohr indicates, "when you don't mythologize, you pathologize."[4] When we don't mythologize, all we have left is our own little story. When it goes awry, we get therapy and recover. After that, what then? Recovery alone is not the point. We need a mythology

---

4. Rohr, *Quest for the Grail*, 23.

for a bigger, better world to which we can "recover." A mythic universe holds the individual and the group soul together, by giving it purpose and meaning. Its primary base of operation is our unconscious, that part of us best awakened by the arts. If we don't find deity here and now, most likely we never will. As Elizabeth Barrett Browning noted, "Earth's crammed with heaven, And every common bush afire with God. But only he who sees it takes off his shoes; The rest sit round it and pluck blackberries." (*Aurora Leigh* 7.820).

INSTITUTIONAL EMBODIMENT

In *Walking on Water* I spoke of Chautauqua Institution, and how over a thirty-five-year period it had been for me a place of enrichment and inspiration. A 2,070–acre gated community on a promontory by Chautauqua Lake, Chautauqua Institution is located in the rural southwestern corner of New York State, eight miles south of Lake Erie and some thirty-five miles east of Erie, Pennsylvania. Two enterprising visionaries, Methodist Bishop John Heyl Vincent of Plainfield, New Jersey, and industrialist Lewis Miller from Akron, Ohio, founded the Institution in 1874.

Lewis, a wealthy inventor in the mowing and harvesting business, was a prominent figure in the spiritual life of Akron. A proponent of close Bible study, he combined a passion for continuing education with a love of nature. As superintendent of the Akron First Methodist Church Sunday School, he expanded the curriculum, creating a semicircular interior plan for the new school building and adding a comprehensive music program, all prototypes for Chautauqua's amphitheater. In addition to his thriving business and active church leadership, he served as president of the Akron board of education and was active on the board of directors of nearby Mount Union College, the first college in America to give equal educational rights and privileges to women and men, and also the first to establish a four-year course of study.

In 1872 he joined the board of directors of the Chautauqua Lake Camp Meeting Association, assembled at Fair Point, on the southwestern shore of Chautauqua Lake, strategically located midway between New York City and Chicago. Small spring and summer evangelistic camp meetings had convened in tents at Fair Point for about a year.

Miller had met Vincent originally in 1868, at which time the two began a lengthy debate over the best way to train Sunday school teachers and enhance the Sunday school experience. Miller, the wealthy layman, was a progressive cultured generalist who was convinced that the study of literature, music, and the fine arts was not out of place in the church. Vincent, the eloquent speaker and church leader, focused on providing laypeople with responsible religious instruction. A bishop, Vincent also served the church as secretary of the Sunday School Union and as editor and publisher of the influential Methodist *Sunday School Journal*, with a circulation of well over 100,000 readers.

At some point Miller, ever the inventor, envisioned a plan for a Convention or Assembly, where people interested in Sunday school work could meet annually for Bible study and general instruction. This would include musical entertainment, lectures, and recreational activity. Eventually this plan led to the establishment of Chautauqua's four pillars: religion, education, recreation, and the arts. Miller shared his vision with Vincent, and the two spent the winter months of 1872–1873 debating the idea. Vincent imagined using the Akron Methodist Church as the model site for a wintertime Bible school, a prolonged course of study for Sunday school teachers from congregations across the land. These enrichment courses could then be taught on a moveable basis, traveling from city to city. Miller, however, wanted a permanent site in a natural rural setting, with emphasis not only on the Bible but on a variety of topics, to include lectures by renowned experts. To sell Vincent on the idea, Miller took him to Fair Point by steamer late in the summer, after the camp meeting had closed for the season. The following year, the Chautauqua Assembly met for the first two-week season. Only invited speakers were allowed on the platform. Liquor and card playing were forbidden, but so also evangelistic altar calls.

Thanks to Vincent's *Sunday School Journal*, some 4,000 participants a day converged on the 80-acre site from 25 states during the first several seasons. Every year Chautauqua grew in size, as tents gave way to 500 wooden cottages. Bishop Vincent built a topographically correct scale model of the Holy Land by the lakeside, in his mind now transformed into the Mediterranean coast. Shops and homes were added, including the great, colonnaded Hotel Athenaeum, its broad front porch a favorite spot for visitors to sit and enjoy the lawns, gardens, and lakefront. Benches set among the trees for audience seating were eventually replaced by a magnificent amphitheater seating 5,000, and by additional venues including the Hall of Philosophy, the Hall of Christ, and the Hall of Missions.

Fourth of July celebrations attained high priority, featuring brass concerts and culminating with an orchestral concert at night featuring Tchaikovsky's "1812 Overture," climaxed by cannon shots produced by audience participation, members popping paper bags at designated moments in the concert. The evening ended with lantern lighting and fireworks around the lake. Eventually Founder's Day celebrations, called Old First Night, complemented the Fourth of July, including a children's parade, graduation ceremonies, concerts, and an annual three-mile race along the perimeter of the gated community. In time, Chautauqua proved a safe haven, a slice of Americana where the plain citizenry integrated conservative respectability with progressive ideals. It was this integrative aspect of the Chautauqua experience that led U.S. President Teddy Roosevelt to call Chautauqua "the most American thing about America."

A scientific congress was convened during the 1876 American Centennial season. Classes in foreign languages, photography, art, and calisthenics were added to the burgeoning curriculum, and a Scientific and Literary Circle was established, precursor of continuing education at a university level of study, including a four-year reading and correspondence course for home study. Eventually a symphony was formed, primarily as a summer home for professional musicians from around the country, initially from prominent orchestras in New York, Cleveland, and Buffalo. Later schools of music, art, drama, dance, voice, opera, and a writing center were added to the performing arts, complemented by a library, bookstore, denominational houses, restaurants, churches, a daily newspaper, a music theater, and practice shacks for instrumental and vocal students. One of these shacks was used by George Gershwin in 1925 to compose parts of his famous Concerto in F.

In 1885, a scant decade after its founding, Thomas Edison arrived at Chautauqua to court Mina Miller, daughter of Lewis Miller. By this time, Chautauqua's grounds had grown to 130 acres. A steamboat landing and pier bordered upon Miller Park, near the Miller Bell Tower that came to symbolize the Institution. By this time, a railroad station complemented the highways leading to Chautauqua, its grounds lined with gardens, groves, and paved avenues. The two-week season stretched to seven weeks. By the mid-1890s, the Chautauqua season had expanded to nine weeks, and had become the setting for a College of Liberal Arts and a month-long Teachers' Retreat, not to mention the first subterranean community sewer system in America.

By Edison's visit, Vincent's national Chautauqua movement had begun. More than three dozen independent Chautauquas had emerged across the land, from Siloam Springs, Arkansas, to Canby, Oregon. Post-Civil War mainstream American culture was ready for a workable forum, where spirituality, emerging ideas, and the performing arts could offer society at large a holistic and integrative foundation for the second industrial revolution's (1850–1914) extensive technological, economic, and social change.

By 1904, the Chautauqua movement expanded from idyllic settings into much of America with the establishment of educational and entertainment circuits known as "traveling Chautauquas." These tent shows enabled rural families to gather in small settings to obtain culture and build character. In this way, the edifying mission of Chautauqua reached a broad audience, providing an affordable experience for people across the ideological, social, and economic spectrum. During its peak season of 1924, as many as 40 million people attended a traveling Chautauqua in over 10,000 towns across America.

As we can imagine, not everyone viewed these traveling Chautauquas as progressive or valuable. In its twentieth-century incarnation, critics saw it as little more than a commercial pandering to "infantile minds." One such critic was Sinclair Lewis, whose novel, *Main Street*, presented a harsh critique of traditional small-town life, including portraying the traveling Chautauqua as little more than a tent show, combining "vaudeville performance, YMCA lecture, and the graduation exercise of an elocution class." While circuit Chautauqua's perceived flaws cut at the heart of a movement concerned with keeping small-town values and community alive, the Chautauqua experience, as demonstrated by Chautauqua Institution, proved resilient because it was able to adapt and evolve. With a symphony, opera, theatre, dance, writer's center, visual arts center, and a renowned music school, Chautauqua Institution continues to produce a programming mix not found elsewhere.

Chautauqua Institution's commitment to theological, denominational, gender, racial, and ethnic diversity is evident in balanced programming as well as in ministerial context. Not only are women ministers regularly featured as Chautauqua's daily worship leaders, but rabbis, including female rabbis, have also served as worship leaders at Sunday ecumenical worship services. Chautauqua has 19 different faith-based organizations and 11 denominational houses. These include the African American House, Baha'i Faith, Catholic, Orthodox, Quaker, Unitarian Universalist

Fellowship, and a weekly Muslim Jummah prayer service. Of the 150,000 people who attend the 9-week session from late June through late August, about 20 to 25 percent are Jewish. Three Jewish organizations are on the grounds, the Zingdon Chabad Jewish House, the Hebrew Congregation of Chautauqua, and the Everett Jewish Life Center. Members and guests of these groups also attend and support the daily interfaith lecture series at the Hall of Philosophy. Chautauqua's Department of Religion also sponsors the Abrahamic Program for Young Adults, established in the 1990s to educate young adults about the shared heritage of the three Abrahamic traditions: Judaism, Christianity, and Islam. In addition, the Mystic Heart Program provides opportunities for Chautauquans to practice universal techniques of meditation, contemplative prayer, and related disciplines drawn from the world's religious and wisdom traditions.

From its inception in 1874, Chautauqua Institution has been at the vanguard of a new way of thinking about how faith can inform and improve people's lives. Earlier we mentioned the brilliant vision of Miller and Vincent, who cofounded the Institution as a place where religion, education, recreation, and the arts together could become building blocks for a spiritual community. In the following half century, two of America's most brilliant and daring theologians—William Rainey Harper and Shailer Mathews—spent many summers preaching, teaching, and using Chautauqua as a testing ground for ideas that eventually became the backbone of modern spiritual thought.

A child prodigy, Harper earned his PhD from Yale University at the age of eighteen. In 1891, John D. Rockefeller appointed him to serve as the first president of the newly reconstituted University of Chicago, where he served until his death in 1891. In 1883, Vincent heard him speak and invited him to teach at Chautauqua. For the next fifteen years, Harper taught at Chautauqua Institution, serving as principal of the College of Liberal Arts and in charge of all education at Chautauqua.

Harper, in turn, hired young Baptist theologian Shailer Mathews to teach at Chicago. Eventually serving as dean of Chicago's school of divinity, in 1912 Mathews followed Harper's example, becoming director of religion at Chautauqua, a position he held each summer until 1932. By this time, Mathews was a well-known theologian, committed to the Social Gospel movement. Mathews's understanding of Christianity was based on two pillars: (1) liberalism (taking a historical and scientific approach to religious knowledge), and (2) the Social Gospel, a movement that applied the teaching of the gospel to political, economic, and social issues of the day, filtered through the biblical principles of justice and loving mercy. Applying the gospel to the four most pressing issues of his time—poverty, immigration, women's rights, and war—Mathews viewed the gospel as a force for change in society.

Such view were considered extreme and controversial in the early twentieth century, condemned by religious fundamentalists as modernist but viewed by Mathews as "a new reformation in which the methods of the modernists are being carried into religion." For Mathews, religion must be practical, applying its values to the benefit of all human beings, particularly those marginalized by society. By the time Mathews left Chautauqua in 1934, religious modernists had prevailed over fundamentalists in the teaching of theology in America. Significantly, Chautauqua's current religious and intellectual leadership is in the hands of President Michael Hill and Senior Pastor and Vice President of Religion Rev. Gene Robinson, both outspoken members of the gay community.

On June 27, 2021, Bishop Robinson preached the opening sermon of Chautauqua's 147th Assembly Season. He began his sermon with a story about a water pump on a seldom-used trail in Nevada's Amargosa Desert. Tied to the pump, in a baking powder can, was a letter with directions for using the pump. Though the pump was in working order, the washer was prone to dry out, and in order for water to flow, the pump needed to be primed. Desert Pete, who wrote the letter, had buried a bottle of water under the rock nearby so the water would not evaporate. There was enough water to prime the pump, but not if some water was drunk before doing so. The letter suggested that a desert traveler pour about one quarter of the water on the washer to get it wet, and then the rest of the water into the pump suction to get it started.

"Pump hard and the water will keep flowing," Pete wrote, "but you have to prime the pump first and then you will get all the water you need. When you have enough, fill the bottle and put it back under the rock for the next person."

"This is our faith-works connection," Robinson said. "One without the other is not useful. Faith without work get us nothing, and work without faith will not get us where we need to be. It takes the balance of all four pillars of Chautauqua (religion, education, recreation, and the arts) to provide the water for a journey through the wilderness. The arts," he added, "can prime the pump during the desert journey."

Over the years, Chautauqua has been faulted for being overly conservative, yet not conservative enough, too progressive, yet not progressive enough. When you are criticized socially, politically, and religiously that way, you must be doing something right. Defying dualistic thinking and living, authentic spirituality is always holistically healthy and wholesome.

QUESTIONS FOR DISCUSSION AND REFLECTION

1. Explain and assess the merits of the author's argument that the doctrine of incarnation is more determinative to Christian theology than the doctrine of resurrection.

2. In your own words, explain the difference between *the* incarnation and "incarnation."

3. In your own words, explain the difference between the incarnation in Jesus and the incarnation in Christ.

4. Explain and assess the merits of the author's explanation of the "third incarnation."

5. In your estimation, what did the apostle Paul mean when he wrote, "If anyone is in Christ, there is a new creation" (2 Cor 5:17)?

6. In your religious journey, have you tended to focus more on "ecstasies and thrills" or on "transformation and enlightenment"? In your own words, explain the difference between these approaches to spirituality.

7. Explain the merits of the author's statement, "The heart of all yearning is . . . wholeness." In this chapter, what does the author mean by "wholeness"?

8. In your estimation, what does the author mean by the statement, "When we buy into sacred/secular dualism, we lack trust in God"?

9. Explain and assess the meaning of the metaphor of the return to the Garden.

10. Explain and assess the merits of Richard Rohr's statement, "when you don't mythologize, you pathologize."

11. Explain and assess Chautauqua Institution's emphasis on religion, education, recreation, and the arts together as building blocks for individual and communal spirituality.

12. In your estimation, what is the primary insight gained from this chapter? Explain your answer.

Chapter 3

THE DUALIST DILEMMA

LIFE IS GRAND—A GIFT OF nature, society, and family, but above all, of our Creator. As we age, we look backward, nostalgically, idealistically: the highs seem higher, and the lows smaller and shallower. And that's the way it should be. For we are blessed, and our backward glance should be filled with gratitude, not with regret.

Human existence is filled with mental and emotional tension, much of it caused by conflict and polarity. In fact, one cannot live without conflict, and the secret of life is learning to embrace and somehow reconcile one's polarities. To do so successfully requires spirituality. Without spirituality, human beings find themselves trapped in cycles of boredom, irritation, and discontent. By spirituality, I don't mean religion, though they are related.

Speaking of polarities, we need to distinguish them from dualistic thinking, a feature in human consciousness manifested in conventional religious thought. Unlike polarities evident in logic and morality, dualistic thinking refers to a mindset that perceives reality as divided into opposing metaphysical entities such as good versus evil, spirit versus matter, and God versus Satan. Nondualist or holistic thinking does accept the existence of opposites or distinctions in nature, such as maleness and femaleness, lightness and darkness, active and passive, but they are viewed on a continuum and thus, as interrelated.

This ultimate relatedness of all things in the universe is best exemplified by the striking Eastern concept called the Tao (pronounced dhow), which speaks of "the way" of reality, the orderly movement of the natural world according to the principle of yin and yang. This is best depicted by the famous Chinese symbol of a circle divided by a backward or reverse S into light and dark (or red and yellow) areas. According to Taoist teaching, yin is the negative force in nature. Understood as passive, it is seen in darkness, coolness, dampness, and femaleness, and is represented by earth, specifically by the moon. Yang is the positive force in nature. Understood as active, it is seen in lightness, warmth, dryness, maleness, and is represented by heaven, specifically by the sun.

All things are on a continuum between yin and yang. For instance, all males have some yin, and all females some yang. These forces are not confined to humans, nor are they static. A rotting tree is said to be losing yang and becoming damp and therefore more yin. No value judgment is given to yin and yang, for neither is better than the other, and neither is solely good or solely evil. Except for a few objects, such as the sun and the earth, which in their totality are yin or yang, the rest of nature, and even events, are a combination. When the two forces work together in harmony, life is as it should be.

Because human brains are hardwired to think in binary or dualistic ways, religious scholar Cantwell Smith distinguished between "conflict dualism" and "complementary dualism." In ancient Mesopotamia, as evident in Zoroastrianism and Manicheism, we find the ideology of conflict dualism, where opposites such as good and evil or God and Satan are locked in constant war. Such ideas influenced Judaism, Christianity, and Islam, based on Greek and Western logic, in which opposites cannot be reconciled. Eastern logic, as exemplified in Taoism and certain forms of Hinduism and Buddhism, emphasizes complementary dualism (nondualist thinking).

The brilliant word, nonduality (*advaita* in Sanskrit), is used by many different traditions, both Eastern and Western, to distinguish from monism, a perspective that erases all diversity and difference, reducing all things to one sameness. Nondualism celebrates difference and affirms diversity. It simply refuses to see this diversity as anything other than the greater unity of a singular Reality.

When referring to nondualism, Cantwell Smith spoke of complementary dualism, but the underlying reality is the same. In nature, things appear as opposites not to conflict with one another but rather to complement each other. In everything they see, think, and experience, nondualists find the dimension of the other.

C. S. Lewis seems to have had this in mind when he identified universal truths in concepts such as the Tao (the Way) in ancient China and *rita* (divine Law or Truth) in early Hinduism.[1] In Hinduism, *rita* is the principle of natural order that regulates and coordinates the operation of the universe and everything in it. Likewise the Chinese speak of the Tao as the essence of reality or the Way of the universe. The ancient Jews conceived of Torah as way, truth, and life. The author of the gospel of John seems to allude to this notion of a universal principle of natural order when he speaks of Jesus as the Logos (the divine Word) in John 1:1, 14 and as the Way, the Truth, and the Life in 14:6.

Two necessary paths move us forward in life: a journey outward and a journey inward. To live adventurously means to take risks, to try new things, to embrace uncertainty, to remain forever open to newness—outwardly and inwardly, physically and spiritually. At birth, a lifetime of adventure beckons. Initially, most of us focus on the tasks at hand: establishing an identity, a home, career, relationships, friends, community, and security, all foundational for getting started in life. If we have good health and financial means, we add travel to the mix. Later in life, many focus increasingly on the inward journey. However, the sooner and the more authentically we live out our spirituality, the better the results.

Our society is deeply divided, not only by politics, race, gender, lifestyle, culture, region, country of origin, social standing, and economic status, but also by religion. When Americans of different faiths disagree, they tend to distrust one another, and even conservatives and liberals of the same denomination are known to regard one another as ignorant, misguided, or diseased. I use that last word intentionally, for people across the denominational spectrum often view those theologically different from themselves—even fellow Christians—as possessing a dangerous and potentially contagious virus destined to bring America to ruin.

Religion, the one factor capable of restoring harmony, unity, and vitality, seems the most divisive and flawed. Designed as a vehicle of hope and grace, religion is being used today to vilify those with alternative lifestyles and views: Protestants versus Catholics, conservatives versus liberals, fundamentalists versus progressives, religionists versus secularists, devout

---

1. Lewis, *Abolition of Man*, 27–29. In an appendix, "Illustrations of the Tao," Lewis examines eight examples of the Natural Law found in legal and religious texts across cultures of antiquity, 95–121.

versus nones, literalists versus metaphorists, believers versus atheists, saved versus lost.

OUR BRAIN'S BINARY LENS

There is a common belief that human brains are hardwired to think in binary or dualistic ways, a view I assumed earlier in this chapter. The ubiquity of digital computers, coupled with smart phones, nanotechnology, and the rise of artificial intelligence, seems to confirm this way of thinking about the brain, since technological forms of intelligence are related to binary code sequencing, meaning they store data and perform calculations using only zeros and ones. Hence, according to Boolean logic, a single binary digit can only represent True (1) or False (O).

Binary thinking, also known as dichotomous thinking, happens when concepts, ideas, and problems are simplified into being true or false. Other options, such as gray areas in the middle, are ignored or go unnoticed. Binary thinking is useful in situations of threat or danger, when instant decisions are required. Even when humans are not under direct or perceived threat, binary thinking provides a sense of certainty. Such thinking is particularly useful regarding identity, and is a factor affecting gender, race, culture, social class, and religious belief.

While binary applications help us understand certain types of digital computation, the analogy between digital computers and the brain is often misleading. While spiking neurons in the brain may be binary at base, human nervous systems also contain neurons with graded responses. While action potentials are usually binary, synoptic communication between neurons in neural pathways are essentially not binary. Most synapses work by neurotransmitters, meaning they provide chemically mediated graded response. Thus, while neural action potentials are often binary, communication between neurons most often is not binary, since potential firing can involve the integration of synoptic information from many different neurons. Viewed in this way, the brain as a whole cannot be reduced to a binary system, though not all experts agree.

For example, John von Neumann, the famous computer scientist, addressed this idea in his book, *The Computer & the Brain*. Focusing on the behavior of neurons to either fire or not fire, he landed on the side of the brain being a binary system. While that is an important observation, particularly significant for people trying to create artificial brains within computer systems, it is clear that whatever definitions one chooses to work with in terms of brain input and output will affect the outcome. However, the brain within a living human being cannot be reduced to a binary system, for to do so overlooks the comprehensive nature of the human brain, including the interaction between personality, emotions, upbringing, education, experience, and spirituality. In terms of artificial intelligence, any degree of inaccuracy in the starting state of the binary system will cause the behavior of that system to diverge completely from the behavior of the specific brain being modeled. Hence, it is reasonable to conclude that on the macro scale, no particular human brain can be reduced to a binary system, for no binary thinking is final.

NONDUALITY AS WHOLENESS

Perhaps you are familiar with Modest Mussorgsky (1839–1881), a soldier by trade and a Russian musician associated with the nationalist movement known as "The Five." Famous for his opera *Boris Godunov*, Mussorgsky also composed a set of piano miniatures called "Pictures at an Exhibition." Originally written for solo piano but later orchestrated by the French composer Maurice Ravel, the work refers to a memorial exhibit of pictures by a friend of Mussorgsky who had recently died, the Russian painter Victor Hartman. Like Mussorgsky, Hartman cared deeply about incorporating Russian "themes" into his work, themes such as the Russian nutcracker or gnome, a ballet, the witch Baba-Yaga, and the great gate at Kiev. To provide thread or unity to the set of ten different musical pieces, Mussorgsky hit upon an ingenious plan, creating a theme called "Promenade," thereby depicting the composer strolling around the picture gallery. The theme returns several times in free variations to show the viewers' change of mood as they contemplate Hartman's varied work.

Like "Pictures at an Exhibition," *Wading in Water* has a "promenade" theme called "nonduality." Why "nonduality"? Because duality thinking, also called polarity thinking or all-or-nothing thinking, is the bane of spirituality. More than with any other personality trait in our lives, all-or-nothing thinking causes huge mistakes and bad judgments. It results in withholding love, misinterpreting situations, and hurting both others and ourselves. This pattern of dualistic or polarity thinking is deeply entrenched in most of us, despite its severe limitations. Dualistic thinking is not wrong or bad in itself—in fact, it is necessary in most situations. However, it is completely inadequate for the major questions and dilemmas of life.

In *The Heart of Centering Prayer*, American theologian and contemplative teacher Cynthia Bourgeault presents three approaches that help clarify what Western Christians mean by nonduality:

1. The simplest and most straightforward approach to nonduality is to view it as a person's capacity to bear paradox and ambiguity. Viewed practically, dualistic thinking is characterized by insistence on either/or, reductionist solutions to life's dilemmas. By contrast, nondual thinking designates the capacity to hold the tension in opposites without the need for resolution. According to Bourgeault, the capacity to tolerate paradox and ambiguity represents only a preliminary phase of nonduality, confined to rationality, and while this capacity marks an advancement in basic psychological and moral development, it is only the first step to spiritual nondualism.

2. Another approach equates nonduality with mystical experience, much like "seeing heaven in a grain of sand" or in the sense of finding oneself at one with everything. The problem with this approach, as with most mystical experiences, is that this unitive realization tends to be temporary. In addition, people interpret intuitions of oneness according to the stage of consciousness they have attained. The apostle Paul is a classic example, his extraordinary sense of being "taken up into heaven" coexisting with harshly dualistic pronouncements such as "women should keep silent in church."

3. What if nondual mystical experiences were to continue indefinitely in a permanent state of consciousness? This assumption defines a third major approach to nonduality, for it points to a level of spiritual attainment classically known as "the unitive state." Here we think of Western mystics such as Julian of Norwich, Meister Eckhart, Teresa of Ávila, and John of the Cross. In Eastern traditions, such experience tends to be monistic, meaning that one's deepest essence or nature is viewed as identical with Ultimate Oneness, whereas in the West, the unitive state is viewed as relational, more like a mystical marriage whereby one is joined to God in love. Here one does not become God, for nondual realization is one of union ("two become one"), not

identity. In Western spirituality, humans are made in God's image; we are in God, and God is in us, but we are not God.[2]

However, what if this "close but not identical" approach is more a shift in perception, a level of consciousness rather than actual nondual attainment, a shift not primarily in *what* we see but in *how* we see? This allows us to look at the concept or experience of nonduality not through the lens of spiritual attainment, but through the lens of continuing evolution of consciousness. At this level of consciousness, we see oneness because we see from oneness.

Because the discussion of nonduality contains serious misconceptions, it might be helpful to use a via negative approach to nonduality, clarifying what nonduality does not mean. Nonduality does not and should not remove our capacity for critical thinking. Nondualism does not suspend the head, but rather anchors the head in the deeper ground of the heart, situating it somewhere deeper than in the realm of abstraction and intellect.

Furthermore, Christian nonduality is not the same as philosophical monism, a Hindu tradition which stipulates that because all beings and things begin in the One, all return to the One. This perspective views complexity and differentiation as *maya*, namely, as part of the illusions of the material world. While this perception is certainly nondual, Christian nondualists posit an essential metaphysical difference between materiality and spirituality. The two are not synonymous. It is still possible to look upon the world from a nondual vantage point and affirm the reality of change, evolution, distinction, and uniqueness. According to Western nonduality, one simply sees situations, persons, and things from the perspective of oneness. There is no implicit need to reduce multiplicity to a primal unity in order to lay claim to nondual perception. Even some schools of Hinduism suggest that the unitive state is "not one, not two, but both one and two." This, then, is Western nondualism, a way of seeing that is "both/and" rather than exclusively "either/or."

As I note in *Refined by Fire*, my guide to rethinking essential teachings in scripture, a helpful way to think about religious truth is by distinguishing between an image of a circle and of an ellipse. Most questions religious people ask become hurdles to faith because they are framed incorrectly from the start. The implication behind our questions, the deficiency in our thinking, is that something is true or false, literal or fanciful, revealed

2. Bourgeault, *Centering Prayer*, 43–52.

or invented, divine or human, particular or universal. The problem with either/or questions is that they promote either/or answers. Such dichotomous forms of thinking set a trap, for the structure of either/or thinking implies that the options presented exhaust all other alternatives: either the Bible is divine or it is human; either one believes there are proofs for God's existence or one is an atheist; if one religion is true, others are false, and so on. Either/or thinking is intolerant of religious pluralism, impatient with both/and resolutions, and dissatisfied with anything less than all-or-nothing answers. It accepts only absolute answers and dismisses uncertainty as a sign of unbelief.

When I teach a course on Christian theology, I draw an image of a circle and an image of an ellipse, and I explain how an elliptical approach to such concepts as the nature of God, an understanding of sin and salvation, and the relation between faith and reason, provides a more helpful result than approaches that rely on the model of a circle for theological understanding. A circle, of course, has a single center, and everything is determined by its relation to the center. The ellipse, by contrast, is a figure that can be described only in relation to two foci, which cannot be resolved into one.

For example, some people are unable to think elliptically (dialectically) about the question, "Where is God?" so they eliminate the tension between immanence and transcendence by deciding in favor of one polarity, that of supernatural theism—a model that conceptualizes God as "out there" and totally separate from nature. This understanding of God is reductionistic, for it allows for only one correct perspective on the presence of God; if God is "out there," God cannot be "here with us," or vice versa. The symbol of a circle takes us back to "either/or" thinking, a simplistic stance that settles on only one possibly correct answer.

The elliptical model, however, makes it possible to view God as simultaneously transcendent and immanent, for both views are biblical and both are essential to religion. The truth is in the polarity between the two foci, and in the area of overlap; the truth is not one-dimensional but dialectical. When one polarity is emphasized to the detriment or exclusion of the other, religion becomes rigid, intolerant, and increasingly confrontational.

Another way to clarify the difference between dual and nondual thinking is by distinguishing monovision from univision. Let me explain what I mean by these terms. As I learned recently, while undergoing radiation to reduce the effects of a tumor in my eye, I am one of a small percentage of the human race that has a form of vision known as monovision. The term "monovision" is synonymous with "blended vision," and simply means that one human eye is focused at a different working distance to the other. In the vast majority of monovision cases, one eye—the dominant—is focused for distance vision while the non-dominant eye is focused for near vision. People with monovision enjoy the best of both worlds: adequate distance vision and the ability to read without glasses.

To view truth as singular or one-dimensional is like riding a bicycle with only one pedal or like paddling a kayak with only one blade. Two pedals are better than one, two blades better than one. Likewise, two eyes are better than one, especially when they work harmoniously. As two eyes improve one's sight, two ears one's hearing, two legs one's ability to walk, and two halves of the brain one's perception, so it is with truth. I believe truth is dialectical and dialogical, meaning that it is not primarily cognitive (knowledge-based), outward, static, or certain, but rather relational, inward, discovered, affirmed, dynamic, and tentative. Furthermore, I believe that humans arrive at this truth not so much individually but corporately, in dialogue with others (by which I mean not simply through conversation, though that is where it might begin), but by commitment to and with others to the principle that in loving, serving, and respecting others we love and serve God.

Dualistic people use knowledge, even religious knowledge, for the purposes of ego enhancement, shaming, and the control of others and themselves, for it works very well in that way. Nondual people are both courageous and creative. Seeing reality with a new eye and heart, they use knowledge for the transformation of persons and structures, but especially to experience transformation. They are "yes/and" thinkers who avoid getting trapped in the small world of "either/or," except in the ways of love and courage, where they are "all in."

Spiritual counselors and psychotherapists stress the importance of embracing "wholeness" as a dimension of health and spiritual wellbeing, which affirms an individual's "oneness" without needing to eliminate or perfect any part of themselves. Embracing "wholeness" not only reinforces individual wellbeing, but it generates the same goodwill toward others. In other words, wholesome self-love leads to greater love for others and for all of life.

The harmonic of the universe is wholeness, not perfection; specifically, it is a wholeness that involves differentiation. Unlike fusion, which sacrifices differentiation, wholeness retains differentiation. Without wholeness, our various parts create dissension, confusion, and cacophony. Wholeness, however, produces the purity of a single tone, while allowing the harmonics of differentiation.

How do we know if we are on a path that leads to increased wholeness? We will hear harmony, not simply the cacophony of a fragmented self. We will also sense the energy of the larger whole. We should, however, occasionally experience the thrill of being a small part of a larger cause, for such participation can lead to the realization that all humans are intertwined. In reality, what we do for another, we do for ourselves. Love passed on to others becomes the most meaningful form of self-love, and care of the earth and its inhabitants becomes care of self.

We have wholeness when we tell our story and, through it, discover a deeper sense of being part of a greater whole. We live wholeness when we know we belong to others, to the earth, the cosmos, and to God (however named). We live wholeness when we know that what we have is sufficient, and that our responsibility is to use it resourcefully.

Wholeness and love are inseparable. Living wholeness is participating in the dynamism of love that encounters others, not as strangers, but as extensions of ourselves. When we enter into the heart of love in this way, we enter the field of relatedness and come to experience the greater unity and consciousness that comprise our deepest calling and truest belonging. According to Franciscan theologian Ilia Delio, our challenge today is "to trust the power of love at the heart of life, . . . to create and invent ways for love to evolve into a global wholeness of unity, compassion, justice, and peacemaking."[3] Loving this way is living wholeness.

NONDUALITY AS ONENESS

Our world is caught in a swirl of deep and divisive crises—social, political, ecological, and religious, certainly, but also profoundly spiritual. The key to human survival and wellbeing is nurturing belief in human connectedness, acknowledging the spirit that flows within and between all human beings on earth.

The Christian gospel teaches that the divine image and dignity are inherent in every human being. Each of us has the freedom and privilege of choosing whether to grow in our unique likeness of this image. To

3. Delio, *Wholeness of Being*, xxv.

understand more clearly oneness or unity, the Christian gospel requires operating from a level of nondual consciousness. Jesus is a clear example of this path, for he modeled inclusive, nondual, compassionate living and being.

If this is true, we ask, why, then, did Jesus tell stories that showed harsh judgment, such as casting rejected people into "outer darkness" and "eternal punishment"? (Significantly, most of these references are in Matthew's gospel; see 5:22; 13:42; 18:9; 25:41, 46.) Do these instances undo the mercy and forgiveness Jesus demonstrated in his life and elsewhere in his teaching? Let me explain how I see it.

We often think that affirming oneness means refraining from taking a stand on issues of importance. However, to practice nondual thinking doesn't mean fuzzy thinking. In our journey toward nondual living, we must build on well-trained minds and balanced spirits. Once we have a firm, first-half-of-life foundation, we can begin to respond holistically (with body, heart, mind, and soul). Holistic being is at the heart of mature spirituality, unlike imposing purity and conformity in practice and belief, which results in frustration, confusion, and dissension.

Some of us are good theoreticians, easily identifying boundaries and norms and prophetically asserting ideals, finding fault, and naming problems, but we remain stuck in idealized boxes. Others speak too quickly of love, forgiveness, and fellowship while remaining trapped in inability and inaction.

When Jesus spoke out against social, political, and economic injustice, he did so harshly, in damning and dualistic ways, because this is where "powers and principalities" are most resistant. "You cannot serve God and wealth" (Matt 6:24); "it is easier for a camel to go through the eye of a needle than for someone who is rich to enter the kingdom of God" (Matt 19:24); or the clear dichotomy in Matthew 25 between sheep (who feed the hungry, welcome the stranger, clothe the naked, care for the sick, and visit the imprisoned) and goats (who don't do these things).

For Jesus, the context is important. Jesus' foundational and even dualistic bias is always against false power and in favor of the powerless. Unfortunately, Jesus' followers often avoid what Jesus taught so unequivocally and with dualistic clarity, such as nonviolence, sharing resources, living simply, and loving enemies.

History shows that Christians regularly compromise or avoid the gospel issues of justice, power, money, and inclusion. Thankfully, a growing number of awakened Christians are learning the contemplative response to social evils, simultaneously practicing the artful balance of clear-headed critique and open-door compassion. Those people recognize the need for restitution, making amends, and public accountability, depending not only on human resources but also on the divine capacity for patience and forgiveness. The gospel requires justice *and* compassion. If either are sacrificed, we do not have the full gospel. While it is a small minority who do both, they are the hope for a better future.

Mystics recognize the inherent oneness of life—that all life is one and all humans are tied together; prophets proclaim that creatures are created and sustained by one just, sovereign, and loving God; and social activists work to combine mystical vision and prophetic voice into reality. The vision of oneness makes possible human and social wellness, and this experience of wholeness brings us back into relationship with oneness. The mystical worldview creates an ethical mandate, and it offers a new way to enact social transformation—from the position of oneness rather than dualism. Nondualism shifts our paradigm, first spiritually, then religiously, socially, politically, and economically. Prophets, mystics, and social activists remind us that God is against all social and metaphysical dualism, and anything that thwarts the oneness of Life ultimately cannot stand.

As Christians, we struggle to believe that we are children of God and co-heirs with Christ (Rom 8:16–17). Simply put, this reality is best expressed in community. It is being together in our wholeness with the entire body of Christ that makes us realize our goodness and uniqueness. Individually, we all possess a small part of this greater glory, for, as Paul tells us in 1 Corinthians, each of us has our own gifts of God's Spirit: "To each is given the manifestation of the Spirit for the common good" (12:7). Paul's word for this is "charism"—a gift that is given to each person, a gift that is maximized when used to build up society. For the greater good, all we need to do is discover our particular gift, even if it is just one small thing, and use it for the good of others.

Paul uses the brilliant metaphor of the body to show how unity is created out of diversity (see 1 Cor 12:12, 27). As individuals, we are imperfect and incomplete. However, in our corporate wholeness, we are the presence of God, the goodness of God, indeed, the glory of God. Individually, we are no people; together, however, we are "a chosen race, a royal priesthood, a holy nation" (1 Pet 2:9–10). Jesus' image for corporate wholeness is the kingdom of God; Paul's image is the church, the body of Christ; and John's image is the journey into mystical union where "I and the Father are one" (John 10:30). All of these are images of communal harmony, a participatory image of what God makes possible through Christ.

Unity, however, is not the same as uniformity or conformity. Unity is the reconciliation of differences, differences that must be maintained. Spiritual unity requires distinguishing and setting aside qualities, traits, behaviors, and preferences, often at a cost to ourselves, before we can achieve wholeness. According to Ephesians 2:11–22, Jesus has broken down the dividing walls between Jews and Gentiles, that he might create in himself one new humanity in place of the two. Through his life and death, Jesus has put to death the hostility between those who are far from God and those who are near, giving both access to the Father through the one Spirit. The great wisdom of Pentecost is the recognition through God's Spirit of our underlying unity amidst numerous differences. Paul makes this universal principle clear in 1 Corinthians 12:4–6. We see this principle also in our word "universe," where two Latin words, *unus* and *versus* are brought together to mean "to turn around one thing," or "to revolve around one center."

Already in biblical times, the apostle Paul and others spoke of the unity of the one Spirit, by which believers are "all baptized into one body [and] . . . all made to drink of one spirit" (1 Cor 12:13). This is not some naïve "everything is one" unity, but the deeper ecumenical unity described by the fourteenth-century mystical visionary Julian of Norwich, who spoke of God's love as a power so great that it creates "such a unity that, when it is seen correctly, nobody can separate himself from anybody else" (*Revelations*, 65).[4]

The letter to the Ephesians, written by a devoted admirer of Paul during the last two decades of the first century, is influenced by a dominant concern, namely, the unity of the church under the headship of Christ. The church at this time had become predominantly Gentile and was in danger of losing its sense of continuity with Israel. The author of Ephesians, desiring to underscore the larger history and tradition that defined Christianity, as well as the mystical unity of believers in Christ, portrays that oneness in three predominant images: the church is (1) the body of Christ (1:22–23), (2) the building or temple of God (2:20–22), and (3) the bride of Christ (5:23–32). The church's solidarity, Paul makes clear in Galatians 3:28, has social implications, namely, challenging racial, social, and sexual barriers.

---

4. Armstrong, *Visions of God*, 216.

Because Christ is one, church members are united. Because Christ is one, church members are equal. Because Christ is one, church members are free to serve one another. In Ephesians, love is not a commandment but a new reality in human relationships that has been initiated by God's prior love through Jesus Christ. The church is a fellowship of love, the highest endowment of God's Spirit (see 1 Cor 13:13; 1 John 4:7–21).

Children enjoy this unity at a prerational level, and mystics enjoy it consciously at a transrational and universal level. Thus, what is now being called "deep ecumenism" is not a variant of classic pantheism or even of unfounded New Age optimism. Instead, it is the method, energy, and goal by which God ushers in a recurring "new age" (see Matt 19:28). Jesus' final prayer is that his followers consciously perceive and live this radical union now (John 17:21–26). Our task is not to invent, discover, or even prove this reality, but only to retrieve what has been discovered and rediscovered repeatedly by the mystics, prophets, and saints of all religions.

The Buddhist monk and peace activist Thich Nhat Hanh illustrates the mysterious interconnection of all things that he calls "interbeing" by speaking of perspective, that is, of how and what we see. If we think mystically, for example, we perceive a cloud when we see a blank sheet of paper. Without a cloud, there is no rain; without rain, trees cannot grow; and without trees, we cannot make paper. The cloud is essential for paper to exist. Hence, we can say that the cloud and the paper "inter-are" or "inter exist." In addition, when we look at a sheet of paper mystically, we see sunshine in it. For without sunshine, trees cannot grow. Thus, sunshine is also in paper; the sunshine and paper "inter-are." If we see deeper, we also see wheat, and loggers, and loggers' parents. Looking more deeply, we can see ourselves in a sheet of paper, because it is part of our perception. As the paper is in the universe, so the universe is in a sheet of paper. Directly and indirectly, all things co-exist. As I am in the universe, so the universe is in me. As God is in me, I am in God. We all "inter-are."

QUESTIONS FOR DISCUSSION AND REFLECTION

1. Explain the merits of the author's statement, "the secret of life is learning to embrace and somehow reconcile one's polarities."

2. Explain the difference between "polarities" and "dualistic thinking." In this regard, assess the merits of the Chinese concept of the Tao.

3. In your estimation, what must we do as citizens of this world to move from conflict dualism to complementary dualism? In your experience, is such a move helpful, or even possible? Explain your answer.

4. In your own words, explain the author's distinction between the journey inward and the journey outward. In your estimation, how are these journeys different, and how are they similar?

5. After reading this chapter, what did you learn about the human brain's binary lens?

6. (a) In your own words, explain the difference between duality and nonduality thinking. (b) Explain the relation between nonduality and wholeness. (c) If possible, provide examples of duality and nonduality in your own experience.

7. In your own words, explain the difference between Christian nonduality and philosophical monism.

8. Explain and assess the author's distinction between circular and elliptical approaches to theology.

9. Are you on a path to increased wholeness? Explain your answer.

10. Using Jesus as exemplar, explain the difference between dualistic and nondualistic consciousness.

11. In your own words, explain the difference between uniformity and conformity, and how this distinction can be helpful in the drive for human connectedness and religious unity.

12. In your estimation, what is the primary insight gained from this chapter? Explain your answer.

Chapter 4

LEVELS OF MEANING

FROM TIME IMMEMORIAL, IN EVERY age, nation, culture, and society, a set of questions has persisted, perplexing human beings. Who am I? Why am I here? Where did I come from? Where am I going? They have been called life's existential questions; philosophers speak of them as "ultimate questions," for they are the ones that never go away.

While we know there are no final or absolute answers to existential questions, they must be asked, especially early in life. At some point we realize that the answers, however given or explained, are not as important as the questions. Nevertheless, the questions must be asked, if for no other reason that they have an integrative function, helping individuals learn how to process information, how to conceptualize, how to interact with others, and how to understand themselves and their place in the grand scheme of life.

As we age physically and progress morally, emotionally, and intellectually, we discover four paths to meaning. To simplify, we can list and rank them as follows:

1. literal or factual

2. symbolic or metaphorical

3. allegorical or parabolic

4. mythological or mystical

As is clear, the most superficial and therefore least effective level of knowing is the factual or literal. We cannot downplay this level, for it is the foundation upon which the first half of life is built. A factual understanding of an event or a discipline is a doorway. Such an approach gets us in the ballpark of thinking, understanding, and living, but it remains superficial. Shallow knowledge gives us confidence, like a child going ankle deep at the beach or wearing floaties in a pool, but it is not swimming. Such knowledge can lead to arrogance and deception. Perhaps you have heard others indicate how, when they read a book, heard a lecture, or attended a seminar, they thought they knew a great deal, only to read additional books or hear other points of view and discover how little they knew about the subject. If you've had this experience, you have something in common with Einstein, who acknowledged, "The more I learn, the more I realize how much I don't know."

While a literal reading of scripture or factual knowledge of religion is a good starting point to spirituality, it is the least effective and least transformative way to live, think, and "know." According to Joseph Campbell, valued in his day as the world's foremost interpreter of mythology, metaphor, whether expressed symbolically, allegorically, or mythologically, is the most suitable language for religion, for it alone is honest about Mystery. "Metaphors only seem to describe the outer world of time and place," he noted; however, "Their real universe is the spiritual realm of the inner life."[1] Authentic religion masters metaphor, transporting from the known to the unknown. Mythology, the most profound and effective level of understanding, certainly the most integrative, helps individuals discover life's meaning in four ways:

1. *Symbolic function.* Mythology influences us subconsciously, helping us approach our questions intuitively, at nonverbal, preconceptual, and pre-emotional levels.

2. *Scholastic function.* Mythology guides individuals through the stages and transitions of life. Mythology's tutorial or explanatory function provides harmonious ways through the inevitable crises of life.

3. *Sociological function.* Mythology supports and validates social order, helping individuals discover their place and role in society.

1. Campbell, *Thou Art That*, 7.

4. *Synchronous function.* Mythology opens the mind to wonder and the heart to transcendence, pointing out the ultimate mystery in which all things participate. Mythology's unifying function links human beings to society, one another, nature, and the cosmos.

FOUR POINTS OF VIEW

Does reality consist of permanence or change? In antiquity, the pre-Socratic Greek philosopher Parmenides argued for the former, and Heraclitus for the latter. If life is reduced to either/or perspectives, one side is right and the other wrong. But is there a third alternative? Plato thought there was, and so he introduced his famous compromise, a dualistic perspective in which there are two competing realities, a world of permanence (a supernatural or ideal realm), perceived by human reason, and a world of change (a natural or real realm), perceived by the human senses).

In modern times, the philosopher G. W. F. Hegel argued for a state of reality he labeled "synthesis," the result of a historical, dialectical process whereby an entity called "thesis" is negated by an opposite entity called "antithesis," the two polarities then fused to form a higher state known as synthesis.

The Hegelian dialectic can be applied to most categories or disciplines. In politics, the two polarities or competing parties are "conservatives" and "liberals," with an intermediary stance called "moderates." Interestingly, on the political spectrum, one can be a moderate conservative or a moderate progressive, with additional gradations possible and present. The same possibilities also hold true in other disciplines or perspectives, such as social, philosophical, and religious.

In the field of philosophy, the German philosopher Immanuel Kant, like Plato, brought together preexisting polarities, in his case elements of rationalism (the view that knowledge requires reason) and empiricism (the view that knowledge requires sense data), to posit a revolutionary epistemological synthesis based on a sharp dualism in reality between an unknowable noumenal (supernatural) realm beyond the senses and a phenomenal (natural) realm known and experienced by the senses. Seeking to unify reality, Kant argued for the necessity of transcendent realities, which, while not corresponding to any object of experience, are posited by reason to unify human knowledge. For Kant, the transcendent ideas forced upon us by "pure" reason are the self, the cosmos, and God. Without the unity these ideas provide, no human or scientific knowledge would be possible.

Likewise, regarding morality, Kant distinguished between two kinds of knowledge: (1) knowledge of what is, by which he meant scientific knowledge, given to the understanding through sense impressions, and (2) knowledge of what ought to be, by which he meant innate moral knowledge.

As we know, people are divided morally, epistemologically, cosmologically, politically, and religiously by competing points of view. On the one hand are those who focus on absolutes, opposed by those who argue for progress and change. Others, noting the dualistic impasse between polarities, argue for synthesis, seeking compromise as a solution. This is what Franciscans mean when they call their movement "alternative orthodoxy," a heterodoxy somewhere between conformity and nonconformity on the theological spectrum, or what the eminent biologist Theodosius Dobzhansky meant when he wrote, "I am a creationist *and* an evolutionist."

Do these three options exhaust the possibilities? Is another alternative possible, a quaternary point of view? There is a fourth alternative, one espoused by sages, mystics, and saints throughout history. In the Bible, we find the fourth face of God in YHWH, in the "I Am" of God, the unspeakable absolute oneness of God (see Exod 3:14). This is the face of God that, according to Exodus 33:20, no one can see and live, the God we know through unknowing. This is why there are four ways of reading scripture (literal, tropological [moral meaning], allegorical, and anagogical [eschatological meaning]) or according to Lectio Divina, four ways of praying scripture (*lectio, meditatio, oratio,* and *contemplatio*), why nature has four seasons (spring, summer, fall, and winter), and why a deck of cards is composed of four suits (hearts, diamonds, spades, and clubs). It is also

1. what Hinduism means by four paths to God (the path of works, devotion, knowledge, and self-actualization).

2. what Jesus meant by loving God with our heart, soul, mind, and strength, (which correlates with feeling, intuition, thinking, and sensing, the four functions of personality used by the Swiss psychiatrist Carl G. Jung and later utilized by the Myers-Briggs Type Indicator [MBTI] to determine personality type).

3. what John F. Haught calls the four components of wholesome religion (sacramental, mystical, silent, and active).

4. what Peter Tufts Richardson calls the four spirituality types (the journey of works, devotion, unity, and harmony).

5. what Arthur Holmes calls four schools of spirituality (sacramental, charismatic, mystical, and apostolic).

6. what Huston Smith means by four levels of reality (terrestrial, intermediate, celestial, and Infinite) and four levels of selfhood (body, mind, soul, and spirit).

7. what theologian Brian McLaren calls the four stages of faith (simplicity, complexity, perplexity, and harmony).

8. what Jungian analyst James Hollis calls the four larger phases of life (childhood, adolescence or first adulthood, second adulthood, and mortality), each with the power to define a person's identity.

9. what depth psychologist Bill Plotkin means by the Wheel of Life, an eightfold modification of the four stages of human development (childhood, adolescence, adulthood, and elderhood).

10. or what Cynthia Bourgeault means when she suggests that we replace binary systems of understanding with ternary perspectives, such as are present in the Christian Trinity. In this case, the third force is not a product of the first two, as in the classic Hegelian synthesis, but is independent and coequal with the others.

According to Bourgeault, the interweaving of the three forces produces a fourth realm of possibility. In contrast to binary systems, which seek completion in stability, through the balance of opposites, ternary perspectives create a synthesis at a completely new level, seeking completion in newness. In *The Holy Trinity and the Law of Three*, Bourgeault advises that we not limit this metaphysical principle to one triad (Father, Son, and Holy Spirit), but rather that we envision the Holy Trinity as one of many triads, each revealing different facets of the divine wholeness. Such a way of conceptualizing is made easier if we stop thinking of the doctrine of the Trinity as about three *persons* and envision it in terms of metaphysical *process*, as three functions or forces rather than three identities. The result is not a compromise, like changing the score in a ballgame, but what Bourgeault calls "an arising," namely, a completely new ballgame.

Most of Christianity's metaphysical paradigms are binary systems. For example, to think of God in masculine or feminine categories is to reduce reality to paired opposites. Ternary systems, however, present a distinctly different mix. The interplay of two polarities calls forth a third, thereby generating synthesis at an entirely new level, which results in new realms of possibility. Think of the agricultural process of planting and sowing. A seed, as Jesus said, "unless it falls into the ground and dies, it remains just a single grain" (John 12:24). If *seed* (the first force) meets *ground* (the second force), which must be moist, nothing happens without a third or reconciling force, *sunlight*. When these three forces interact, they generate a *sprout*, which is the actualization of the possibility latent in the seed. Unlike binary systems, ternary systems are not about paired opposites but about threefold process, which leads to new fields of possibility, because the fourth force is not a final and stable completion but "the new arising that inevitably emerges from the dynamic interplay of the three."[2]

Is it possible to utilize all four levels of consciousness simultaneously? Yes, because spirituality enables and encourages such plasticity. According to mystics and sages, humans consist of body, mind, soul (heart and emotions), and spirit. Don't we humans live out of our fourfold nature simultaneously?

In her song, "Both Sides Now," Canadian singer-songwriter Joni Mitchell examines aspects of nature (clouds) and of human nature (love) "from up and down," that is, imaginatively or realistically, realistically or pessimistically, concluding with "something's lost, but something's gained, in living every day." Yes, there are at least two ways to see things, but these do not exhaust the possibilities, for there are more than two sides or possibilities to moods, experiences, and things.

This idea of double and triple entendre is evident in other popular music as well. Take, for example, Paul McCartney's "Fixing a Hole," sung by the Beatles in their 1967 album, *Sgt. Pepper's Lonely Hearts Club Band*. That song, said to be a tribute to marijuana and to the joys of allowing one's mind to wander, can also be seen as a homage to individual freedom and the need to be guided by one's internal compass or life force. As McCartney noted, he wrote perplexing lyrics to communicate double meaning.

Of course, that's true of all art—from music to painting, literature to theatre—and of all spirituality. Art, like spirituality, is intended to draw outsiders in, using notes, words, pictures, and acts to transport viewers and readers not only into the artist's world, but also as pathways to their own souls. In art, the levels of meaning are limitless, the possibilities inexhaustible.

---

2. Bourgeault, *Holy Trinity*, 19.

Huston Smith was clearly on the right track by dividing reality into four levels (terrestrial, intermediate, celestial, and Infinite) and in showing how the inner self (composed of body, mind, soul, and spirit) parallels external reality, the microcosm (the self) mirroring the macrocosm (the cosmos). The ancient Greeks believed matter was composed of four elements—earth, water, air, and fire. For two thousand years, this idea served as the cornerstone of philosophy, science, and medicine.

Smith's tiers correlate in such a way that higher levels of reality correspond to deeper levels of the self:

- the terrestrial tier (also called the material, physical, sensible, corporeal, and phenomenal) corresponds to the body.

- the intermediate tier (also called the subtle, psychic, or astral) corresponds to the mind.

- the celestial tier (this realm views God as personal; here one speaks of God's attributes and personality) corresponds to the soul.

- the Infinite tier (this realm views God as transpersonal; this level is best spoken of through analogy, in negative terms, or through paradox) corresponds to the spirit.

The highest and deepest tiers, Infinite and Spirit, are, according to Smith, without limitation; while the Infinite is unbounded externally, the human Spirit is unbounded internally. These two (undifferentiated) levels, therefore, are in fact the same.

We speak of two halves of life, but in reality there are at least three, if we add the interim period called "midlife," and likely more. James Hollis, a Jungian analyst, notes that beyond the many subphases of life, there are four larges phases, each with a power to define the person's identity.[3] The first identity, *childhood*, is characterized by dependency of the ego on the world of the parents. The second identity begins at puberty. During *adolescence*, the emerging ego is malleable and prey to the influence of peers and pop culture. This phase has as its primary task the solidification of the ego, whereby a youth gains sufficient strength to leave parents, go into the larger world, and struggle for survival and the achievement of desire. Hollis calls the period from roughly twelve to forty the first adulthood. This identity, which may extend throughout one's life, is a provisional existence, lacking the depth and uniqueness that makes a person truly an individual.

3. Hollis, *Middle Passage*, 23–27.

The third phase of identity, the *second adulthood*, is launched when one's projections dissolve. In this crisis, one has the opportunity to become an individual, beyond the determinism of parents and cultural conditioning. Tragically, the repressive power of the psyche, with its reliance on authority, often keeps a person in thrall to cultural and parental complexes and thereby freezes development. Second adulthood is only attainable when the provisional identities have been discarded and the false self has died. The pain of such loss may be compensated by the rewards of the new life that follows, but the person in the midst of the midlife crisis may only experience the dying. The fourth identity, *mortality*, involves learning to live with the mystery of death and accepting its reality.

Another way to look at these shifting identities is to classify their different axes. In the first identity, childhood, the operative axis is the parent-child relationship. In the first adulthood the axis lies between ego and world. The ego struggles to project itself into the world and create a world within the world. In the second adulthood, both during and after midlife, the axis connects ego and Self. It is natural for consciousness to assume that it knows all and is running the show. When its hegemony is overthrown, the humbled ego then begins the dialogue with the Self, defined as the mystery within, concerned with the purposiveness of the organism. The fourth axis is Self-God or Self-Cosmos. This axis is framed by the cosmic mystery that transcends the mystery of individual existence. Without some relationship to the cosmos, we are constrained to lives of transience, superficiality, and aridity. Since the dominant culture offers little mythic mediation for the placement of self in a larger context, it is all the more imperative that the individual enlarge his or her vision.

According to psychologist Erik Erikson (1902–1994), psychosocial development proceeds by critical steps, described as infancy (birth to 18 months), early childhood (2 to 3 years of age), preschool (3 to 5 years), school age (6 to 11 years), adolescence (12 to 18 years), young adulthood (19 to 40 years), middle adulthood (40 to 65 years), and maturity (65 to death). Each stage is marked by crisis, connoting not a catastrophe but a turning point, a crucial period of increased vulnerability and heightened potential. At such points achievements are won or failures occur, leaving the future to some degree better or worse but in any case, restructured

In his book *Nature and the Human Soul* (2008), depth psychologist Bill Plotkin takes the four stages of human development—(a) childhood, (b) adolescence, (c) adulthood, and (d) elderhood—and develops an eight-stage model of human development called the Wheel of Life, an eight-fold pathway from egocentricism to soulcentrism, a nature-based model that fully honors the deeply imaginative potentials of the human psyche. A wilderness guide and self-styled "agent of cultural evolution," Plotkin uses his model to show how healthy and holistic lifestyles should be rooted in a childhood of innocence and wonder, sprout into an adolescence of creative fire and mystery-probing adventures, blossom into an authentic adulthood of cultural artistry and visionary leadership, and finally ripen into an elder-hood of wisdom and grace, tending both the social and natural world. His premise is that true adulthood is rooted in mystical affiliation with nature, experienced as a sacred calling, embodied in soul-infused work and mature responsibilities. This mystical affiliation is the very core of maturity, and it is precisely what Plotkin believes has been overlooked or even suppressed by mainstream Western society.

According to Plotkin, the eight stages, together with the passage from one stage to the next, are not defined by chronological age or social status but by the progress made with the developmental tasks encountered at each stage. Each transition involves loss and pain and entails a crisis for the conscious self. The stage of adolescence—beyond which most adults never move—holds the key to both individual development and human evolution. In this stage individuals develop their distinctive ego-based consciousness, which represents both their greatest liability as well as their greatest potential. If they are to become fully human and move to the stages of genuine adulthood, people in the adolescent stage must undergo an initiation process that requires letting go of the familiar and comfort-able while submitting to a journey of descent into "the mysteries of nature and the human soul." Individuals who remain within the constraints of a largely adolescent world regress into "pathological adolescence," charac-terized by materialism, sexism, competitive violence, racism, egoism, and self-destructive patterns. Patho-adolescent societies are perpetuated by leaders and celebrities described as self-serving politicians, moralizing re-ligious leaders, drug-induced entertainment icons, and greedy captains of industry. If society is going to develop soulcentrically, it must be overseen by councils of wise elders, not by assemblies of adolescent politicians and corporate officers.

Plotkin's stages, while correlating ideally with chronological, bio-logical, and evolutionary age, are not primarily based on such phenomena, since people can remain locked in any of these stages, unable to progress further until they successfully complete the task(s) of that stage. According to Plotkin, one cannot skip a stage only to return later in hopes of moving on.

Committed to promoting a global ecological citizenry, the Wheel of Life provides a model for the human life cycle based on eight acts, offering a map for reaching the destination of becoming fully human. The Wheel, ecocentric in that it models individual human development from the perspective of nature's cycles, rhythms, and patterns, is also soulcentric in that it envisions the principal goal of maturation to be the conscious discovery and embodiment of soul. Understanding the human soul as being the very core of human nature, the eight developmental stages—early childhood, middle childhood, early adolescence, late adolescence, early adulthood, late adulthood, early elderhood, late elderhood—together constitute a single story, the story of a deeply fulfilling but nevertheless entirely human life.

In his book *Faith After Doubt*, theologian Brian McLaren proposes a fourfold model of faith development in which questions are not the enemy of faith but rather a portal to a more mature and fruitful kind of faith. Doubt, it turns out, is the passageway from one stage to the next. Without doubt, there can be growth within a stage, but growth from one stage to another usually requires us to doubt the assumptions that give shape to our current stage. Each new stage, like a ring on a tree, embraces and builds upon the previous stage, while growing beyond its limits. Alternatively, each stage includes and transcends its predecessors. McLaren labels the four stages: Simplicity, Complexity, Perplexity, and Harmony.

As it turns out, McLaren developed this framework earlier, having introduced it in *Naked Spirituality*, where he compared his stages to the four sequential seasons of spring, summer, fall, and winter, likening Simplicity to the springlike season of spiritual awakening, Complexity to the summerlike season of spiritual strengthening, Perplexity to the autumnlike season of spiritual surviving, and Harmony to the winterlike season of spiritual discovery.[4] Like living with nature, the point is not to stay in spring or summer forever, nor is it the point to get to (or through) winter as soon as possible, any more than the point of life is advancing from infancy to old age as soon as possible. Rather, the point is to live each stage fully, to learn well what each day and season has to teach, and to live and enjoy life in companionship with God and others through all of life's seasons.

---

4. McLaren, *Naked Spirituality*, 26–27.

Those who reach Stage Four (Harmony) do not experience certainty, however, for that is the concern of those in Stages One and Two. Stage Four people never feel they have arrived. They are not obsessed with misguided notions of certainty or supremacy—more the opposite. Committed to the faith journey, they know there is no such thing as certainty in faith. Faith, like all creativity, flourishes not in certainty but in questioning, not in security but in venturing.

Those who reach Stage Four can look back and see that each stage contributed to Harmony. No stage was bad because it wasn't Stage Four (that would be a Stage One thing to say). Neither was any stage a distraction, delay, or obstacle to success because it wasn't Stage Four (that would be a Stage Two thing to say). Nor was any stage futile and in vain because it wasn't as mature and complete as Stage Four (that would be a Stage Three thing to say). Rather, each stage makes a vital contribution, appropriate for a time, which makes possible what follows, and each stage remains a central element of what follows. No stage is the destination, for each plays a vital role in the journey toward and into Harmony.

QUESTIONS FOR DISCUSSION AND REFLECTION

1. In this chapter, what did you learn about the four paths to meaning?

2. Select what for you is one of life's "ultimate" questions, and explain how each approach or path to meaning can provide helpful ways to deal with this existential issue.

3. Explain and assess the four ways by which mythology can help us decipher religious "truth."

4. In this chapter, what did you learn about the importance of the fourth point of view? In this regard, explain the difference between binary and ternary systems or perspectives.

5. Explain and assess how ternary systems lead to new fields of possibility and new ways of thinking about problems.

6. Explain and assess the merits of Huston Smith's fourfold model for understanding the human self and its correlation with external reality.

7. In your own words, explain James Hollis's distinction between the two halves of life. In your estimation, can there be more than two halves of life? Explain your answer.

8. Explain and assess the merits of Bill Plotkin's eight stages of life, and his view of "pathological adolescence."

9. Explain and assess the merits of Brian McLaren's fourfold model of faith. Do you agree with him that doubt "is the passageway from one stage to the next"? Explain your answer.

10. In your estimation, what is the primary insight gained from this chapter? Explain your answer.

Chapter 5

Spirituality and Liminality

It is no secret that our world is in a state of crisis. The prognosis is bleak and the conditions may be irreversible. The tip of the iceberg, evident to almost everyone nowadays, is the environmental fate of our entire planet. During the second half of the twentieth century we learned that deterioration in the quality of the air we breathe, the water we drink, and the soil in which we grow our crops seriously threatens our continued life and well-being on this earth. Despite changes made by numerous governments across the globe, the prognosis remains bleak.

In addition to environmental degradation and anticipated ecological factors such as unpredictable weather patterns, increasing number and severity of storms, and sea-level rise, we can add pandemics and the outbreak of new diseases, species extinction, malnutrition and widespread famine, terrorism, violence and crime, the breakdown of the family, increased addictive behavior, unemployment, corporate scandals, an increasing income gap between rich and poor, religious fanaticism and sectarian wars, and the list goes on and on.

The current crisis involves many factors: ecological, political, economic, sociological, and ethical. At its core, however, the problem is spiritual. The crisis of spirit, dubbed "the impoverishment of soul" by Matthew Fox, is particularly evident in our Western civilization today. It is characterized by imbalance, or more accurately, by dissociation between the spiritual and physical realms of life.

The current generation outpaces all others in history in terms of wealth, health, education, and convenience—yet it doesn't seem to be happier or more content than preceding generations. Perhaps, in our passion for acquiring things, we have actually lost something profound—something so valuable that we would never knowingly sell it or trade it away. Some may refer to values, standards, or patriotism, but what it comes down to is the loss of the sacred.

Rather than being rooted in a spiritual worldview and in principles espoused by the traditions of the world's great religions, particularly in their mystical approaches to reality, modern humans see the world through the lenses of crass materialism, scientism, and positivism. In his thoughtful volume, *Man and Nature: the Spiritual Crisis in Modern Man* (1997), Islamic scholar Seyyed Nasr takes the reader through history and explores the causes of the desacralization of nature in the West and the resultant ecological crisis we face today. He demonstrates how the West, by divorcing science from spirit, has wrecked havoc on our planet. He also argues that the Christian faith helped accelerate this process when it removed elements of its metaphysical doctrines that kept nature as a part of the divine.

Whether the current crisis is curable is debatable, but it will clearly require massive cultural reorientation. More importantly, it will require a transformation of the human spirit and a commitment of will. Only a relationship of genuine harmony with nature and a love of nature's God can transform humans from consumers to caretakers. When historians look back at the start of the twenty-first century, it is hoped that they might remember it most for two commitments: as a time when the peoples of the world made a profound commitment to one another and made an equal commitment to nature.

GLOBAL CITIZENSHIP

The central defining characteristic of spirituality is an individual's sense of connection to a much greater whole. At its heart, spirituality involves an emotional experience of awe and reverence. As such, it's something that is highly desired, fervently sought, endlessly disagreed upon, and thoroughly fascinating.

The world we live in today is the world we know through scientific observation, a much different world from the classical world where Western civilization first emerged. At that time, there was greater continuity between religion, culture, and nature. Today, however, we are experiencing a discontinuity unequaled in its order of magnitude. That is why there is suspicion and misrepresentation among the religions of the present time and why we are experiencing new fundamentalisms: Islamic, Jewish, Christian, Buddhist, Hindu, and Shinto.

Fundamentalism is a defensive tactic. It is one reason why few of the religions of the world are dealing with the ecology issue on a widespread scale. They simply do not feel equipped to deal with this new challenge. By not accepting responsibility for the fate of the earth, there is a failure of religious responsibility to the divine, as well as to the human. We seem not to realize that as the outer world becomes damaged, our sense of the divine is degraded correspondingly.

Why did our ancestors have such a wonderful idea of God? Because they lived in an awesome world. They wondered at the magnificence of whatever it was that brought the world into being. This led to a sense of adoration. This adoration, this gratitude, we call religion. But now, as the outer world is diminished, our inner world is drying up.

Religion involves the sense of God, of the human, of creation, and of revelation. All of these aspects belong together, and they cannot be treated separately. We would have no sense of the divine without creation. Speculatively, we could talk about God as being prior to or outside creation or independent of creation, but in actual fact there is no such being as God without creation.

Pagans are seen as idolatrous because they worship the forces of nature and depict the divine in natural images and forms. But the divine always appears in some embodiment; no one ever worshiped matter as matter. Whatever is worshiped is seen as a mode of divine presence. Prior to the advent of monotheism, the divine was experienced by peoples generally as an all-pervasive presence of mysterious power in the universe. Biblical people drew together this all-pervasive presence in a transcendent, divine, personal creator related by covenant to a special people. People in the West, who inherited this outlook, gained a great deal, including a historical perspective, a sense of personal identity, and a sense of community. But they gradually lost the outer world, and when the outer world is lost, much of the inner world is lost as well.

Christianity allows for both the immanence and transcendence of God. The two polarities, however, must be maintained in tension. Excessive emphasis on the immanence of God can limit the divine to the range of purely natural phenomena. Excessive emphasis on the transcendence of God, however, can lead to apathy toward nature or even to misuse of its resources, thereby contributing to the destruction of the planet.

Of course, we have to recognize that immanence—this divine presence in creation—is understood differently in our present historical context than by our primal ancestors. Primal peoples related to nature immediately and intuitively; they simply observed and admired the natural world about them. Time was eternal—it moved in ever-renewing, seasonal cycles of change—and the universe existed as it always was and always would be. Humans could not really interfere with that or change it.

In the biblical world, however, a new sense of history came into being, an awareness that the universe emerged into being at a definite moment. Modern science, though it perceived the universe through a different set of intellectual lenses, with the aid of microscopic and telescopic instruments, reinforced the biblical perspective. Gradually, the Western world came to understand that the universe is not simply a given, and that it did indeed have a beginning in time. And time, we have discovered, is irreversible. Our modern scientific view of the universe thus coincides with the biblical realm rather than with the non-biblical world.

There is something very important about the origin of the universe as we now know it. The beginning of the universe, we now understand, involved articulated energy constellations bound together in an inseparable unity. The various parts of the universe, while outwardly differentiated, were once inwardly bonded together in a comprehensive intimacy of each particle with every other particle.

Ecotheologian Thomas Berry indicates that at the beginning of the universe there were two forces: an expansive force, which resulted in a diversification process, and an attractive or gravitational force, which pulled things together in profound intimacy. While this attraction that everything has for everything else is vital, nobody knows its nature. Isaac Newton (1642–1727), who noted the laws of gravitation, said he did not know what gravitation was, and to this day no one can tell us what gravitation is. But we do know that these antithetical forces, the attractive force and the explosive force, together constitute what is called the curvature of the universe. According to Berry, "Everything that exists comes into existence within this context, the curvature of space. If this rate of emergence had been a trillionth of a fraction faster or a trillionth of a fraction slower, the universe would have either exploded or collapsed. . . . If the attraction overcame the expansion, it would collapse. But if the expansion overcame the attraction, then it would explode."[1] Gravitation, built into this process, binds everything together so closely that nothing can ever be separated from anything else. Alienation, therefore, of one human from another or of humans from nature, is only a perception, for it is a cosmological impossibility.

As Berry points out, the other thing that is so important to this process is the relationship of origin: everything in the universe is derived from the same source. Science indicates that, and so does theology. If that is so, then everything in the universe is cousin to everything else. There is literally one family in the universe, one bonding. Community is not something we humans invented. And if the planet is a single community of existence, then all living beings are interconnected and all things are vital. In a universe where everything is related by origin, nothing is unimportant, nothing is marginal.

The current crisis of humanity is, in essence, a crisis of a lack of relationship. Humans are out of touch with themselves—with one another, with nature, with their past, with their future—but also with the Creator, the God of the universe. As this crisis grows, so does the yearning for relatedness. And that is the good news. Crisis precedes transformation and actually fuels or serves as a catalyst for transformation.

In the journey of life upon which we have all embarked, the most important task is to cultivate a sense of trust. Nothing will serve us better than a profound and ever deepening trust in the Creator, the sovereign power that keeps the vast panorama of universal existence moving along. Yes, the world is in poor shape, and many of its problems grow worse with each passing day. We must do what we can, but we must not fall into despair. If we focus on the big picture, we will realize that the universe is in a continual state of change. And we must remember that our planet is only a small part of the whole, that our crises are but fleeting instants in the eternity of time. There is perfection to the order and flow of this grand universe that is not absent from our tiny earth or our present time.

THE SACRAMENTAL SENSE OF REALITY

John F. Haught, professor of theology at Georgetown University, argues that when it is wholesome, religion maintains four components: sacramental, mystical, silent, and active. Each of these dimensions suggests a distinct

1. Cited in Dunn and Lonergan, *Befriending the Earth*, 14.

"way" of being religious, he argues, "but religion is most healthy and alive when it blends all four ways harmoniously. And it begins to dissolve into something other than 'religion' whenever any of the four aspects is isolated from contact with its three partners. In the actual world of religious life, such sundering of one aspect from the others is not unusual. But when this splintering occurs, religion rapidly decays into magic, escapism or obsession with esoteric teachings, or into cynicism, iconoclasm or vacuous activism."[2] When, on the other hand, religion concretely preserves the four components in a balanced way, it will function in an ecologically supportive way.

What fascinates me most about these aspects is the sacramental dimension. Religion is sacramental in the sense that it can speak of unspeakable mystery only through the use of symbols, or what theology calls sacraments. A sacrament, in its broadest sense, includes any object, person or event through which religious consciousness is awakened to the presence of sacred mystery. Historically, most of religion's sacraments have been closely related to nature. For example, the luminosity of sunshine, dawn, and dusk; the experience of wind or breath; the purifying power of clean water; the fertility of soil and life—all of these natural phenomena, and many more, have been used by religions to symbolize the way in which ultimate mystery affects us.

Since nature provides many of the fundamental sacraments of human religion, it is easy to see how the conservation of nature is indispensable for the survival of religion. If we lose the environment, we lose God as well. And it is equally true that when religion loses touch with its sacramental origins, it begins to grow indifferent to the natural world. A sacramental vision, Haught reminds us, makes nature, at least in a fragmentary way, transparent to divinity. In this sense it concedes to nature an inherent value without allowing it to become a substitute for God. According to this Christian perspective, nature is worth saving not because it is sacred, but because it is sacramental.

Of course, religion can exaggerate its sacramental side. It does so when it loses its association with mysticism, its essential polarity, as well as silence and action, another set of opposites that exists in a sort of tension with sacramentalism. When mysticism is lost, the sacrament becomes an end in itself, losing its symbolic value. But mysticism alone, if it diminishes the value of nature by looking exclusively beyond the natural order, can

2. Haught, *Promise of Nature*, 73–75.

decay into sheer escapism. Occasionally it has even gone to the extreme of hating the earth and everything natural. Mysticism and sacramentalism are necessary, as are silence and action, but they need to be delicately balanced. Mysticism dissociated from a vigorous sacramentalism promotes the doctrine of "cosmic homelessness," whereas sacramentalism without the mystical aspect of religion collapses into idolatry or pure naturalism (the view that nature is all there is).

In his book *The Luminous Dusk*, Professor Dale Allison explores the loss of wonder in Western society and its negative impact on our relationship to the cosmos. Arguing that early Christians favored the desert to the city, finding it natural to practice Christianity in solitude and silence, he laments that modern people forsook the wilderness and filled the cities. As a result, they have lost soul, for the closer humans came to themselves, the more cynical they became.

Allison mentions a poll of scientists taken some years ago, whose object was to gauge their belief in God. Although few acknowledged a belief in God, of those that did, there was a significantly higher percentage of cosmologists than biologists, and a significantly higher percentage of biologists than psychologists. The results led Allison to conclude that the closer one's profession takes one toward human beings, the less belief in God there is.[3]

REVISITING THE GRAIL QUEST

In the beginning God said, "Let it be," and from that fecund singularity emerged incredible diversity, resulting in a universe filled with galaxies containing trillions of stars. In one such galaxy, called the Milky Way, there evolved on a planet called earth millions of species, one of its species, *homo erectus*, proliferating into astonishing billions of human beings, further dividing into families, tribes, clans, nations, cultures, social classes, races, and religions.

As perception developed, human beings used senses, reason, and experience to divide and separate reality into component parts, using binary categories to categorize and distinguish one thing from another. Primal peoples and children, it seems, retain the ability to think holistically, to intuit and envision the original unity underlying reality, a quality many people recapture in old age. In the interim, however, beginning with puberty and continuing through adolescence and well into adult life, the

3. Allison, *Luminous Dusk*, 13.

primal unifying vision, corrupted by fear, stress, insecurity, and the need of security and success, became lost.

That, of course, is the meaning of the Grail, often associated with Christ's passion.[4] According to one Christian version, the Grail was brought from heaven by neutral angels. Envisioning a war in heaven between good and evil, God and Satan, one medieval writer built on biblical imagery to describe how some angelic hosts sided with Satan and others with God. In this sense, the Grail represents the unifying spiritual path between pairs of opposites such as fear and desire and good and evil.

The backdrop to the Grail quest is that the country, the land, indeed the whole territory of concern, has been laid waste. It is what life looks like when reality is viewed dualistically, the spiritual superseding the natural. The nature of this wasteland is a way of living characterized as inauthentic, where people do as they are told, living like those around them, conforming to the status quo, with little courage or imagination to be unique. It is a way of living selfishly, forever climbing the ladder of success, oblivious or immune to the needs and suffering of others. This is what T. S. Eliot spoke of in his poem *The Waste Land*.

The earliest surviving version of the Grail legend is *Perceval, le Conte del Graal*, composed about 1180 by Chrétien de Troyes, who declared that he adapted the tale from a book given to him by his benefactor Count Philip of Flanders, shortly before the departure of Count Philip for the Holy Land in 1190. The Grail quest, while inclusive and harmonious with the whole, adopts the resources of the whole to live authentically, with vision and courage. The Grail represents the fulfillment of the highest spiritual potentialities of the human consciousness.

In Chrétien's Grail romance, Perceval finds two kings in the Grail Castle, the Grail King and the Fisher King. The Grail King, clearly a God image, he sees only briefly but describes as "the most beautiful person he ever beheld." Perceval never sees the Grail King again, but he cannot forget what he saw. In the outer chamber of the castle is the wounded king. His name is Anfortas, from an old French word meaning Infirmity or "without strength." The two kings are the two parts of the human soul, the godly part and the broken part. The godly king is the one that holds the castle together, that accepts the gospel, that always says "Yes" to God. The broken king is

---

4. The Grail quest is the subject of chapters 10 and 11 of my book, *Walking on Water*. Some ideas are repeated in this segment either as review for readers of that book or to provide perspective for new readers.

the part that feels obsessed, neurotic, and sick. Both parts are in us. The hero's task is not only to discover his True Self, but also to bring the two kings, the two parts, together.

As a young man, the Fisher King, like all adolescents, exhibits great potential, but he has not yet earned the position of King. He rides forth from his castle with the cry "Amor!," appropriate for youth, but not for the guardianship of the Grail. As he rides forth, a pagan knight emerges from the woods. The two level their lances at one another and attack. The lance of the Fisher King kills the pagan, but the pagan's lance castrates the Fisher King.

What this means is that religious and rationalistic dualism—highlighted by the Christian separation of matter and spirit, of secular and sacred life, of natural and supernatural grace—has castrated Western civilization. The European and American mind and life, as it were, have been emasculated by the separation. Vital spirituality, which results from the union of matter and spirit, has been killed. This, for me, is one of the insights of the nursery rhyme, "Humpty Dumpty sat on a wall, / Humpty Dumpty had a great fall. / All the king's horses / And all the king's men, / Couldn't put Humpty together again." While the original meaning may have alluded to the death of England's King Richard III, whose brutal reign ended in 1485, or to a large cannon that fell from a castle parapet and shattered, Humpty Dumpty is often drawn as an egg and interpreted as a symbolic reference to human or social fragility. Viewed spiritually, human brokenness can only be healed by integrating matter and spirit.

In the Grail romance, the pagan represents Nature, a person from the suburbs of Eden and thus an idealization of spirituality and union. On the head of his lance is written the word "Grail," which is to say, that nature intends the Grail, intends authenticity, integration, and wholeness. Spiritual life is not an add-on to life, not a supernatural virtue imposed upon it, but the flowering and fulfillment of human life. The sense of the Grail is that Nature intends the Grail; the impulses of nature are what give authenticity to life, not rules imposed from an alien supernatural authority. Nature and spirit yearn for one other, and the Grail legends long for the union once again of what has been divided. The Grail is a reminder of the original singularity from which all life emerged, and our job—the task of those on the Grail quest—is to take God's original "Let It Be" and find ways to participate in the evolutionary fallout of creation by living, thinking, and proclaiming that message in our own experience.

The Grail quest symbolizes an authentic life that is lived imaginatively and uniquely, in terms of its own volition, a way of thinking and living that carries itself midway between the opposites of good and evil, light and dark, wounded and healed. When Perceval, naïve yet noble of heart, comes to the Grail Castle, he meets the Fisher King, who is brought in on a litter, wounded yet kept alive simply by the presence of the Grail.

The court fool had prophesied long before that the Fisher King would be healed when an innocent fool arrived in the court and asked a specific question. It may shock us that a fool should have to undertake such a crucial role. However, what the myth is telling us is that only the naïve part of our being will heal and cure our Fisher King wound. It also tells us why the Fisher King cannot heal himself, and why, when he goes fishing, his pain is eased though not cured. For people to be truly healed, they must allow something entirely different from themselves to enter their consciousness and change them. They cannot be healed if they remain in the old Fisher King mentality. That is why the young fool part of ourselves must enter our life if we are to be cured. We must look to a foolish, innocent, part of ourselves for our cure. Many legends put our cure in the hands of a fool or someone most unlikely to carry healing power. The inner fool—someone or something most unlikely to carry healing power—is the only one who can touch our Fisher King wound.

Perceval enters the Grail Castle and beholds the wounded King. His compassion moves him to ask, "What ails you?," but he fails to ask the question because he had been taught by mentors that a knight does not ask personal or unnecessary questions. So he follows the rules, and the adventure fails. It takes Perceval years of ordeals, setbacks, and embarrassments (his entire adolescence, it seems), before he returns to the castle and asks the question that heals the King and heals society. The question is an expression of compassion, not of legalism, political correctness, or religious propriety. Compassion is the natural opening of the human heart to another, but it is also the inner fool healing his own Fisher King wound.[5]

The wasteland results when the rules and boundaries of the first half of life keep us locked in immature adolescent patterns, preventing us from our authentic second half of life. We humans live in two worlds, not only ideologically, but also developmentally. We live in the external world, the socialized world given to us by others, and we live in our own inner world.

---

5. Perhaps this is what Jesus meant when he spoke the proverb, "Doctor, cure yourself!" (Luke 4:23).

Spirituality helps us achieve a harmonious relationship between these polarities. As members of society, we must learn to live by the rules of society. However, we cannot allow the external to control the internal. The internal world must be valued and nurtured as well, even if this impetus violates the expectations of others.

When we ponder the Grail quest, many dualities come to mind, including social, psychological, cosmological, philosophical, and religious. Those acquainted with the history of Christianity are aware that during its first five centuries, there were many Christianities, many ways of being Christian. Eventually, in the late fourth century, the only religion allowed in the Roman empire was the Christian religion, wedded to the remnants of Roman imperialism in what became known as Christendom. The West's conversion to Christianity required the demise of paganism, and with it, the demise of nonduality as a way of thinking and living.

One of the interesting aspects of the Grail legends as we remember them is that they developed about five centuries after Christianity was imposed upon Europe. Properly understood, these legends represent a coming together of two traditions, Celtic pagan and non-Celtic Christian traditions, an amalgam not unlike the earlier Canaanite pagan and Israelite traditions, or the later Judeo-Christian and Greco-Roman synthesis.

THIN PLACES

The way back to the biblical Garden, to the underlying unity and harmony of the universe, requires us to become co-creators with God, to embody God's creative "Let It Be" program, thus becoming citizens of God's eternal kingdom. To return to the Garden, to become what Jesus called kingdom people or what Paul called co-heirs with Christ, we need to rediscover liminality, the creative, rejuvenating spirituality that lies both within and beyond time and space. Liminality often presents itself to us in times of silence, meditation, and rest, sometimes in the still of the night, but more often at twilight or dawn, in times and places that transcend locality and temporality, singularities known as "thin places." According to the biblical record, Jesus went to deserted places to pray, doing so regularly (see Matt 14:23; Luke 5:16; 6:12; 9:28; 22:39–46). As we discover, the times and places may change throughout our life. Liminality requires flexibility, even spontaneity. However, engaging with liminality is not about lacking focus or being lazy. This is holy work; at stake is our salvation.

"Thin places," a metaphor taken from Celtic spirituality, refers to places, objects, events, persons, and other phenomena that are understood as being transparent to the divine. The concept has its home in an understanding of reality that affirms at least two layers or dimensions of reality: (a) the visible world of ordinary experience and (b) the sacred, understood as the source of all things but also as a presence interpenetrating everything. In "thin places" the boundary between the two levels becomes diaphanous and permeable.[6]

As "places" of beauty, fascination, and intrigue, thin places stir the imagination; as "places" of honesty and courage, where truth and justice prevail, they call us to action and selfless service; as "places" of conviction, inspiration, and empowerment, they challenge us to transformation; as "places" of insight, wisdom, and discernment, they call us to spiritual renewal.

Thin places are paradoxical: they are places of power and weakness; they provide weal and woe, bliss and pain; they are found in crosses and cancers but also in resurrection and remission; they may be ordinary, or extraordinary; sometimes they delight us, other times they perplex us; they are places of wonder but also of terror. When they surround us, we are enraptured, and when they fade, we experience despair. Thin places fuel the imagination, foster risk-taking, feed the spirit, and foment human transformation. They have the ability to alter our way of thinking, transform our character, and renew our souls.

Why do they intrigue us? Why do they grip us like a vice? In his influential study, *The Idea of the Holy*, Rudolph Otto put forth the view that religious experience relies upon a deep sense of the "numinous." Coined from the Latin *numen* (holy, sacred), the term expresses a natural human response to the experience of the sacred developed prior to rational and moral notions about it. Experiencing the numinous as ultimate mystery, people feel a strong sense of awe and reverence. The holy is also *fascinans* (fascinating); it exerts an irresistible attraction because it is recognized as profoundly familiar and essential to humanity. The experience of the sacred has always involved wonder and fascination.

Thin places are liminal spaces—in-between spaces, windows, doorways, thresholds, intersections, portals, transitions—that usher us from one state or space to another. They signify boundaries, beginnings, and becomings that open the way to something new, expanding our awareness

6. Borg, *Meaning of Jesus*, 250.

and providing unity to our reality. For Christians they encompass activities, events, persons, objects, and experiences by which the Father speaks, in which Christ is present, and through which the breath of the Spirit blows freest. Thin places are transparent to the divine because God is there: through-and-around-and-over-and-under-and-behind-and-before-and-within them.

C. S. Lewis, one of the twentieth century's foremost Christian authors, knew about "thin places." He wrote about them in the *Chronicles of Narnia*, a set of seven children's classics in which he created a land of wonder and enchantment called Narnia. Following this publication, Lewis rigorously defended the fairy tale against those who claimed that it gives a false conception of life. The fairy tale, he argued, like the myth, arouses longing for more ideal worlds but at the same time gives the real world a new depth. While Lewis's Narnia *Chronicles* remind us of other works, such as the Alice-in-Wonderland-like opening of *The Lion, the Witch and the Wardrobe* or the voyage made by the *Dawn Treader*, which is akin to the voyage of Odysseus, Lewis blends Christian themes with events created from the rich world of fantasy. A dominant idea in his stories is that of an earlier time when reality was more harmonious and unified. It was Lewis's hope that upon reading these stories, children (and adults) would return to the "real world" with a new perspective, their minds opened to the possibilities of an unseen spiritual world and to the limits of merely human intellect and undeveloped imagination.

Lewis was referring to "thin places" without using the term. He knew, as children of all ages discover when they read his Narnia *Chronicles* or J. K. Rowling's Harry Potter books, that our world is alive with liminalities (threshold spaces between the sacred and the mundane); pictures, closets, fireplaces, train stations—any object, event, or person can open our minds to the possibilities and transport us to an unseen spiritual world.

While we are intrigued by the proverb, "Physician, heal thyself," what does it mean? How can we heal ourselves? The answer, at least in part, is this; we need to find sacred time and sacred place, meaning, we need to discover liminality. While liminality can best be experienced in silence and times of rest such as daydreaming, gazing, pondering, meditating, worshipping, singing, and individual and small-group Bible study, it can also be experienced in creative arts such as music, painting, and writing, and through activities such as yoga, tai chi, gardening, swimming, kayaking, cross-country skiing, hiking, running, cycling, and numerous other rhythmic and aerobic activities that ground and connect us with the larger whole. Anything therapeutic is holistic, for what is good for the body is good for the mind, and what is healthy for the body and mind connects us to the soul and spirit within. Such interaction, even in its initial stages, enhances spirituality, for spirituality is at work in all holistic endeavors.

To explain liminality, the ancient Greeks told the story of Apollo and Daphne, a myth retold by Hellenistic and Roman authors. Apollo, the Greek sun god, was also a great warrior. At one point he mocks Eros, the god of love, for his use of bow and arrow, as Apollo was also the patron of archery. Bragging about his own skills, Apollo insults Eros, who retaliates by preparing two arrows, one made of gold and the other of lead. Shooting Apollo with the gold arrow, Eros instills in him a passionate love for the river nymph Daphne. Subsequently, he shoots Daphne with the lead arrow, instilling in her a dislike for Apollo.

Having taken after Apollo's sister, Artemis, Daphne spurns her many potential lovers, preferring instead woodland sports and solitude in the forest. Ignoring her dedication to perpetual virginity, her father, the river god Peneus, pressures her to marry and give him grandchildren. She, however, begs her father to let her remain unmarried, and he eventually complies.

Apollo, enamored by Eros's arrow, follows her, chasing her repeatedly while never able to catch her. They are evenly matched in the race until Eros intervenes, helping Apollo gain the advantage. Seeing that Apollo is about to reach her, Daphne calls upon her father for help, whereupon she is transformed into a laurel tree. Apollo, despondent in love, uses his powers of eternal youth and immortality to render Daphne evergreen.

While later authors fashioned this story into an amorous tale, it was originally a myth, not about love between the gods, but about a daily ritual in nature, Apollo, the persistent sun, chasing Daphne, the elusive dawn. While we can interpret the myth as a phenomenon of nature, it also speaks of liminal time (dawn and twilight) and space (thin places), and of the longing for union not only between male and female, but also between heaven and earth, the secular with the sacred.

QUESTIONS FOR DISCUSSION AND REFLECTION

1. While the world's current ecological state is perilous, there are no easy answers, if any. If there is a spiritual solution (beyond the apocalypse), what might it be?

2. In your estimation, is there any connection between global citizenship (humans profoundly committed to one another) and our commitment to nature? If so, how are these commitments related to spirituality?

3. Explain and assess the merits of religious fundamentalism, if any.

4. Explain what ecotheologian Thomas Berry meant by "the curvature of the universe," and what this teaches about global citizenship.

5. Explain what John Haught meant by a sacramental sense of reality. How can such a perspective be gained, and how lost?

6. In this chapter, what did you learn about the Grail quest?

7. In your own words, explain the concept of a wasteland in the context of the Grail quest.

8. In the Grail quest, explain the positive correlation between Christianity and paganism.

9. Explain and assess the merits of the concept of "thin places." How is "liminality" important to spirituality?

10. In your estimation, what is the primary insight gained from this chapter? Explain your answer.

Part II

SPIRITUALITY
AND THE ARTS

Chapter 6

THE POWER OF POETRY

ART IS A BROAD AND ambiguous word. Is art a painting, a clay pot, or a photograph? Is art a poem, a short story, or a novel? Is art dance, a musical composition, or a set of lyrics? Is art a play, a movie, or a theatre production? The answer, of course, is yes. But what about a mathematical theory or equation, or a chemical compound or an alloy? Is it art when a scientist finds a new way of understanding something, or when a doctor finds a cure? Art is a process as well as a product; it finds expression in creation. Art is the meeting of mind and soul, head and heart. There are no limits to art, for art is the place where the rational mind meets the subconscious, where the natural meets the supernatural.

Defining art is like defining love, or God. Perhaps it is time to put all three debates to rest and concede that, in all three cases, we are trying to define absolutes using relative terms. To do so is to end up with questions answerable only with more questions, with definitions only expressed in negatives: art is not this, love is not that, and God is never this or that. Another approach is to produce an endless list of attributes that never get at the essence of something, but simply help us to wrap our limited minds around concepts that arise from deeper levels of consciousness, that of spirit, not of mind.

All art is communication. To a painter or sculptor, the canvas, clay, marble, or bronze is the paper; their brushes and chisels are the pens and ink; and shapes, colors, and textures are their words. When these "words" are assembled, arranged, and given form, something emerges that we call their art. To the writer or poet, the paper is a blank canvas, and the words are the colors and shapes arranged and formed by the writer's brush or chisel. To the musical composer, the notes and lyrics are the words, and the canvas is the instrument, the orchestra, or the singers. Likewise the playwright has the stage for a canvas, with lights and scenery, dialogue, costume, music and dance as colors and shapes to combine into coherent forms. The actors provides life for the characters, interpreting their characters holistically. Dancers or choreographers can be the most spiritual of all artists, for they use every part of the human being—body, mind, soul, and spirit—to create poetry or tell a story, painting their picture with movement, props, and costumes, becoming, through their skill, the art form itself. Artistry occurs when artists are able to translate their spiritual consciousness to others on a level that transcends the medium, the technique, even the limits of human expression and comprehension. Great artists communicate an understanding of aspects of the human experience that cannot be expressed through ordinary means.

Art is holistic and integrative, each art form a slice of the pie, a piece of the whole. Fragmenting reality into bits and pieces, isolating and separating things into unrelated parts, is not, of course, a modern invention, but we moderns have become adept at fragmentation and specialization. Think, for instance, of how we view cosmology. Until recently, we lived in a universe; now, however, we live in a multiverse. This change is also reflected in how we view higher education. Prior to the 1950s and '60s, we were educated in universities; now, however, we attend multiversities.[1] Though often confused or conflated, the approaches are distinct. Their difference is based on contrasting views of reality. The traditional view, that of the university, arose at a time when the world was believed to be a coherent whole—a universe.[2]

Within that unified worldview, the aim of scholarship was to describe reality and all its aspects coherently, so that although scholarship was specialized, the various disciplines were seen as coherently related, united by their common reference to unified values. Parts of reality could be studied individually, that is, described as accurately and fully as possible, but always in relation to the whole, of which they were members. No part was thought

1. The term "multiversity" was coined by Clark Kerr in his 1963 book, *The Uses of the University*. The relation between the word "university" and "universe" is more accidental than deliberate, for originally the word "university" meant a whole unit or single community engaged in practice, and only gradually a scholarly community.

2. McCully, "Multiversity and University," 514–15.

to be fully intelligible by itself, in isolation from the whole, because in reality all things were related. Taken together, the disciplines comprehensively explained all reality, as it was known. That, at least, was the ideal pursued by the scholarly community.

In scholarly communities, teachers and students would individually and jointly pursue various interests, and would attempt, at least occasionally, to refer their conclusions formally and systematically to their colleagues and to the entire community, that is, the university of learning. Discoveries in one field would be tested not only with respect to that field, but also with respect to the others. Cross-fertilization and inter-departmental collaboration was a common occurrence. Because achievements in one field could be brought to bear on other fields, the whole body of scholarship would be raised to a higher order and power. The educational program of the university was liberal education—meaning education that was all-embracing or universal in emphasis; its aim was the full development of one's human potential. In Greco-Roman times, the education was called "liberal" because it was worthy of free individuals, by contrast with the "mechanical arts," viewed as more appropriate to slaves, who simply did as they were told.

During the Middle Ages, John of Salisbury, a leading scholar of the twelfth century, wrote that the liberal arts were the primary aid to those who loved wisdom (philosophy), and that students in the liberal arts were to be elevated to understand all things, empowered to solve problems on their own rather than to rely on the help of others to understand the meaning of books or to find solutions to questions that arose. Such people were free, thus, in that they were intellectually self-reliant.

During the twelfth century, in a span of some eighty years, four great universities were founded in Europe: Bologna in 1119, Paris in 1150, Oxford in 1167, and Cambridge in 1200. The thirteenth century, however, has been called the most Christian in history, for it expanded that foundation. With the building of great cathedrals came a new emphasis of education. Since cathedrals (churches of the bishops) were located in cities, their schools to train parish priests were in time opened to all. The great cathedrals gave birth to medieval universities, for the supreme task of the university was to understand and explain God's revealed truth. During this period, worship came to be understood as more than an act, and liturgy as more than ritual; together they were a way of life, requiring the totality of one's being, body and soul, heart and mind.

The curriculum of the cathedral school began with grammar, rhetoric, logic, arithmetic, geometry, music, and astronomy—the seven liberal arts—and then moved on to the advanced study of law or theology, the professional schools that prepared leaders for church and state. The first part of the liberal arts was the *trivium* (grammar, logic, and rhetoric), followed by the *quadrivium* (arithmetic, geometry, music, and astronomy). To this should be added philosophy, regarded as the entry point into theology.

In strong contrast to both the university and to liberal education stand its modern descendants, the multiversity and its programs of general and specialized education. When Clark Kerr coined the term "multiversity" in 1963, he meant to suggest that modern American institutions of higher learning are composed not of one community but of many, whose interests are varied and even conflicting, whose interrelations are procedural rather than substantive. Knowledge, under this new understanding, is fragmented, and scholarship is divided into specialized and autonomous departments. This disintegration replaces the traditional university of learning, which attempted to describe the world as a coherent whole, by describing the world as fragmented and compartmentalized into divisions such as arts, humanities, business and economics, and the social and physical sciences and further subdivided into specific disciplines of study. The final legacy of the university tradition, liberal education, has become general education, relying on the ancient liberal arts while replacing variety for coherence, which is no longer viewed as feasible.

While the multiversity is here to stay, we need to find ways to strengthen and revitalize its "liberal" core. Our desperate need for a modern understanding that the world is one—for unity as a nation and as individuals in the world—must be harmonized with our respect for uniqueness, variety, and diversity. Only by combining the old and the new, the university with the multiversity, the communal with the individual, the spiritual with the secular, can we rediscover the moral and spiritual core of reality to guide and inspire us, to make us more fully human.

In our age of specialization and sub specialization, we distinguish between fields of study such as the fine arts and the humanities, although in academia, the arts have traditionally been considered part of the humanities. They certainly have similarities. For example, both utilize *logos* (logic, analysis, and reason) and *mythos* (fantasy, imagination, and myth), two forms of knowing associated with right- and left-brain thinking, though the arts generally focus on practice and the humanities more on theory and analysis. Should they be distinguished? This is not a debate we can or should attempt to solve, but it is interesting to raise the question, especially from the perspective of spirituality, which focuses on wholeness, inclusivity, and integration.

When we think of the fine arts or of creative art in general, most of us think about painting or perhaps music. But what about literature in general, or poetry? Aren't they equally creative, similarly artistic? While classification is always questionable, contemporary thinking groups seven disciplines as fine arts: painting, sculpture, architecture, music, theatre, dance, and literary arts (including fiction, drama, poetry, and prose), to which can be added cinematography, photography, textiles and fashion, culinary arts, communication, and oral storytelling, among other emerging fields, and seven arts in the humanities, including history, linguistics, literature, religion, philosophy, ethics, and logic, including those aspects of social sciences that have humanistic content and employ humanistic methods, such as archaeology, anthropology, area studies, classical studies, sociology, and jurisprudence. These employ skill and imagination to produce objects, performances, convey insights and experiences, and construct new environments and spaces. The practice of modern art is a testament to shifting boundaries, improvisation, experimentation, and questioning that art must undergo. As both a means of expression and as ends in themselves, the arts can be equally pragmatic and creative, simultaneously responsive to the world and expressive of our inner values and goals. As noted in the preface, ancient Greeks gave this considerable thought, approaching the matter mythologically through the concept of the Muses, who were nine in number. Together, they inspired not only poetry, music, and dance, but history and astronomy as well.

The arts encompass not only multiple and diverse modes of thinking, but also of doing and being as well. While expressive in nature, they often require sustained study, training, and theorizing within each tradition. Together, they are a vehicle through which human beings cultivate distinct social, cultural, and individual identities, while transmitting values, impressions, judgments, ideas, visions, meanings, experiences, and patterns of life.

THE ARTS AND SPIRITUALITY

As all arts and sciences are interrelated, so also all of us are interrelated, sharing a language of spirit that connects us at the most primal level. The artist seeks to tear down the barriers imposed by the limitations of language, thereby relating to the underlying spiritual sense of form present in all of us. By giving form to the formless, extracting the essence of the absolute, and providing us forms and symbols to represent those inexpressible but substantial concepts, the artist is a channel for the divine; ideally, God's interpreter.

Art is spirituality, and spirituality is art; the two cannot be distinguished. If art doesn't express a spiritual idea, then it is a craft, and not art! Among many interests and concerns, art seeks to represent the absolute. While we cannot define the absolute, we can, at least, define its absoluteness, and suggest what it is not. Emily Dickinson, among others, frequently employed negative simile and metaphor—"this is not." Son of a Baptist minister, the painter Malcolm Parcell represented God as a closed box in the sky in one of his works, effectively communicating the mystery of the divine, indescribable rationally yet achieving expression in the arts. Like the mystery of love, the mystery of God is beyond our capacity to comprehend. Human beings may be unable to look directly on God's face, but art grants us glimpses of God's back.

On many levels, the arts cohere, for in a cumulative sense, they transform abstract sensation into expressible form. Artists are creators, giving life to their characters, scenes, and compositions. In this respect, art is both mother and midwife, active in the birthing process. The artist creates and breathes life into new creatures, for an artistic creation is a living creature. The true artist possesses a vision and is able to translate that vision so others can share it. But where does that vision originate? If we say that we are created in the image of God, then we can become creators as well. As humans, one of our greatest gifts is the ability to share in the ongoing creative stream. Art can be both a means for God to speak and a sacramental vehicle whereby artists and their audience can become unified with God and one another in a sacred act of creation.

When materialism, power, and success narrow the areas of our concern, poetry reminds us of the depth and richness of our existence. If by spirituality we mean the incorporeal—the unseen essence of all we believe, hope, and experience—then we are speaking of that which is vital and central to human life. Spirit literally means breath, wind, and air. As such, spirit includes our thoughts, feelings, desires, and our creativity. Spirituality is the animating principle that gives us life, who we are on the inside.

The arts, it seems, are a two-way street, for they give voice to one's spirit while also acting as a means of stimulus for that spirit, equally a vehicle of expression and of sustenance. Over the years, spirituality has been the subject of songs, plays, novels, and musical compositions, but poetry has been the most effective way to explore and express spirituality. Many have found this to be true in the poetry of the Sufi mystic Rumi, whose spirituality centered on love. Known as "the Bridge," Rumi captured the bliss of spirituality found in love, compassion, meditation, and nature.

As we learn from archaeology, art has been a feature of every civilization, and poetry has been integral to art and culture since the inception of writing. The reason for its ubiquity is that poetry, like music and art, has been composed to express what is both knowable and unknowable. Poetry is a form of communication. If we want precise information, we resort to straightforward or direct speech, the sort of language we find in essays, news reporting, and scientific journals, whereas if we want to communicate attitudes, feelings, and interpretations, we might resort to metaphor, myth, and poetry. Both communicate information, but in each case, the subject and means of communication differ significantly. Art doesn't represent reality as such, but rather perceived reality.

For example, when a factually minded individual wishes to pledge commitment to his beloved, he might say, "I love you," whereas when a romantically minded person wishes to convey affection to her beloved, she might say, "My love is like a red, red rose." For a literalist, red is red, but for a lover, red becomes a red rose, something real, alive and dynamic. To the skilled artist, the red rose may not even be a rose; it may be a coded reference to secrecy or beauty. Because poetry is an art form, it extends beyond speech to include the vision and voice of the artist. As art goes beyond reality, giving color and shape to vision and perception, so poetry uses words to express what words alone cannot express. Lyrics can be poetry, as in the work of artists such as Stevie Nicks or Bob Dylan. Musical notes, likewise, conjure colors and shapes, language and movement; musicians such as Duke Ellington and Louis Armstrong regularly created poetry with musical notes.

POETRY: ITS NATURE AND PURPOSE

Poetry is the language of the soul, not of the mind. Poetry is language that emerges through the mind, but it originates in the soul. Poetry best expresses our inner self because poetry compresses profound meaning into a few words. Poetry can be put to song, stir the imagination, and used as a form of prayer; it can provoke, entertain, and even heal. Poetry taps into the universal flow; creating depth, it also connects us to something transcendent, to nature, and to the universal whole.

Poetry is a powerful form of expression that gets to the heart of life's issues. Poetry reaches deep within us to confront and answer questions about the meaning of life. Part of what makes us who we are is our experiences, both past, present, and future. This experience connects us with poetry, because poets write to convey those experiences.

While there are many definitions of poetry, perhaps Emily Dickinson defined it best, "If I read a book and it makes my body so cold no fire ever can warm me, I know that is poetry." As generally understood, poetry is a form of literature that uses aesthetics and often rhythmic qualities of language to evoke meaning, awareness or experience, or emotional response. Such definitions may be helpful, but in the end, what best defines poetry is its unwillingness to be defined.

Poetry has been described as "chiseled marble of language" and likened to a painted canvas, only the poet uses words instead of paint, and the reader as canvas. One of the most definable elements of the poetic form is its economy of language. As in all effective communication, careful selection of words for conciseness and clarity is essential. However, poets go beyond this, considering a word's emotive qualities, its etymology and use, its musical value, its double- and triple-entendres, and even its spatial relationship to the phrase, line, or sentence.

Unlike prose, poetry often has an underlying purpose that goes beyond the literal. Poetry is evocative, typically provoking in the reader intense emotion. Poetry has the ability to surprise the reader by providing revelation, insight, and deeper understanding of elemental beauty and truth. As John Keats said, "Beauty is truth. Truth, beauty. That is all ye know on earth and all ye need to know." To borrow a phrase, "Poetry is a riddle wrapped in an enigma." An ever evolving genre, poetry shirks definition at every turn, for like all creative arts, it is kept alive through continual evolution.

Let us not forget, poetry is meant to be recited. When recited, it unites language with music, the rhythm, meter, spacing, and punctuation all parts of a musical score for the instrument that is the spoken word. Some prose can be read as poetry. For example, Dylan Thomas's "A Child's Christmas in Wales" was intended to be read aloud, and it comes alive when read with proper inflection and enunciation. The storyteller's art predates the written word, and possesses a special magic all its own. This is the art of the bards and of Greek theatre, both forms equally inspiring and inspired. With poets of all backgrounds and nationalities writing poetry today, your study of poetry need never end, especially if you find someone's work that sends electricity up your spine. Who knows, perhaps you might write such poetry yourself!

EXPERIENCING POETRY

Poetry is one of life's greatest mentors. It has much to teach us, not only about our world and others, but also about our lives, hopes, fears, joys, and experiences. It also has much to teach us about reality, those parts we find accessible and particularly those we find inaccessible, such as our soul's intimacy with God.

Reading poetry is easier for some people than for others. While most people are intrigued by poetry, having studied it in school and having memorized poems in part or in whole, many of us find poetry confusing, even inexplicable. Part of this frustration comes from our modern sense of impatience, combined with our need for instant gratification. Surrounded by instant information, instant news, even instant entertainment, we avoid confusion, uncertainty, and silence, elements congenial to poetry.

A helpful way to read poetry is meditatively, as we read scripture. In this regard, a reading approach with a long history of practice in the Christian tradition is called Lectio Divina, a simple yet profound way of engaging the scriptures that transcends mental processing. Those who utilize this approach today emphasize a meditative, not a scholarly or literary approach, with the intention of learning what God has to say to us about the true meaning of life for themselves and for the world. In Lectio Divina, one works intensely with a short scriptural passage (or poem) following four distinct steps called *lectio, meditatio, oratio,* and *contemplatio.* While these steps are usually presented as sequential, seasoned practitioners often experience them as circular, with the steps unfolding in any order.

1. *Lectio* (reading). Read the poem or text slowly and attentively, pausing for a moment of silence before reading the passage again. The point of *lectio* is to gain an initial impression.

2. *Meditatio* (reflection). In the second step, engage with the poem through focused mental reflection, using reason, imagination, memory, and emotions to work with the text. The process may differ with each poem. Sometimes the poem may trigger a memory, or it might stimulate your thinking through a certain term, phrase, or compelling image. The point of *meditatio* is analytical, but in a way that allows the poem to resonate with your own heart.

3. *Oratio* (prayer). In this step, engage with the text through the feelings it produces or memories that might arise. As feelings arise, ponder them quietly, insightfully. If possible, you may shape your feelings into a prayer, using words of petition, gratitude, or concern. This is the moment when, in Paul's words, the Spirit prays within you. A prayer, of course, doesn't have to be in words; the feelings themselves can be the prayer. If the poem causes no such response, do not to force a response but simply move to the next step. The point of *oratio* is emotional response.

4. *Contemplatio* (contemplation). This step in the mystical tradition denotes "resting in God." At this stage, suspend all mental and emotional activity and simply "abide" or "rest" in the fullness of the experience. The point of *contemplatio* is to allow the poem to work on you subconsciously, that is, below the level of your conscious mind.

Devoting half an hour a day to this practice, or even half an hour several times a week, will produce dramatic difference in your understanding of poetry. Like lyrics of songs, words and images that arise during one's time of "experiencing" poetry will percolate beneath the activities of your day, shaping what you see and do in remarkable ways. Incidentally, the poem you read need not be long. Some readers focus on a sentence or a single word—sometimes for days—until the poem reveals its hidden treasure. If you have time, begin Lectio Divina by applying it to the following poem by Emily Dickinson: "Few, yet enough, / Enough is One - / To the ethereal throng / Have not each one of us the right / To Stealthily belong?" (no. 1639).[3]

---

3. The numbering system I use for Dickinson's poems follows R. W. Franklin's authorized version, *The Poems of Emily Dickinson*. This version, which appeared in 1998,

Imagine yourself, bound in time, space, and individuality, united with God and all reality. Take a few moments to experience this unity alone, in the privacy of your "special" space; then experience it in a crowded space, surrounded by others. Experience this unity at dawn and at sunset, in a quiet walk on a sunny day and while walking in the rain or in stormy conditions. Then imagine God, unbound by time and space, experiencing immediately and eternally each of us and all reality simultaneously. Now try experiencing nature that way, communing with animal and plant life as God does, fully, reverently, creatively, lovingly. Engaging poetry's liberating and unitive possibilities is experiencing spirituality.

THE FIVE VOICES OF POETRY

In our time, it is common for each person to think of him/herself as having "voice," that is, of having valid perspectives and opinions that merit attention. In this respect, we also think of poets and authors in general as having voice, that is, of speaking with power and conviction. In previous eras, however, poets were not recognized for their "voice," but rather for their "thought." In his "Essay on Criticism" (1711), in which we find the famous lines, "To err is human, to forgive divine," and "Fools rush in where angels fear to tread," Alexander Pope famously described the poet's task as that of producing "What oft was thought but ne'er so well expressed." The poet's task, in Pope's time, was to make consensus memorable through the expressive power of genius, not to substitute his or her individual voice or intention for those of convention.

Since Pope's time, poetry as thought was gradually supplanted by poetry as voice, until, in the twentieth century, poets as diverse as Robert Frost and William Carlos Williams would have found themselves in agreement on little other than the idea of poetry as the presentation of individual voice. In "The Three Voices of Poetry," written for the National Book League Annual Lecture of 1953, Anglo-American author T. S. Eliot attributed three voices to poetry: (1) the first voice is the voice of the poet talking to him/herself—or to nobody; (2) the second voice is the voice of the poet addressing an audience, offering a message; (3) the third voice is the poet creating a dramatic character to address social issues.[4] These days, with the exception

---

restored Dickinson's order, unusual punctuation, and spelling choices.

4. In the remainder of this chapter and in chapter 7, we examine Eliot as exemplifying the second poetic voice and Emily Dickinson and Elizabeth Barrett Browning the first

of opera, there is little of contemporary verse drama in the United States, while the domain of Eliot's first voice has expanded considerably. The private voice is common in poetry today. Is it possible that poetry began to lose its audience not when poets began talking to themselves or to no one in particular—poets have always done that—but when they began doing it as though there was no other choice?

While I find Eliot's essay illuminating, I wonder if there are not more than three poetic voices. Perhaps we should speak of a fourth voice, the poet's subconscious inner voice, itself infusing the other voices but hardly detectable or knowable to the poet, for it works beneath the poet's cognitive grasp or possession. This voice may be likened to that of scripture, "sharper than any two-edged sword," as the author of Hebrews states, "piercing until it divides soul from spirit, joints from marrow" (Heb 4:12). This, to me, is poetry's subliminal power, its most compelling voice.

Thinking about voice allows me to approach poetry with greater openness, with anticipation and even with reverence. As Eliot reminds us, "If you complain that a poet is obscure, and apparently ignoring you, the reader, or that he is speaking only to a limited circle of initiates from which you are excluded—remember that what he may have been trying to do, was to put something into words which could not be said in any other way, and therefore in a language which may be worth the trouble of learning."

When reading poems like Eliot's *The Waste Land* or *The Four Quartets*, poems difficult to read, I can't help but feel a deeper appreciation for his third and fourth voices, the openness to multiplicity and polyphony that they represent. These poems, while long and complex, show Eliot attempting to swallow life's meaning and message, not because he is able to digest them, but because he is voraciously hungry, curiously perceptive, and humanly incomplete. Perhaps Eliot felt, for all his verbal experimentation, that even his most evocative poetry had failed to break out of his first or second voice, that he was not fully able to write even in his third voice. Perhaps even the construct of dramatic plot and characterization cannot truly escape the soul's point of view.

In addition to these four voices of poetry, a fifth voice must also be acknowledged, the voice awakened in the reader. In his 1933 essay, *The Use of Poetry and the Use of Criticism*, Eliot spoke at length of his poem *The Waste Land*, discovering special authority in his own poetry, noting that "the poet does many things upon instinct, for which he can give no better

and third voices respectively.

account than anyone else." Noting that his intention in *The Waste Land* had remained undetected by the critics, he declared that "what a poem means is as much what it means to others as what it means to the author; and indeed, in the course of time a poet may become merely a reader in respect to his own work, forgetting his original meaning—or without forgetting, merely changing."[5]

Regardless of whether we believe in the possibilities of a poet's fourth or fifth voice, it seems evident that awareness of poetic voice allows readers to explore new ways of perceiving and expressing internal and external reality. Ultimately, the possibility of third, fourth, and fifth voices—voices that enhance our capacity for universal and unifying global vision—is galvanizing.

T. S. ELIOT MEDIEVAL MODERNISM

Perhaps the most celebrated poet of the twentieth century, T. S. Eliot (1888–1965) was also a playwright, literary critic, and editor. Considered a leader of the Modernist movement in poetry, he is best known as the author of such works as *The Love Song of J. Alfred Prufrock* (1915), *The Waste Land* (1922), *Murder in the Cathedral* (1935), and *The Four Quartets* (1943). His importance comes from his ability to capture feelings and attitudes of the early twentieth century. His literary work exemplifies Modernism in both content and style, reflecting the influence of modern life, individually and societally. Eliot excelled in using stream-of-consciousness to show the chaos, alienation, and fragmentation of the modern mentality.

Although Eliot is known as a modernist poet, he has been depicted as a "medieval modernist" because of his admiration for the spirituality of the Middle Ages together with his "impersonal" conception of art. While exhibiting medieval themes and style, his works are also rooted in the modern orientation of literature. The point is that Eliot seemed to have nostalgia for the medieval tradition, centered on religious vision and cultural integration, together with an interest in contemporary issues.

The tension become clear in *The Waste Land*, where Eliot shows his discomfort with modern life by contrasting it with medieval traits. He shows the difference between the integrative force of medieval life and the lack of spirituality in modern life. In theme and intent *The Waste Land* can be considered a modern fundamentalist text. The primary Modernist

5. Eliot, *Use of Poetry*, 130.

element is its clear reliance on images, many of them fragmented, to depict the feeling of cultural and personal loss. Although the untrained reader understands few of these images, the intent is to help readers derive meaning from fragmentation. The fragmented images, the stream of consciousness, and the many other odd stylistic features in the poem intentionally help convey the poet's message, that modern life is chaotic, illogical, and fragmented.

A trained philosopher with a Harvard PhD in philosophy, he knew about the unstable self, a phenomenon portrayed in *Prufrock*. More thoroughly educated than any other twentieth century poet, Eliot studied a daunting range of subjects, from Sanskrit and advanced mathematics to Japanese Buddhism and classical Greek. Modernity is complex, and Eliot knew that poetry in a modern age had to reflect its complexity. Adding to this was Eliot's need to reach back in time to something primal, something instinctive and holistic. The result was *The Waste Land*, now considered by many to be the single most influential poetic work of the twentieth century. Because of his complex imagery and odd style, Lewis included notes to his poem, not as a reader's guide, but as part of the poem itself, one more riddle to interpret. As seems likely, the notes and much else in the poem was inspired by James Joyce, whose *Ulysses* was published soon thereafter.

After *Waste Land*, Eliot's reputation grew exponentially. By 1930 and for the next thirty years, he was the most dominant figure in poetry and literary criticism in the English-speaking world. Much of *Waste Land* was written during the aftermath of World War I, and Eliot's poem became a lament for modern European civilization, an articulation of modern cultural trauma. Later readers who engaged with Eliot's work became fascinated by continuity and disruption in their own and in other cultural histories.

With the publication of *The Waste Land*, it is as though a curtain was raised, and Eliot began describing his political and social views as "reactionary and ultra-conservative." In 1928, he wrote in a preface to a book of essays that he considered himself "a classicist, a royalist, and an Anglo-Catholic." Having been raised a Unitarian,[6] a religious perspective that rejected key Christian doctrines such as the Trinity and the divinity of Jesus,

---

6. Though he spent most of his life in England, T. S. Eliot was born in St. Louis, Missouri. The Eliots originally hailed from Somerset in England and settled in America in the late seventeenth century. They began as a Boston family, but Eliot's grandfather, William Greeleaf Eliot, moved to Missouri in 1834 to preach as a Unitarian minister. Over his life, T. S. Eliot struggled with his Unitarian heritage, finding his family's religious tradition flawed and inadequate.

by the mid-1920s he came to believe that only orthodox Catholic Christianity presented a persuasive solution to the cultural and personal trauma of the post-War world. However, the Roman Catholic Church in England represented what he called a sect, and his loathing of sectarianism and his conviction that the culture and faith of a people should be intertwined led him to the Church of England. That body, he recognized, was also deficient, having an unsatisfactory mixture of Protestantism and Catholicism in its beliefs and practices but being, from the viewpoint of the Catholic Church, not Catholic at all.

Eliot's solution was to align himself with the Anglo-Catholic movement in the Church of England, which saw itself as part of the universal Catholic Church from which it had regrettably separated at the Reformation. Maintaining the validity of its orders and sacraments, Anglo-Catholicism aspired to return in full to Catholic communion, a position rejected by Rome. Initially, or perhaps as a result of his personal trauma due to a failing marriage, his sense of cultural dissolution in The Great War, his failure to find consolation in philosophy, his study of Eastern religions, and his disillusionment with Unitarianism and Protestantism in all their varieties, he wrote some of his most distinguished poetry. This led to the conviction that poetry comes out of suffering; apparently, so, too, his faith.

The poet of The Great War, Eliot became one of the greatest poets of the Second World War, not because he fought in it, but because he registered so fully its struggle and destruction. These are some of the elements that power the final poems of *The Four Quartets*, written during the Nazi air raids on Great Britain, in the period before the United States entered the war and while Britain was facing defeat. Due largely to these four interrelated poets, Eliot remains one of the greatest religious poets in the English language.

"Burnt Norton" (1936), the first poem of Eliot's *Four Quartets*, introduces the central theme of time and salvation.[7] Here, Eliot emphasizes the need of the individual to focus on the present moment while recognizing a universal order. Understanding the nature of time and the order of the universe, individuals are led to recognize God and seek redemption. While it is easy to focus on the poem's unity and beauty, in Eliot's mind these are but vehicles to a greater purpose and good. Like many of Eliot's works, the poem was compiled from fragments that he had reworked over many years.

---

7. The poem's title refers to a manor house Eliot visited in 1934, its rose garden a focal point.

"East Coker" (1940) follows the theme of time, focusing on the disorder that results when human beings follow science apart from God.[8] Leaders are described as materialistic and as unable to understand reality. The only way to find redemption is through pursuing the divine by looking to spirituality within and without, that is, by affirming our spiritual nature and the interconnectedness of humanity.

During the writing of "The Dry Salvages" (1941), which continues the theme of time, Eliot first envisioned a unified set of poems, thinking of a fourth, as yet unwritten poem to complete the set.[9] According to Eliot, within each person is a connection to the whole of humanity. If we accept reality solely as experienced by the senses, we will continue drifting upon life's sea, only to end up broken upon the rocks. What we must do is understand the patterns of the past to see where meaning can be found. Through moments of revelation, such as given in Christ, we can experience signs of eternity, for only the divine can free us from the limitations of time.

"Little Gidding" (1942), the fourth and final poem of the set, serves as a summary to views Eliot expressed throughout the series.[10] The poem discusses death and destruction, things unaccomplished, and regret for past event. In this poem, the spiritual journey is made circular, for in our beginning is our end, and in our end is our beginning: "We shall not cease from exploration. And the end of all our exploring will be to arrive where we started and know the place for the first time."[11]

In his lecture on *The Music of Poetry*, Eliot acknowledge the debt he owed to the art of music in his solution to the problem of finding a form for his four-part poem. Each poem in the set contains what can be described as five sections or "movements," each with its own inner structure. The first poem contains two contrasting but related themes, like the first and second

8. The poem's title refers to a small community that was related to Eliot's ancestry, a place Eliot visited in 1937. East Coker was home to St. Michael's Church, which later housed Eliot's ashes.

9. The poem's title comes from the name of a marine rock formation off the coast of Cape Ann, Massachusetts, where Eliot spent time as a child.

10. The poem's title refers to a small spiritual community in England established by Nicholas Ferrar in 1626, an informal community that followed High Anglican practice. Eliot had visited the site in 1934. Unlike the other localities mentioned in the titles of the other poems in the set, Eliot had no direct connection to this site. As such, the community is said to represent any spiritual community.

11. Although the theme of time, central to *The Four Quartets*, preoccupied Eliot throughout his career, he likely first conceived the theme of time in 1910–1911, while he was in Paris attending lectures by Henri Bergson on the philosophy of time.

subjects of an opening movement in musical sonata form. We see this form developed throughout the poems, for instance, in the treatment of river and sea images in "The Dry Salvages," or in the symbols for two different kinds of time: the time we feel in our personal lives and the time we become aware of through our imagination. In general, it is fair to say that the first movements are built on contradictions, later reconciled.

Eliot's second movements are constructed on the opposite principle of a single subject handled in two contrasted ways. The effect is like that of hearing the same melody played on a different group of instruments, or differently harmonized, or through elaborate variations. In the third movements, readers are less conscious of musical analogies. Eliot's third movement is the core of each poem, an exploration of previous themes now reconciled. After a brief fourth lyrical movement, the fifth movement recapitulates the themes of the poem with personal and topic applications that offer resolution to the contradicting themes in the first movement.

The Four Quartets depend on form in a way that *The Waste Land* does not. In the former, Eliot took the Grail myth for his ostensible subject or starting point. In that poem, coherence came not from poetic form but from its underlying myth,[12] to which constant reference is made, and of which the varied incidents and personages are illustrative. However, in *Four Quartets*, the title of the whole poem tells us nothing of its subject, and the titles of the separate poems tell us very little.

Central to each poem in the set of "quartets" are the four elements, described by ancient Greek philosophers as air ("Burnt Norton" is a poem about air, essential to life and the medium of communication), earth ("East Coker" is a poem about earth, of which we are made and to which we shall return), water ("Dry Salvages" is a poem about water, out of which the material world arose and which limits and encroaches on the land), and fire ("Little Gidding" is a poem about fire, the purest of the elements, by which some people think the world will end, fire that both consumes and purifies). For Eliot, fire, described in a manner similar to Julian of Norwich's writing about God's love, is related to the purgation of the fire of Pentecost.

In her study of *The Four Quartets*, Helen Gardner notes that while the set of poems is about the four elements, the possibility exists that Eliot had in mind a fifth element, "unnamed but latent in all things: the quintessence,

12. In the Grail myth, the Fisher King, the king of the Grail Castle, is wounded. His wounds are so severe that he cannot live, yet he is incapable of dying. As a result, his land and subjects are in desolation, for the kingdom mirrors the condition of its ruler, a wasteland inwardly (spiritually) and outwardly (sociologically).

the true principle of life, and that this unnamed principle is the subject of the whole poem."[13] While the possibilities are intriguing, if such an option exists, could it be *agape* (divine, unconditional, self-sacrificing love), or spirit?

Another unifying aspect in this cycle of poems is the cyclical pattern of nature's season, for "Burnt Norton" is about autumn, "East Coker" about summer, "The Dry Salvages" about winter, and "Little Gidding" about winter passing to spring. Additionally, theological elements distinguish the set of poems, beginning with grace in "Burnt Norton," faith in "East Coker," hope in "The Dry Salvages," and love in "Little Gidding." Eliot's final poem concludes by explaining how sacrifice is needed to allow individuals to die into life and be reborn, and that salvation should be the goal of human life. In addition to the theme of suffering and renewal, the image of the rose garden at the end of this poem is the image that began the first poem, only now we learn that "the fire and the rose are one."

QUESTIONS FOR DISCUSSION AND REFLECTION

1. In a sentence or two, define the word "art" or "arts."

2. In your own words, explain the interrelationship between the arts.

3. In your estimation, how does spirituality counter our modern tendency to fragmentation, compartmentalization, and specialization?

4. Explain and assess the meaning of the statement, "If art doesn't express a spiritual idea, then it is a craft, and not art."

5. In your estimation, how can the arts help us represent and understand absolute things and the absolute realm? Can you provide specific examples?

6. Explain and assess the meaning of the notion that art is a two-way street, able to give voice to one's spirit while also acting to nourish that spirit.

7. Explain and assess the merits of the statement, "Poetry is the language of the soul, not of the mind."

8. In your own words, explain the meaning of the statement, "Poetry is a riddle wrapped in an enigma."

13. Gardner, *Art of T. S. Eliot*, 45.

9. Explain and assess the merits of the author's distinction between reading poetry and experiencing poetry.

10. In your estimation, assess the merits of reading poetry as scripture, utilizing the four distinct steps of Lectio Divina.

11. Explain and assess the author's concept of "the five voices of poetry."

12. Using T. S. Eliot's *Four Quartets*, explain why literary critics depict him as a "medieval modernist."

13. In your estimation, what is the primary insight gained from this chapter? Explain your answer.

Chapter 7

POETIC EXEMPLARS

THIS CHAPTER CONTINUES THE DISCUSSION on poetry and spirituality, examining poetry's double function, equally a vehicle of expression and of sustenance for our inner spirit. Here we examine the contributions of Elizabeth Barrett Browning (1806–1861) and Emily Dickinson (1830–1886), two remarkable women exemplars of spirituality and the arts, both among the greatest poets in the English language. Contemporaries, one British and the other American, E. B. B. (as Elizabeth called herself) was an inveterate traveler who spent much of her married life living abroad, while Emily remained unmarried, living reclusively at home. Afflicted physically but resolute and expansive in mind and spirit, both died at the relatively young age of 55.

ELIZABETH BARRETT BROWNING: LONGING FOR DIVINE LOVE AND JUSTICE

Elizabeth Barrett Browning is one of the greatest poets of the nineteenth century. By the time of her marriage to Robert Browning in 1846, she was recognized internationally for her innovative and challenging verse and was heralded as one of the most accomplished poets of the period. Today, her fame rests chiefly upon her love poems, *Sonnets from the Portuguese*, and her epic poem *Aurora Leigh*, the latter now considered an early feminist text. In these poems, she mastered the poetic second and third voices respectively, namely, addressing an audience with a message and creating dramatic characters to address social issues.

Born in Durham, England in 1806, Elizabeth was the oldest of twelve children and the first in her family born in England in over two hundred years. For centuries, the Barrett family members had lived in Jamaica, where they owned sugar plantations and relied on slave labor. Educated at home, Elizabeth was a precocious youngster, familiar with the works of Shakespeare and Milton by the age of ten. By her twelfth year, she had written her first "epic" poem, which consisted of four books of rhyming couplets. Two years later, she developed a lung ailment that plagued her for the rest of her life. The following year, while saddling a pony, she suffered a spinal injury. Despite her ailments, throughout her teenage years she continued her education, learning Greek to read the Greek classics and Hebrew to read the Old Testament in its original language. At the same time, she was active in church life, developing passion for her Christian faith.

At the age of twenty, she anonymously published a collection of poems. Shortly thereafter, her mother died, and the growing support for the abolition movement in England, coupled with mismanagement of their Jamaica plantations, depleted the family income. In 1832, Elizabeth's father sold his rural estate, and by 1835, the family settled permanently in London. By this time, Elizabeth gained attention for her translation of *Prometheus Bound*, by the Greek dramatist Aeschylus. Life at home became unbearable for Elizabeth, due, in part, to her father's domineering personality and his sending of Elizabeth's siblings to Jamaica to help with the family business. Elizabeth bitterly opposed slavery, and made her voice known. In 1838, she wrote *The Seraphim and Other Poems*, expressing her social concerns in the form of classical Greek tragedy.

Due to her weakening disposition, Elizabeth was forced to spend a year at the seacoast town of Torquay, accompanied by her brother Edward, who drowned later that year while sailing. Elizabeth returned home emotionally broken, becoming an invalid and a recluse. She spent the next five years in her bedroom at her father's house. She continued writing, and in 1844 produced a collection entitled *Poems*. This volume gained the attention of poet Robert Browning, six years her junior, whose work Elizabeth had praised in one of her poems.

Browning wrote her a letter, and over the next twenty months, the two exchanged 574 letters. Due to opposition from her authoritarian father, who did not want any of his children to marry, in 1846 the couple eloped and settled in Florence, Italy, where Barrett Browning bore a son, Robert. In 1859, Barrett Browning published her *Sonnets from the Portuguese*, dedicated to her husband and written in secret before her marriage. The term "Portuguese" in the title is misleading, for it was simply a reference to Browning's nickname for his wife. Barrett Browning's *Sonnets*, written in an Italianate sonnet form influenced by Petrarch, are considered by critics to be her best work. Compared to the sonnets of Shakespeare, over time, Barrett Browning's *Sonnets of the Portuguese* brought her lasting fame.

Given her strong Christian faith, is it possible to read her lyric poetry as love not just for her beloved Robert, but perhaps more deeply as love of God? When she writes in poem 43, "How do I love thee? Let me count the ways," she resorts to the language of spirituality. Her spiritual love for God is not diminished by her human love for Robert, but reframed and enlarged.

Following her move to Italy, Barrett Browning confronted contemporary political issues, as she had done earlier with English social problems, speaking out against injustice. In *Casa Guidi Windows* (1851) and *Poems Before Congress* (1860), she expressed intense sympathy for the struggle for the unification of Italy. It was in Italy that Barrett Browning first knew freedom, and her emotions swept into her poetry.

In 1856, E. B. B. published the long epic "novel" *Aurora Leigh: A Poem in Nine Books*, generally understood as a portrayal of male domination over women. Considered her magnum opus, it was this work on which Barrett Browning wished her reputation to rest. *Aurora Leigh* remains a vital, highly original, and outspoken feminist statement. If not autobiographical, it contains her theories about life and art, with particular reference to the life of a woman artist. *Aurora Leigh* traces two careers, one female, one male; one artistic, one philanthropic. Written to explore experience, inspiration, and independence, the poem traces processes of self-liberation through informed confrontation and questioning. The poem ends confidently with vision of a new dawn reflecting its heroine's name, a new Day "which should be builded out of heaven to God" (9.957).

The poem received hostile reception from many early reviewers, some traditionalists criticizing it for its length and others for its subject matter, viewed by them as shamefully immoral and couched in language unsuitable for respectable women to read. The public disagreed. The first edition quickly sold out and lending libraries rationed their subscribers to two days each. Demand continued, so that by 1860 five editions had been published. Young progressives in art and literature endorsed it, among them the English poet A. L. Swinburne, who called it "one of the longest poems in the world and there is not a dead line in it." The eminent Victorian critic John Ruskin, prominent among the British avant-garde, told E. B. B. that he considered *Aurora Leigh* "the greatest poem in the English language and the first perfect poetical expression of the Age." Unfortunately, Barrett Browning did not live to enjoy more than a glimpse of the new age dawning social and spiritually, an age she welcomed and embraced, for she died in Florence on June 29, 1861.

As a novel, *Aurora Leigh* has a theme, the characters develop, and clues are laid to hold the interest and point to what is coming. In the first two books, the main characters, Aurora and her cousin Romney are shown in their arrogant youth. Aurora, a half-Italian orphan adopted by an English aunt, is full of spiritual pride, convinced that the world can be saved by art, and that she is to be the savior. Romney, in love with her, is equally obstinate in his conviction that he must save the world, only not by art, which he tends to despise, but by social service. He asks Aurora to marry him, but she refuses. Their aunt is angry in the refusal, for she sees in the marriage a safeguard for her ward's future. Shortly after, the aunt dies, unable to leave any income to Aurora, as without a male heir the Leigh estate goes to Romney. He attempts to give Aurora money, but she refuses it, deciding to go to London to make her living as a poet.

In Book 3, Aurora writes popular poems for magazines, which earn her an enthusiastic following, but she is dissatisfied, longing for a great work of art that will bring her lasting fame. At the same time, Romney carries his social conscience to the extreme by offering to marry Marian Erle, a girl he has rescued from a sweatshop. Book 4 tells of the wedding. Romney in his naivety invites both his society friends and Marian's neighbors. Aurora also attends. As an onlooker, she notes that the society women behave worse than the slum-dwellers. The wedding is delayed, and Marian never turns up. Believing that Romney has abandoned Marian, the wedding guests attack him, and Aurora rushes to try to save him.

In the fifth and following books, the plot thickens as Romney is pursued by the socialite Lady Waldemar, who persuades Marian to give up Romney, offering to give her money for the fare to Australia. Marian consents to go, only to find herself trapped and confined in a brothel in Paris. The field is now clear except for Aurora, whom Lady Waldemar senses as a rival with more insight than Aurora herself shows.

Aurora, tired of London fame, decides to visit Italy and on the way stops in Paris, where she catches a glimpse of Marian, who now has a baby son. When Aurora learns that the child was born not through seduction but through brute force at the brothel, she offers to take Marian and the child with her to Florence. There Aurora relaxes in her congenial surroundings, enjoying news of the great success her magnum opus is having in London, a manuscript she had sold to get to Italy. Content to rest on her laurels, she becomes an observer of Florentine life.

One evening, while sitting on her terrace, she is startled to hear the voice of Romney. She assumes that he has married Lady Waldemar, for a letter with news that there had been no marriage had never reached her. They talk until she invites him to sit down, whereupon the reader learns, gradually, that Romney is blind, a fact not yet clear to Aurora. Romney tells Aurora that he has read her book and believes it to be good and true Art. Romney tells Aurora he still considers himself bound in marriage to Marian, who, on overhearing this, comes forward to declare she does not wish ever to marry. Romney feels Aurora still does not love him and prepares to leave. At last, Aurora realizes that Romney is blind, and his blindness changes everything. She had loved him all along and now is ready to devote her life to him and, as it were, to pool their ideals—her art and his good works—for the benefit of the world. "Art is much," she declares, "but Love is more" (9.656). Love—first God's, then that between "wedded souls" (9.881–82), heralds the New Jerusalem come to earth.

ELIZABETH BARRETT BROWNING AND THE RELIGIOUS IMAGINATION

In an age when many were giving up the Christian faith, E. B. B. identified herself as a Christian poet. However, unlike Lewis or Eliot, she was a Congregationalist, a denomination in England associate with the "Independents," a group that rejected any authority apart from the Bible, including creedal dogmas and fixed patterns of liturgy, both central to the Church of England.

Spurning sectarianism, however, Barrett Browning claimed to believe in a "universal" Christianity, for throughout her lifetime she remained open to a variety of theological perspectives. In an early volume of verse entitled *An Essay on Mind* (1826), Elizabeth declared there was "unspeakable poetry in Christ's religion."[1] Her wide scriptural knowledge influenced many of her early diary entries, and, having learned Greek and Hebrew, she welcomed the historical-grammatical approach to scriptural interpretation while maintaining, against deists, spiritualists, and nonconformists, the absolute authority of scripture as the unique source of divine truth.

Despite dissenting voices, the concept of separate spheres and even of separate modes of being for men and women defined the nineteenth century, shaping cultural roles, expectations, and contributions of both groups. Numerous studies have familiarized us with the configuration of men as intellectual and rational by nature and women as emotional. These assigned roles also had implications for the type of language each was expected to use, whether written or spoken. Already by the third decade of that century, women writers were constrained by the expectation that they choose sentiment over intellect in their work, relegating most women's religious verse to emotive language. Hymn writing was a preferred means of religious expression, and in pursuing her own poetic voice, Elizabeth experimented initially with that form. She titled or subtitled several of her early religious poems as hymns, even resorting to the metrical structure and devotional voice of the hymn in poems not titled as such. She also understood that hymns performed some measure of theological work, and she became increasingly skilled in using her own hymns for scriptural interpretation.

However, despite early success, Barrett Browning seems to have chafed against the limitations of this form. After 1838, she wrote no new hymns. Though in future work she sometimes cast the female poet as prophet to contest standard gender roles, she also engaged in another model for the poet, that of preacher, whose primary rhetorical means was not the hymn but the sermon. In midcareer poems and particularly in *Aurora Leigh*, Barrett Browning's poetry demonstrated the sermonic mode by becoming more explicitly social in dimension. Already in 1843, she had written, "if a poet be a poet, it is his business to work for the elevation & purification of the public mind."[2] From the mid-1849s through the end of her life, she worked for the "elevation" and "purification" of the public mind by addressing social, political, and religious issues.

In 1843, she gave sustained attention to the words Truth and Love, which expressed her vision of the church. For her, Truth and Love were coterminous. In her mind, truth did not come from indoctrination, but

---

1. Kelley et al., *Browning Correspondence*, 3:179.
2. Kelley et al., *Browning Correspondence*, 7:21.

from critical reflection. "The more thought and enquiry," she wrote, "the better for Truth. Error is the result of half-thinking." To accept the church and its dogma as interpreter of scripture, rather than responsible thought, dismayed her. Acknowledging that thought and enquiry might lead to disagreement in the short term, in the end they would only produce a better understanding of Truth.

Important for Barrett Browning's later thinking about the poet figure, Congregationalists did not explicitly exclude women from the position of church officer or preacher. In the United States, a woman named Antoinette Brown was ordained as a Congregationalist minister in 1853. Hence, when Barrett Browning began to envision the woman poet as preacher, she was engaging in a concept that was centered on a democratic rather than a gendered model, though such views were not yet widely accepted.

Though Barrett Browning formulated her poet-as-preacher paradigm before her marriage, her conception as to its relevance for poetry did not change during her married period. The implicit dialogic form of the sermon, its emotional appeal, and the grassroots figure of the Congregationalist preacher retained for her powerful potential for a religious poetic aimed at Truth and Love, though later in life these models failed to meet her expectation. After her marriage, when she and Robert lived in Italy, she became disappointed by cathedral sermons, finding them lacking in inspiration, "having the sun but no light." For E. B. B., the way for Truth and Love was through language that combines intellect with feeling. To such a task she aspired, creating a distinct poetic sensibility as a means to that end.

Over her lifetime, Barrett Browning used poetic form to explore issues central to her imagination. The question of a poetic voice at once instructive and democratic, knowledgeable and emotive, involve her in experiments with a range of generic forms, from hymnic to lyric to dramatic epic. Eventually abandoning the hymnic form, she turned instead to dramatic and epic genres. These genres allowed her to place the individual in dialogue with a community. These genres also enabled her to challenge gender norms.

Her midcareer dramatic poems and particularly *Aurora Leigh* featured women in key roles. At first tentatively and then more confidently, Barrett Browning cast women as poet-preachers—that is, as informed speakers with sophisticated interpretive and linguistic skills. In *Aurora Leigh*, she succeeded in creating a sophisticated woman poet-preacher who was able to use language effectively, valuing the cognitive in the emotive and the emotive in the cognitive, and helping others (men) value this interpenetration as well. Endorsing the role of the emotive in knowledge by criticizing social work not based on love, in this work Barrett Browning lived up to her definition of poetry as "truth in relation, perceived in emotion."[3]

In *Aurora Leigh*, Barrett Browning illustrates her mature concept of the poet-preacher and the value of the democratic and dialogic over the authoritative. She does so by depicting Aurora's shift from a naïve perspective of the poet as seer to a humbler view of the poet as necessarily engaged in a communal effort to discover the right and the good. The prospect of being the lonely prophet in the wilderness does not ultimately appeal to her. She desires dialogue, not pronouncement. By Book 7, Aurora begins to acknowledge that no solitary speaker, of either sex, can ascertain truth on his or her own. She specifies, "truth is neither man's nor woman's but just God's" (7.753). Eventually, Aurora gives over her earlier exclusivist claims and asserts "poet and philanthropist . . . may stand side by side" (6.199). Neither poetry nor philanthropy can save the world, but each needs the other in conversation, in community.

Aurora can only serve as an interpretive guide for others after she has first acknowledged her own need for guidance through inquiry and conversation. To underscore this understanding of the poet, Barrett Browning employs biblical language and poetic speech in *Aurora Leigh* more subtly and perhaps more effectively than ever before. First, by using blank verse rather than rhymed lyrics, which brings speaking voices more in line with everyday speech patterns, and also by having Aurora as reflective and interpretive narrator use biblical language more often than the youthful Aurora. Not only does Aurora's religious speech develop in tandem with her better understanding of the poet, but her words also effect change in others, particularly in Romney. His early biblical allusions tended to be cynical or misapplied, whereas by the end, he learns from Aurora that social duty without love has no results and no rewards.

EMILY DICKINSON: LONGING FOR DIVINE LOVE AND INNER COHERENCE

Grouped by literary critic Howard Bloom with Walt Whitman, Wallace Stevens, Robert Frost, T. S. Eliot, and Hart Crane among the six major poets engendered by the United States, Emily Dickinson is not only America's

---

3. Kelley et al., *Browning Correspondence*, 10:168.

greatest female poet, but also one of the most original poets of all time. Writing in literary seclusion in western Massachusetts, she mastered the poet's first voice—the voice of the poet talking to herself—inventing a poetry both unprecedented in form and long lasting in impact. A product of the Victorian age, she wrote as if to bid farewell to the Victorians and to incite the Modernists.

In her 1789 extant poems, Emily Dickinson pierced to the heart of the great universal mysteries of life, death, love, and nature, all handled with a personal yet profound spiritual sensibility. She revealed the singular beauty at the core of each theme in a terse, aphoristic, primal style of writing described as spiritual, a language best understood by the soul. Like writers such as Ralph Waldo Emerson, Henry David Thoreau, and Walt Whitman, she experimented with expression in order to free it from conventional restraints. Like Elizabeth Barrett Browning, she crafted a distinct type of persona for the narrator, a profound observer who sees the limitations of society as well as its imaginable transcendence. To make the abstract tangible, Dickinson created in her writing a distinctively elliptical language to express what was possible but not yet realized.

Her family, though not particularly religious, was of Puritan stock. Born and reared in Amherst, Massachusetts, a Puritan stronghold subject to periodic evangelical revivals, Emily never converted to Christ or accepted the doctrine of innate sin—a fact her family and friends were aware of but accepted along with her other eccentricities. Her male ancestors adhered to the Protestant work ethic. Her grandfather, Samuel Dickinson, was the driving force behind the establishment of Amherst College. Her father, Edward, was educated at Amherst Academy and then at Yale. He returned to his father's practice in Amherst, working tirelessly as an attorney, community leader, longtime treasurer of Amherst College, and briefly as state legislator and congressman, until his sudden death in 1874. By contrast, Emily's mother was a frail, uncommunicative, narrowly conventional farmer's daughter, of whom comparatively little is known, but who is often presented as the passive wife of a domineering husband.

Thanks to Edward's drive to succeed, the Dickinson home in Amherst was attractively appointed, and their father's presence on Sundays could be counted on. He regularly read aloud from the Bible, which led to Emily's familiarity with scripture and may have helped to heighten her fascination with aphoristic language and rhetoric in general. In her youth, the Dickinson home was the center of much community and academic activity.

Her father customarily entertained the writers and politicians who visited Amherst College, affording Emily contact with some of the finest minds in nineteenth-century America. If paternal absences and maternal silences were facts of her home life from her earliest years, then perhaps Emily learned the value of unspoken intimacy and of silence. The same interpretive talent also served her concise, intermittent poetic style, valuing silence equally with words.

By the time of Emily's early childhood, there were three children in the household, including older brother Austin and younger sister Lavinia. All three children attended the one-room primary school in Amherst and then moved on to Amherst Academy, only recently opened to girls. By Emily's account, she delighted in all aspects of the school—the curriculum, the teachers, and the students. The school prided itself on its connection with Amherst College, offering a curriculum that emphasized science. At Amherst Academy, Emily had many opportunities to attend lectures by Edward Hitchcock, president of the college, who devoted his life to maintaining the connection between science, the natural world, and religion. While the strength of the Academy's curriculum lay in its emphasis on science, it also contributed to Dickinson's development as a poet. One of her teachers Daniel T. Fiske, described Emily at twelve as "an excellent scholar," yet "somewhat shy and nervous." He found her compositions to be "strikingly original."[4] Receiving the same education as that of their male counterparts, the females' time at school was one of intellectual challenge and relative freedom.

After studying for seven years at Amherst Academy, at the age of seventeen Dickinson entered Mount Holyoke Female Seminary (now Mount Holyoke College). Under the guidance of Mary Lyon, the founder and headmistress, the school was known for its evangelical religious atmosphere. Accompanying the curriculum were weekly sessions with Lyon in which religious questions were raised and the state of the students' faith assessed. The young women were divided into three categories: those who were "established Christians," those who "expressed hope," and those who were "without hope." Much has been made of Emily's place in this latter category, and of the widely circulated story that she was the only member of that group. School records disagree, however, disclosing that thirty students ended the school year with that designation. Years later her classmate Clara Newman Turner remembered the moment when Mary Lyon

---

4. Habegger, *My Wars Are Laid Away in Books*, 152.

"asked all those who wanted to be Christians to rise." Only Emily remained seated. Turner recalls Emily's comment to her at the time: "They thought it queer I didn't rise," adding perceptively, "I thought a lie would be queerer."[5] Whether because of homesickness, ill health, or her defiance toward the church—perhaps because of all three—she returned home after her first year without finishing her studies. Biographer Richard Sewell offers a different explanation. Looking over the Mount Holyoke curriculum and seeing how many of the texts duplicated those Dickinson had already studied at Amherst, he concluded that Mount Holyoke had little new to offer her.

Emily's departure from Mount Holyoke marked the end of her formal schooling. It also prompted a dissatisfaction common among young of the time. Upon their return, young women were to prepare for marriage, and unmarried daughters were expected to set aside their own interests in order to meet the needs of the household. Emily was not amenable to either. Her letters from the early 1850s register disdain for domestic work: "God keep me from what they call households," she exclaims in a letter in 1850. Life for a married women, she declares in her 1861 poem "Title divine, is mine" (no. 194), can be summed in three words: "Born – Bridalled – Shrouded," for married life for nineteenth-century women generally represented indenture and death. Deliberately misspelling "Bridled," she uses sarcasm to equate becoming a "bride" with being "bridled," exchanging a bridal veil for a shroud.

While she wrote a few poems in the early 1850s, it wasn't until 1858 that she began to write mature poems with regularity. The years 1859 through 1865, roughly the years of the American Civil War, were her most productive. During that period, she concerned herself, in one way or another, with the spiritual life, dedicated to "Tell all the truth, but tell it slant" (no, 1263). In that poem, one of her most famous, she explains, "The Truth must dazzle gradually / Or every man be blind."

When Dickinson left school in 1848, she returned to live at home for the rest of her life. Although for a time she continued to pursue a limited social existence, she gradually and famously withdrew until few outside her immediate family circle caught sight of her. Even esteemed guests might be turned away at her doorstep if the moment were not right, though neighborhood children were known to receive baskets of her gingerbread, lowered from a window by the virtually invisible "Miss Emily."

---

5. Poetry Foundation, *Emily Dickinson*, §7.

Although she wrote, at times furiously, from her twenties through her fifties, she chose voluntarily not to publish the poetry. Instead, she circulated it selectively by inserting or weaving her poems into numerous informal notes and longer letters to family and friends. According to Victorian custom, she also bound her poems into stitched packets known as "fascicles," for the purpose of her own editing and revising. As she wrote in an 1863 poem, "Publication – is the Auction / Of the Mind of Man" (no. 788). Distancing herself from "professional" poets and from Romantic authors who wrote lengthy tomes, often for financial gain, Emily wrote succinctly and enigmatically, disdaining the possibility that her poems might be sold between the grammars and dictionaries in the stationary story. Unlike her contemporary Walt Whitman, she expressed herself at a deep level of consciousness, eschewing anything that approached conformity or correctness, including traditional punctuation. From 1858 to 1864, Dickinson made copies of more than eight hundred of her poems, gathering and binding them into forty groups of booklets that Dickinson scholar Dorothy Oberhaus called "a private kind of publication." In addition, she embedded some 500 poems in letters, many completed as semifinal drafts written on odds and ends of paper—the backs of envelopes and discarded letters, bits of wrapping paper, and edges of newspaper. These, added to her 1787 known poems, means she wrote some 2287 poems altogether, or more than one a week for nearly forty years.

When Emily's mother died in 1882 after a long illness, Emily and Lavinia, who also never married, lived together in the family homestead until their deaths. During this period, Lavinia was Emily's primary means of access to the outside world. Emily was also close to her brother, Austin. When he married Susan Gilbert, a childhood friend of the Dickinsons, his new family, living in the house next door, became the center of Emily's existence. As Emily's withdrawal intensified, Emily's principle method of communication was through her letters, which must be considered part of her oeuvre, some letters regarded as poetry in themselves.

Emily Dickinson only published seven poems in her lifetime. When she died in Amherst in 1886, her sister found about 900 of her poems and she undertook to have them published. Emily had instructed Lavinia to burn all letters she had received over the years, a task Lavinia set about immediately, and then later regretted. To her surprise, she came upon a bureau drawer full of hundreds of loose manuscript poems in her sister's hand. Since Emily had apparently left no instructions about poems, Lavinia engaged the support of Mabel Loomis Todd to publish the first selection of her poems in 1890. Unfortunately, a complete volume did not appear until 1955, when Dickinson scholar Thomas H. Johnson compiled, cataloged, and edited all of her poems.

In 1866, Dickinson wrote a poem that poignantly and succinctly declares her life's desire: "If I can stop one Heart from breaking / I shall not live in vain / If I can ease one Life the Aching / Or cool one Pain / Or help one fainting Robin / Into his Nest again / I shall not live in vain" (no. 982). The uniqueness of Emily Dickinson's vision, its ability to fuse the concrete and spiritual, and, finally, to come to terms with death, are splendidly revealed in perhaps her best-known poem, "Because I could not stop for Death, / He kindly stopped for me" (no. 479). In this poem, Dickinson portrays Death as a kind friend who gently stops to take her to her grave. Death is an entity, as distinguished from the moment of death itself. She distinguishes Death from Immortality, whom she represents as a fellow passenger on her journey. The journey takes her past a review of her life. As the sun sets, she senses her life drawing to a close and a chill overtakes her; her gown is thin and gossamer and can protect her no longer. Then Death pauses, allowing her to view her own grave, her new home. Dickinson's image of a woman and her escort, Death, meditating on the prospect of eternity, is neither one of despair nor loss, but of acceptance.

The will to live in the face of death—and the joy this creates—is a theme in many of Dickinson's poems, and is remarkably modern. Emerson, her contemporary and her inspiration, would have found this stance unacceptable. Emerson and the nineteenth-century Romantics believed in the triumph of the transcendental human—a being without bounds, inseparable from nature, by which they meant, from the divine. For Dickinson, the moment of pure, divine, wisdom comes with the acceptance of life, with its fragility, imperfection, and defeat. In her elegy on the occasion of her father's death in 1863 she wrote, "'Tis not dying hurts us so - / 'Tis Living – hurts us more" (no. 528).

Heaven plays no part in poem no. 479, for eternity is achieved through the visionary moment, which exists outside space and time. As she wrote in poem no. 1609, "Who has not found the Heaven – below - / Will fail of it above." Those who can grasp "The Fact that Earth is Heaven / Whether Heaven is Heaven or not" (no. 1435), effectively own a portion of paradise. Dickinson's characterization of heaven as a property to own or rent, as an item of real estate, is indicative of her belief that heaven was susceptible to being possessed. Dickinson's heaven is an earth-heaven; it is the intensity of our lives that offers paradise. Although the inevitability of death makes life far from perfect, death is necessary: Death concentrates life, extruding its transcendent essence. This is the essence for which Dickinson struggled in her poetry. Unlike her contemporaries, she never succumbed to easy solutions or to private desire.

EMILY DICKINSON AND THE RELIGIOUS IMAGINATION

Profoundly aware of the Bible and well acquainted with Christian theology, Emily Dickinson wrote at a time when comparative religion was extremely popular. Therefore, we should not be surprised to discover that religious myths and symbols are essential to understand her poetry, particularly the life of Jesus, in whom she found an experience comparable to her own.

In 1862 Dickinson was at the peak of her creative power. This was the time when many of her most interesting poems with broadly religious themes emerged. It was also the time of intense fighting during America's Civil War. In one of her letters written at this time, she described God as an "eclipse" that her family worshipped every night. This imagery is a small example of Dickinson's ambivalent feelings about religion and religious faith in general. As symbol, an eclipse has a curious meaning. In antiquity, eclipses were worshipped because they inspired fear. Today, they draw our curiosity and wonder. Thus, Dickinson's "eclipse" is both sarcastic and appreciative. While she was sarcastic about unquestioned faith, her disregard was combined with a clear appreciation of religion.

In his work *Nimble Believing: Dickinson and the Unknown*, James McIntosh claims that "the unknown is not so much a subject she takes up as a condition of her poetic existence she perpetually comes up against."[6] Though in her poetry Dickinson demonstrates a personal faith that encompasses doubt, for her, the unknown was the ground upon which one truly encounters God. While she may not have believed in a personal God, her poetry is an expression of her religious faith.

Studies show that Dickinson's Puritan heritage, mixed with the liberal theology emerging in Boston, fused with classical mythology, was a source of her poetic enrichment. In the years after Ralph Waldo Emerson's "Divinity School Address" (1838) called for a new age of "poet-priests," there also emerged beside the mainstream Emersonian tradition another tradition

6. McIntosh, *Nimble Believing*, 125.

that was, in effect, anti-Emersonian because it found poetic language structurally resistant to the idea of transcendence. Emerson's reinvention of religion as a species of poetry was tested and found wanting by many of the poetic innovators whom he addressed.

While Dickinson may have been sarcastic about religion and theology, it is not correct to characterize her poetry as her secular way of being religious or as a replacement for religion, for in her piety she was quite amenable to faith, both as a matter of disposition and as part of an epistemic framework of uncertainty that necessarily includes doubt. Rather, Dickinson's poetry allowed for a particular structuring of thought that helped her (and us) negotiate theological problems. Some of the most pertinent examples of her spiritual journey are found when she explores complexities surrounding loss and return in her own poetic self. There is anguish in Dickinson's religious imagination, but also humor and wit. Poetry makes a place for irreverence in theology even as it challenges it and probes its meanings and doctrines. In this case, religion is more than a context in which to read Dickinson; Christianity gave her the conceptual and emotional vocabulary with which to explore the epistemic problems at the core of her spirituality.

Three poems from 1862 help introduce the tension created between artistic and religious forms of imaging the "beyond." The first, poem no. 436, begins, "I found the words to every thought / I ever had – but One - / And that – defies Me." Here Dickinson suggests she has turned to religion as an artist who understands the animating power of the unspeakable, and yet who feels simultaneously subject to an overwhelming force. The second, poem no. 373, begins, "This World is not conclusion. / A Species stands beyond - / Invisible, as Music - / But positive, as Sound." Here we get a sense of Dickinson's ambivalent feelings about faith and her deep preoccupation with the unknown. In no. 373, faith is personified as a young, foolish, but quite likeable girl, who looks to the flimsy support of natural theology's "Evidence" and asks directions in vain. Dickinson reserves her greatest sarcasm for the habits of the Revivalist church that for all its assertiveness, cannot hide the emptiness that undergirds its own doctrinal surety. The empty gesturing from the pulpit and the congregations "strong hallelujahs" are powerless, Dickinson suggests, to still the questing mind or soul.

The third, poem no. 466, begins "I dwell in Possibility - / A fairer House than Prose" illustrates the connection between the unknown and Dickinson's sense of poetic purpose. It also illustrates the difficulties she saw in poetic and religious journeying. This poem leaves room for optimistic interpretation of poetic possibility as a more welcoming "beyond." The juxtaposition of "Possibility" with "Prose" leads many to see the former as poetry and the latter as the possessive nature of ordinary reality. Taken together, these poems give a sense of the variety of possibilities to be found in the lively discussion Dickinson encourages between religious and aesthetic forms of imagining.

In *Emily Dickinson: Perception and the Poet's Quest*, Greg Johnson argues that Dickinson's career can be understood as a Romantic quest, which seeks to restore a lost or diminished spirituality. For Johnson, the problem of quest is key to understanding Dickinson's life, which he conceives in terms of a myth of isolation and lyric voice. He describes her body of work as a process of self-mythologization, comprising a drama whose theme is the adventure of consciousness, whose goal was a visionary apprehension of spiritual reality, and whose implied heroine is her poetic self. The way in which Dickinson consciously worked and reworked her writings in every stage of her life suggests a mind that was never satisfied and a poetic quest whose object was its own process.

Like Bunyan, Lewis,[7] Eliot, and Barrett Browning, we see in Dickinson a longing for an object that remains perpetually beyond her powers of expression. In Bunyan, Lewis, and Eliot's case, the longing is for an idealized past, present, or future, For Barrett Browning, it is a longing for divine love through external (sociological, communal, national) unity and coherence, whereas for Dickinson, it is a longing for divine love through inner (existential) unity and coherence.

This opens a new way of thinking about Dickinson's sense of her vocation as a quest of self-discovery. Religious narratives gave Dickinson a rich vocabulary for this journey, such as Jacob's struggle at Peniel and Christ's challenge at Gethsemane. Jacob's struggle with the angel at Peniel is reflected in Dickinson's "A Little East of Jordan" (no. 145). Critics argue that Dickinson was drawn to that story because she saw Jacob as a representative individual who confronts divine authority to bring inspiration through his or her work. In one of her letters Dickinson wrote, "Poetry requires pugilism, a struggle with the divine, in order to have the power to bless." Dickinson identified with Jacob because hers is a vocation of power that grants and unleashes creative energy. As a figure for the poet, Jacob draws attention to the agony of the encounter with the divine.

---

7. The religious allegories of John Bunyan and C. S. Lewis are discussed in chapter 8.

Gethsemane, too, was a place of agony. At Gethsemane, Jesus struggled with loneliness and the temptation to abandon his divine purpose. Dickinson, too, struggled with despair, separation, and liminality, forging analogies between her personal struggle and her own poetic project. In "One Crucifixion is recorded" (no. 670), Dickinson narrows the preoccupation of the human quest for self-realization to the inner landscape, situating loneliness and struggle at the core of her being. In "I like a look of Agony" (no. 339), Dickinson emphasizes the final journey from this world to the next; agony emphasizes mortality and human suffering at the point of death. The agony also depicts the uncertainty of the transition or of the "in-between" nature of mortal life, so near yet so far to the other side.

The personal struggle implied in "One Crucifixion" is fleshed out in "I should have been too glad" (no. 283), where she uses the relationship between "circuit" and "circumference" to suggest an analogy with her own poetic project. "Earth would have been too much," she states, "And Heaven – not enough for me." The poet's power, her "new Circumference," arrives unexpectedly and remains precarious until the end: "Faith bleats – to understand!"

As Dickinson writes in 1862 to Thomas Wentworth Higginson, an editor and a frequent contributor to the *Atlantic Monthly* magazine, "My Business is Circumference": a wonderfully compact way of asserting that her poetic project embraced concerns that were relevant to the entire human sphere, not just to herself. Elsewhere, she gave that phrase specificity, noting in a letter to her friend Elizabeth Holland, "My Business is to love. . . . My Business is to Sing." In both song and love, we have an idealization of something boundless, extending across space and time. Even the image of Circumference, one she used repeatedly in her poetry, is of a boundary that suggests boundlessness. When, in Dickinson's terms, individuals go "out upon Circumference," they stand on the edge of unbounded space. Dickinson's use of this image refers to a project central to her poetic work, for the key to her poetry rests in the word "is." In her world, definition proceeds via comparison. One cannot say directly what is; essence remains unnamed and unnamable. To engage with reality, Dickinson resorts to metaphor; defining one concept in terms of another produces new layers of meaning. Her vocabulary circles around transformation, often ending before change is completed. The final lines of her poems might best be defined by their inconclusiveness. Her poetry, like her life, remains open, a gift of her enthralling spirituality.

The nuance that Dickinson brings to her depictions of the religious quest arise from fascination with the conditions of process—struggle, loneliness, and border crossings. Her analogy between the religious and the poetic quests brings such notions into focus as the condition of creativity.

QUESTIONS FOR DISCUSSION AND REFLECTION

1. In your estimation, to what extent is E. B. B's *Aurora Leigh* autobiographical?

2. In your estimation, what is "the new Day" that E. B. B. envisions in *Aurora Leigh*?

3. In *Aurora Leigh*, a major conflict between Romney and Aurora involves the issue of whether the world can best be saved by art or by social service. If you were asked to weigh in on this debate, where would your sentiments lie? Explain your answer.

4. Explain and assess the meaning of E. B. B's line, "Art is much, but Love is more."

5. In your estimation, to what extend did E. B. B's Christian faith influence her literary imagination?

6. For E. B. B., Truth and Love were coterminous. Do you agree? Explain your answer.

7. In your estimation, how did Emily Dickinson's life and upbringing influence her subject matter, poetic voice, and point of view?

8. In your estimation, why did Emily Dickinson never marry? She had male friends, and was clearly in love with some of them.

9. In your estimation, why are Emily Dickinson's poems considered "existential"?

10. In your estimation, what is the meaning of Emily Dickinson's line, "Tell all the truth, but tell it slant"?

11. In your estimation, does Emily Dickinson's poetry represent an authentically Christian point of view? Explain your answer.

12. In your estimation, what did Emily Dickinson mean when she wrote, "My Business is Circumference"?

13. After reading this chapter, what similarities and dissimilarities do you find in E. B. B. and Emily Dickinson's life, priorities, and poetic approach?

14. In your estimation, what is the primary insight gained from this chapter? Explain your answer.

Chapter 8

THE POWER OF ALLEGORY

AFTER THE EASING OF RESTRICTIONS regarding the COVID–19 pandemic, a group of us gathered at a local church for our weekly study of a chapter from my book, *Walking on Water*. I had agreed to attend as a participant and to answer questions regarding the topic that evening, "The Power of Myth." Several members of the group lead individual classes, and on this occasion the leader was Jess Costa. At one point, Jess faced me and asked why I had not included allegory when dealing with metaphor and myth. That question led me to write this book as sequel to *Walking* and to invite Jess to provide assistance in chapters on poetry, allegory, and theatre, dimensions of the arts he is uniquely qualified to explore.

In the field of literature, three categories of allegories exist: (1) *intentional*, that is, allegories envisioned by the author; (2) *potential*, unintended but potentially latent in the author's mind; and (3) *hypothetical*, namely, never part of the author's intention, but theoretically possible. In this chapter, I focus on two literary allegories, *Pilgrim's Progress*, John Bunyan's classic tale, and C. S. Lewis's *Pilgrim's Regress*. Both are clearly allegories of the spiritual journey. As is clear in all spiritual allegory, the goal of life's journey is not perfection but wholeness, a truth underscored by the popular folk saying, "God has a sense of humor; instead of creating a perfect world, God created us."

However, as the Irish poet W. B. Yeats strikingly noted, "Nothing can be sole or whole that has not been rent." This holds true for great love and great suffering—perhaps humanity's greatest mentors—both necessary for healing, wholeness, and spiritual growth. Of suffering, we learn from literary allegory that "what does not kill us makes us stronger." Regarding love, we learn that in the grand scheme of things, a king's loss of a kingdom may well be far less than a child's loss of a doll.

I define allegory as a story, poem, or picture that reveals a hidden meaning, typically a moral or political one. The term "allegory" derives from the Greek *allegorein*, formed from two Greek words: *allos*, meaning "other," and *agoreuo*, meaning "to speak in a place of assembly." The agora is a marketplace or place of assembly. As a compound word, *allegorein* means "speaking about one thing under the image of another." Building on those ideas, an allegory is a figure of speech in which words are used out of their ordinary or literal meaning in order to add beauty or emotional intensity to the reader. Dorothy Sayers once described allegory as "the interpretation of experience by means of images. In its simplest form, [allegory] is a kind of extended metaphor."[1] As C. S. Lewis noted in the afterward to the third edition of *The Pilgrim's Regress*, "all good allegory exists not to hide but to reveal; to make the inner world more palpable by giving it an (imagined) concrete embodiment. . . . When allegory is at its best, it approaches myth, which must be grasped with the imagination, not with the intellect."[2]

Jess and I recall attending an art exhibit that included ceramic works created by a senior student at Washington & Jefferson College, herself a Native-American member of the Zuni tribe in western New Mexico. At that gathering, ceramics professor Pat Maloney explained a significant but often unrecognized detail in Zuni jewelry or pottery, namely, the inclusion of a scratch, or more importantly, of a decorative unclosed line around a pot. The purpose of this imperfection is twofold: (1) it allows the spirit of the pot to join the spirit of the user, so the two may become one. In addition, (2) it allows the spirit of the user to enter the pot and join with its spirit. Such spiritual wisdom is lost to a technological society limited to fixing or discarding what is broken.

This modern obsession with replacement explains my disinterest in keeping up with technological fashion. I appreciate technology, particularly when it improves the quality of life. However, I want things to last. Perhaps this explains why I kept my first car for twenty-five years, or my reaction when I heard that my road bike was no longer repairable. I had cycled across the North American continent on it, and it needed repairs. I

1. Sayers, in her introduction to Dante's *Divine Comedy*, 11.

2. Lewis, *Pilgrim's Regress*, 152.

was not about to part with it, and resented the repairman's verdict: "Your bike is obsolete; you need to buy a new one!" For me, such an attitude is impractical and unspiritual.

Life has much to offer, but also much to teach. However, when we are caught in complexity, we often miss what is most basic or important. When we can't figure out what something means, it helps to simplify. Thankfully, literary mentors exist to help us make sense of things, often in the form of riddles, parables, and allegories. Take, for example, the following three riddles:

1. What is the depth of a river?
2. What kind of tree is in a forest?
3. What is sharper than the tip of a sword?

Like all riddles, they initially appear perplexing, even logically contradictory, but upon further examination, they contain an obvious solution. Notice, for instance, that the first question is not about a particular river, or about a specific spot in that river. Based upon that observation, the answer would be, "the distance between the top and the bed of a river." Likewise, the second question is not about species of trees in a particular forest, but is framed in such a way as to require the answer, "the green and the withered," that is, the living and the dead. Using intuition, the answer to the third question is "understanding," like the other answers, stunning in its simplicity.

Like riddles, parables, and other extended metaphors, the value of literary allegory is obvious. When taken to unexpected levels of interpretation, its deeper wisdom—what we might call its magic—is unleashed, illuminating our blind spots, helping us compare seemingly opposite or unrelated stories to our own lives and journeys. Such wisdom is illustrated by Bunyan and Lewis in their allegorical writings and unexpectedly so in *The Wizard of Oz*, the subject of chapter 9 below.

In *The Allegory of Love*, C. S. Lewis's critical study of the medieval outlook, Lewis developed his theory that allegory is inherent in the human imagination. In his estimation, the essence of thought and language is allegorical—the realization of the insensible in terms of the sensible. When the folk bards first took the links forged by the imagination between the abstract and the concrete and turned them into stories, they became the originators of literature. In his study, Lewis tried to explain medieval sensibility to a generally unsympathetic 1930s audience by claiming that allegory is the most psychologically natural of all literary forms, and that the historical problem is not how the taste for allegory developed, but rather how it deteriorated. The reason, Lewis alleged, was the increasing emphasis on logic and the scientific method. Without dismissing the importance of scientific learning, Lewis believed it had to be combined with the arts and the humanities, which emerged from humankind's deepest instincts and therefore remain the soundest guide to what is truly significant.

JOHN BUNYAN'S *THE PILGRIM'S PROGRESS*

Published in 1678 and begun while its author John Bunyan was in prison, *The Pilgrim's Progress* is one of the most influential books in the English language. In the seventeenth and eighteenth centuries, Bunyan's book was second only to the "Authorized" or King James Version of the Bible in popularity and influence in English homes, owned and studied by educated and relatively uneducated men and women alike. In turn, Bunyan's allegory provided William Thackeray with the title he had long sought for *Vanity Fair* and molded important aspects of Charles Dickens's pilgrimage narratives, *Oliver Twist* and *The Old Curiosity Shop*. Although Bunyan wrote other allegories, including *The Life and Death of Mr. Badman* (1680) and *The Holy War* (1682), none rivaled the inventiveness and popularity of *The Pilgrim's Progress*. Even those unfamiliar with the book have heard of phrases from the book such as Slough of Despond and Vanity Fair.

The son of an itinerant tinker (a mender of pots and kettles), John Bunyan was destined to follow his father's example. Speaking of his home as "being of that rank that is meanest and most despised of all the families in the land," his formal education seems to have been limited to attendance at a nearby grammar school. Despite his humble upbringing, Bunyan became a constant reader of the Bible. Eventually he came upon a worn copy of Martin Luther's *Commentary on the Galatians*, and as a result of these influences and the religious influence of his wife, whose dowry brought Bunyan two used books, *The Plain Man's Pathway to Heaven* and *The Practice of Piety*, in 1653 he became a member of the Open and Particular Baptists. Shortly thereafter, he discovered his ability to stand before others and speak with simple eloquence and conviction. It was the beginning of his remarkable career as a nonconformist religious leader, who by the clarity and fervor of his sermons drew vast crowds to hear him as he preached in the streets and fields, including in small towns and larger cities.

His popularity drew to him the suspicion of the established church and of the government that had officially proscribed the sort of preaching in which Bunyan excelled. It is a tribute to his influence that in 1660, on the return of the king to the throne, he was the first to be prohibited from holding public meetings. Refusing to obey the law, he was imprisoned for a period of twelve years. When, in 1672, he was released with a king's pardon and the right to preach, he carried with him the first part of *The Pilgrim's Progress*.

Lacking a formal education, Bunyan's style is delightful to readers because it is the vocabulary of common people. At all stages of the journey, the pilgrims encounter figures such as Madam Bubble, Mr. Worldly Wiseman, Lord Hategood, Mr. Talkative, and Mrs. Timorous, all recognizable to the reader. Bunyan is possible the only writer who gave to the abstract the interest of the concrete. In the works of many celebrated authors, characters are mere personifications. They present not a jealous individual, but jealousy; not a traitor, but treachery; not a patriot, but patriotism. Bunyan, however, was so imaginative that personifications, when he deals with them, become individuals, and the dialogue he provides between two concepts has more dramatic effect than dialogue between two human beings in most plays. While there were many clever writers in England during the latter half of the seventeenth century, there were only two minds that possessed the imaginative faculty to an eminent degree; one of those minds produced *Paradise Lost*, the other *Pilgrim's Progress*.

A work of allegory and even thought by some to be the first English novel, *The Pilgrim's Progress* is a Christian allegory, meaning that it has two levels of significance. On the surface, the story follows a man named Christian as he leaves the City of Destruction and journeys to a place called the Celestial City, encountering all sorts of roadblocks and fearsome creatures along the way. However, on a deeper level, the book charts the journey of an average Christian who strives to leave behind his destructive, sinful ways and get to Heaven. In 1684, Bunyan wrote Part II of *The Pilgrim's Progress*, in which Christian's wife, Christiana and their children, who earlier had mocked Christian and thought him delirious, likewise travel from the City of Destruction to the Celestial City.

The story of Christian's journey is actually a dream that the book's unnamed narrator is having. In the narrator's dream, Christian is carrying a heavy burden on his back—the weight of his sins—and doesn't know how to get rid ot it. Following the advice of a man named Evangelist, he sets out on his quest for his destination. Christian is pursued by two neighbors, Obstinate and Pliable; the former turns back, but Pliable catches up with Christian, and the two get caught in a muddy bog called the Slough of Despond.

Released with the assistance of a figure called Help, Christian sets out alone to deal with figures such as Mr. Worldly Wiseman, Mr. Legality, and Mr. Civility, hoping to lose his heavy burden. Thankfully, Evangelist finds him again and explains that the advice of these false comrades cannot remove his burden. Passing through the Wicket-gate, Christian stops at the Interpreter's House, where the Interpreter shows him a series of riddle-like symbols of a Christian believer's journey through life. After this, Christian runs to the Cross, where he immediately loses his burden. Three angels, called the Shining Ones, greet him. One of them hands Christian a certificate, which he must present when he reaches the Celestial Gate. Continuing on his journey, he is confronted by a hideous fiend named Apollyon. After a long, fierce combat, Christian wounds Apollyon with his sword. Soon he encounters a fellow pilgrim, Faithful, and together they enter the ancient town of Vanity, which boasts a huge Fair selling every imaginable type of goods. When the pilgrims resist the Fair's attractions, the people of Vanity persecute them, and Faithful is cruelly executed. Christian escapes and is joined by a man named Hopeful, and together they travel toward the Celestial City. After being starved and beaten by a Giant named Despair, they resort to prayer, whereupon Christian discovers a key that releases them from the giant's dungeon.

As they approach the peaceful land called Beulah, which borders the Celestial City, they encounter a man named Ignorance, who believes he will attain Heaven on the basis of his efforts and good intentions. Before reaching the City, they must cross the River of Death by the power of their faith. Christian finds the crossing terrifying, and Hopeful must keep his friend's head above water. Once Christian begins to think of Jesus instead of his own sins, he suddenly finds the crossing easy. The pilgrims hand in their certificates and are joyously welcomed into the Celestial City, which gleams with gold and rings with music.

After watching Christian and Hopeful enter through the gate, the narrator wishes he were with them. Ignorance is shut out of the City because he is without a certificate of entry and is sent to hell. The narrator wakes up from his dream. Ignorance's appearance emphasizes the idea that spiritual progress requires more than simply living a good life and having a natural faith in God. Progress can only be made when action is combined with knowledge and understanding. Ignorance is a likeable pilgrim, but he is only walking toward salvation, not progressing toward it. He cannot make progress like Christian because he has not received revelation, nor does he believe in its value or express any interest in hearing about it. He thinks the revealed word of God is nonsense, and so his travel is only physical, not mental or spiritual.

In the conclusion, the narrator says that he has told his dream and now invites the reader to interpret it. Though he warns of the dangers of interpreting his dream incorrectly, the narrator also warns against the obvious surface content, against being entertained by the tale rather than instructed by it. He says that one must not play with the surface details of his story but look beneath the surface to the essential meaning. The difference is that now the one who must interpret is no longer Christian, but the reader. Christian's quest for understanding is now that of the reader.

In addition to the quest for understanding, Bunyan's *Pilgrim's Progress* may be understood as a quest for freedom from worldly distraction and spiritual destruction. Bunyan was intent on offering a picture of "the merciful working of God upon my soul," and he describes a process of deliverance from both worldly delights and from an acute and painful sense of sin.

Bunyan had at his disposal sermonic treatise and scriptural exposition to convey his Puritan theology, but instead he relied on his own spiritual experience, using a dreamlike, introspective style to forge a highly original style. In this style, body, mind, and soul are so intertwined as to be inseparable. Despite Protestantism's predilection for expounding truth in sermons, Bunyan recognized that the natural mind is not content with factual information alone. Rather, in its search for truth and understanding, the mind must be invited to put aside its doctrinaire veil, turning instead to metaphor and riddle for stimulus and challenge. Indeed, the mind must work for what it understands, for the grail is worth the questing. As a fisher of men and a snarer of souls, Bunyan uses all the devices appropriate to fishing and fowling, challenging readers with imaginative elements such as dream and symbol, metaphor and riddle, to become more fully alive to the wonderful wizardry of art.

As he dramatized in the Vanity Fair episode, the eyes, ears, and heart of this world are so full of earthly vanities that they cannot comprehend God's mystery as it is embodied in Christian and Faithful, who speak a strange language and dress and act peculiarly. This view is artistically exploited on those occasions when the pilgrims are asked to interpret riddles, most notably by the innkeeper Gaius in the Second Part.[3] Small wonder, then, that as the spell of sacred art is cast within us, alert readers will find themselves bound to be vigilant, since they know that allegory, like scripture, is forever reading them. We play strenuously when we play in the field of spirituality.

In the Apology prefacing his work Bunyan writes, "This book will make a traveler out of you . . . It will make the slothful active; and the blind will see delightful things." That's the role of the creative arts. Beauty and goodness in the arts have the capacity to guide the human spirit apart from explanation or rational thought. As transcendent vehicles, they can enhance vision and transform the stubborn heart.

In his Apology, Bunyan attacks the popular misconception that religion and fiction are enemies. Citing Hosea 12:10, "I have used . . . similitudes" (KJV), he acknowledges that the Bible contains various forms of speech, including allegories, metaphors, and fictional parables. In his mind, allegorical language enhances truth, purifies the mind, pleases the understanding, and makes the will submissive. He also notes that when he began *The Pilgrim's Progress*, it was not what he had intended to write. The allegorical approach came upon him suddenly, the multiplicity of ideas arising "Like sparks that from the coals of fire do fly." The result has led some to view the book as the work of a "transcendent genius, as original as anything in literature can be, its innovative fictional realism inexplicable save by reference to its author's own daemon."[4]

Bunyan demonstrates the importance of interpreting indirect meanings by focusing on Christian's experience with the Interpreter. The scene in the Interpreter's house is one of the longest in the book. Christian spends a lot of time with the Interpreter because he has a lot to learn about interpretation. In Bunyan's view, Christian cannot get to heaven by obeying moral rules. Instead, he must figure out how to understand meanings behind objects and events. In the Significant Rooms, the Interpreter shows Christian not just one example of a thing that requires interpretation to be understood, but half a dozen. Some of the interpretation is straightforward, like the portrait of Christ that represents the historical figure. Others require more thought and guidance. Christian doesn't know fire represents the believer's faith and water represents the devil. Nor is it obvious in the dusty parlor that dust symbolizes sin, and that the sweeper is the law of

---

3. Keeble, *Pilgrim's Progress*, 221.
4. Keeble, *Pilgrim's Progress*, xi–xii.

the Old Testament. Christian must be guided to these meanings. In this, Christian is like the reader of *The Pilgrim's Progress*, who must be guided to find meanings behind the obvious layers of the story.

The book's opening portrays the central idea of the work—the journey. Bunyan's allegory is about travel and the meaning that one's quest comes to acquire. The journey is one of discovery and learning new things. Christian is journeying not to return home but to leave home, or rather, to make a new home for himself in an unfamiliar place. Because he believes his town is destroyed, he cannot return home. Instead, he heads for a better place through his journey. Therefore, the geographical wandering across the land is also a mythic advancement, a spiritual development, which is the "progress" referred to in the title. Though joined occasionally by companions, Christian's journey is a solitary experience. In part, his solitude is a necessary aspect of his Protestant faith, which holds that salvation comes not through church attendance and group ritual, but rather through private prayer and introspection. Bunyan shows the reader that faith is individual, so Christian must be alone to practice it.

Solitude, however, reveals a dark side of Christian. One of the disturbing aspects of his character is his relative indifference to the fate of the wife and family he leaves behind. He tries to persuade them to come along but gives us quickly, and he is never shown thinking about them or missing them. Salvation matters more to him than worldly relationships, but his lack of family feeling casts a shadow over his personality.

In Bunyan's quest for understanding, personal experience is an important source of evidence, but alone it can mislead. Only when personal experience is combined with "heavenly witness," that is, with biblical teaching and guidance by the Holy Spirit, can experience become a source of ultimate knowledge. So also, proof texting scripture is unpersuasive, as we see in the case of Talkative, with his knowledge of scripture unattended by conviction, and in the case of Ignorance, with his heartfelt conviction unaccompanied by knowledge. Bunyan's epistemology is clear: common experience is not as trustworthy as is personal experience, but even the latter is suspect if it does not conform to the truth of scripture interpreted by the Holy Spirit within the sanctified believer.

In 1666, while in prison, Bunyan wrote his spiritual autobiography, *Grace Abounding to the Chief of Sinners*. In that work he speaks of a time before his conversion, describing his encounter with a community of radical Christians as meeting people who had found a "new world"; that new world became the subject of *The Pilgrim's Progress*. To portray his own experience of that new world, and to describe how grace alters the perception of one's former world, required the use of allegory. For Bunyan, such allegory had to be derived from scripture. *The Pilgrim's Progress* is allegorical because its subject is a special kind of experience: the process of moving from one kind of reality to another and meanwhile rediscovering one's present reality.

C. S. LEWIS'S *THE PILGRIM'S REGRESS*

C. S. Lewis was one of the most widely read apologists for the Christian faith in the twentieth century, and his influence continues to our time. Since his death on November 22, 1963—missed by many because it occurred on the same day as the assassination of U.S. President John F. Kennedy—sales of his books continue to grow. Part of his popularity results from the variety of his interests, which range from theology and literary criticism to science fiction and fantasy literature. Perhaps his greatest popularity is as author of the *Chronicles of Narnia*, widely recognized as among the best children's literature written in the twentieth century.[5]

Steeped in allegory, particularly in Edmund Spenser's *The Faerie Queene*—in which the landscape of Fairy Land is that of the soul—and fond of Homer, Virgil, Celtic mythology, *Beowolf*, old Norse mythology, and Milton, Lewis wrote appealing literature in large part due to his ability to utilize both halves of his brain, merging *logos* and *mythos* to probe humanity's deepest emotions. For example, in *Till We Have Faces*, Lewis presents a thorough reworking of the legend of Cupid and Psyche. Rather than analyzing the human personality through reason, Lewis portrays our innermost emotions through myth, making the myth come alive through

---

5. While these seven books were written in a certain order, beginning with *The Lion, the Witch, and the Wardrobe* (1948) and ending with *The Magician's Nephew* (1953), looking at the tales in the order of the chronology of Narnia, the *Chronicles* become an allegory of Christian history, beginning with creation in *The Magician's Nephew*, continuing with redemption in *The Lion, the Witch, and the Wardrobe* and the church's golden age in *The Horse and His Boy*, and proceeding through quest-voyages to the apocalypse in *The Last Battle*. In keeping with Lewis's principle of incorporating Christian doctrine, this sequence appropriates the Christian mythos. There is a reason why Aslan is only physically present in the first books, and then is absent for long periods until his reappearance at the conclusion of *The Last Battle*; Lewis is following the biblical storyline. Lewis maintained that he did not write specifically for children, but wrote in the fairy-tale mode because, as the title of one of his essays has it, "Sometimes Fairy Stories May Say Best What's to Be Said."

fictional narrative. However, even in his most fantastic fiction he maintained a logical, analytic approach, and in his most analytical work, he retained an imaginative style. According to Lewis, reality can only be understood by integrating logic and myth. This approach led Lewis to Christianity, which he understood as a marriage of heaven and earth. As he learned from his friends in the literary circle that called itself the Inklings, the heart of Christianity is a myth that is also a fact: Perfect Myth and Perfect Fact.

For Lewis, when divine truth falls on human imagination, myth is born. Myth puts us in touch with Reality in a more intimate way than by knowing what is merely factual. Myth touches our lives at a deeper level than abstract though and, thus, is the best means of divine communication. Lewis believes that one of the functions of the natural world is to provide symbols that point to spiritual reality. Nature supplies the substance for myth; God supplies the meaning. It is this blending of the mythical and the real in a historical occurrence that gives Christianity its greatest argument for validity, for here and only here the myth has become fact: the Word, flesh; God, human.

Lewis considered myth to be the master key not only to literature but also to life. With that key, he opened many literary doors. In his essay "Myth became Fact," Lewis describes myth as "the mountain whence all the different streams arise which become truths down here in the valley. . . . Or, if you prefer, myth is the isthmus which connects the peninsular world of thought with that vast continent we really belong to. Myth is not, like truth, abstract; nor is it, like direct experience, bound to the particular."[6] The Christianity to which Lewis converted became for him the incarnation of God in history, the underlying truth of all ancient myths and legends.

Although membership in the Inklings varied, it regularly included J. R. R. Tolkien, Owen Barfield, Hugo Dyson, Gervase Matthew, and Charles Williams. The author Dorothy Sayers was not a member, but she was closely associated with this group through her friendship with Williams, and the Inklings were deeply influenced by her religious writings.

The group met twice weekly, often to read portions of their works in progress in order to receive praise or criticism. Lewis found the "romantic theology" of Charles Williams particularly appealing. By "romantic" Williams meant, not one who is romantic about theology, but one who is theological about romance, that is, one who considers the theological implications of those experiences called romantic. At the core of Williams's

6. Lewis, *God in the Dock*, 66.

work is the belief that the most serious and ecstatic experiences either of human love, earthly joy, or of imaginative literature have theological implications, that is, are to be subsumed into the Christian vision.

Another Inkling that influenced Lewis was the fantasy writer Tolkien. It was Tolkien's interpretation of myth as fragments of eternal truth that allowed Lewis to see the truth in what he considered the Christian "myth." Tolkien further gave Lewis an appreciation for the uses of fantasy to portray deeper levels of reality. Tolkien also influenced Lewis with his concept that in writing literature, authors are not creators but "sub-creators," who may hope to reflect something of the eternal light of God's creative work in the universe.

The Pilgrim's Regress, published in 1933, was C. S. Lewis's first published work of prose fiction after he converted to Christianity. Lewis's allegory charts the progress of a fictional character named John through a philosophical landscape in search of the Island of his desire. Lewis clearly had Bunyan's late sixteenth century *The Pilgrim's Progress* in mind as he wrote, though he recast it with the philosophical, cultural, and ideological principles of the early twentieth century. As such, the character struggles with communism, fascism, socialism, liberalism, Freudianism, and deficiencies in the Christian Church of the twentieth century, together with other philosophical and aesthetic movements of the time. Partly autobiographical, *The Pilgrim's Regress* describes Lewis's journey from agnosticism to theism and from theism to Christianity. In this work we find many of the themes that Lewis developed during the rest of his life.

In 1954, when he became Professor of Medieval and Renaissance English, not at Oxford—where he had served as a fellow and tutor since the 1920s—but at Cambridge, he told his audience during his inaugural address that for him, the "great divide" in Western civilization was not that between paganism and Christianity, nor the divide between the Middle Ages and the Renaissance, but rather the Industrial Revolution, which separated the "Old Western Culture" from the current "post-Christian Culture." Lewis further argued that paganism and Christianity shared more in common than either shared with a secularized modern world. On another occasion he wrote, "Monotheism should not be regarded as the rival of polytheism, but rather as its maturity." In 1931, Lewis wrote to his longtime friend Arthur Morris that "*real* paganism at its best . . . is the next best thing to Christianity."

As described in his 1955 spiritual autobiography *Surprised by Joy*, much of Lewis's spiritual pilgrimage involved the parallel movements of his intellectual thought with the mystical experience of Joy, or as Lewis preferred—*Sehnsucht* ("longing"). Lewis defined *Sehnsucht* as an unsatisfied desire that is itself more desirable than any other satisfaction. Unlike other desires, however, the object of this desire is often unknown or mysterious. Lewis's autobiography is the account of his search for the object of his longing and his discovery, at last, that the longing is for union with God.

Before examining Lewis's *Pilgrim's Regress*, we need to become familiar with his spiritual conversion—more a journey than an event, more a process of recognition than of cognition, and more about returning ("regress") than advancing, as we shall see. Having been reared in a traditional Anglican home, "Jack" Lewis turned from a Christianity of fear and guilt, led by insincere clergy, to distrust of religion. Viewing all religions as human inventions, the adolescent Lewis came to associate Christianity with "ugly architecture, ugly music, and bad poetry." He was not what we would call an atheist, since he remained open to transcendent mystery and surprise, but he wanted nothing to do with organized religion or Christian religiosity.

Admitted to Oxford at the age of eighteen, Lewis felt duty-bound to enlist in his country's military, fighting near the end of World War I on the front lines, where he was wounded and later discharged. He returned to Oxford, enrolling in the Honors School of Classics known as "Greats." Lewis began to find his literary interests turning more and more toward Christian writers, and even the pagan writers he most enjoyed—Plato, Aeschylus, Virgil—seemed to be the most religious. Still considering Christianity a myth—that is, a human contrivance—he felt it provided a good framework on which to hang his philosophical idealism. At this point in his life he also read George MacDonald's *Phantastes*, attracted by the "romantic" elements in the novel. In addition, Lewis found something new, a "bright shadow" he later discovered to be the voice of holiness, "something too near to see, too plain to be understood, on this side of knowledge." At this time, he also began to read G. K. Chesterton, loving his writing despite Chesterton's Christianity. As Lewis later recalled, he came to feel "Christians are wrong, but all the rest are bores."

Lewis became friends with Tolkien, who was both a Roman Catholic and a philologist, two things Lewis had previously mistrusted. Around this time Lewis experienced anew the state of intense longing he had previously experienced only at crucial points in his boyhood, a longing he described as *Sehnsucht* and translated as Joy.

Thinking of this longing as a form of love, he came to realize that this experience was not an end in itself but a pointer to something else— something far more desirable than the sensations that accompanied this desire. But what was the object of this desire? According to Lewis, if one finds in oneself a desire that no experience on earth can satisfy, the most probable explanation is that one is made for another world. In other words, these "immortal longings" he experienced were "signals of transcendence" or "thin places" that implied the existence of a realm beyond the material world.

At this point, Lewis believed he had committed himself only to the acceptance of "the God of the philosophers," but not yet the God of Christianity. Reading Chesterton's *The Everlasting Man*, the Christian understanding of history began making sense to him. In 1929, Lewis knelt and prayed to a personal God, not yet a Christian but a theist; still, as he later described it, "the most dejected and reluctant convert in all England."

Two years later, in September 1931, Lewis joined Inklings members Dyson and Tolkien for a walk on the picturesque footpath of Magdalen College in Oxford called Addison's Walk, followed by an all-night conversation. The discussion focused on the topic of myth, and how Christianity is true myth. That night was pivotal for Lewis, for it led to his conversion from theism to Christianity. Lewis embedded his understanding of myth in *The Pilgrim's Regress*, written less than a year after he had become a Christian. Modeling his book on Bunyan's *Pilgrim's Progress*, Lewis completed the project during a two-week period, the images and words pouring forth in creative torrents. Though he never used allegory in any of his previous writings, he found that it provided the perfect medium for what he wanted to say. Like Bunyan, his account is set forth as a dream in which the hero undergoes perilous adventures, searching for Joy, which in the end turns out to be a quest for God.

At one point in the story, the pilgrim John, troubled by the mythological nature of Christianity, hears a voice, declaring: "Child, if you will, it *is* mythology. It is but truth, not fact: an image, not the very real . . . But this is My invention, this is the veil under which I have chosen to appear even from the first until now. For this end I made your senses and for this end your imagination, that you might see My face and live."[7] Lewis's view of

---

7. Lewis, *Pilgrim's Regress*, 120.

myth as found in this passage seems to derive in part from the conversation Lewis had with Tolkien on September 19, 1931. On that occasion, Tolkien declared that in making myth, the story teller or "sub-creator" is actually reflecting a splintered fragment of the true light. Pagan myths are therefore never just "lies": there is always something of truth in them. And whatever pagan myths describe, they all became true once—in Christ. As Lewis later wrote in his book *Miracles*, myth is not priestly lying, but "at its best (is) a real though unfocused gleam of divine truth falling on human imagination."[8] Therefore it is true, not in the sense of being verbally or doctrinally accurate, but adequately expressed in the actual incarnation, crucifixion, and resurrection of Christ.

As depicted in *Pilgrim's Regress*, Lewis believed in progressive revelation, namely, that God discloses truth to human beings in the way best suited to their particular stage of development. For pagan culture, divine revelation took the form of mythology. For the Israelites, God spoke through the Law and the prophets. Since they were the "chosen people," the Israelites were the recipients of "chosen mythology—the mythology chosen by God to be the vehicle of the earliest sacred truths, the first step in that process which ends in the New Testament where truth has become completely historical."[9]

The Pilgrim's Regress centers around the main character, John, who as a boy grows up in Puritania under the stern, allusive, and seemingly tyrannical Landlord. At one point, John has paradisal visions of an Island that create indescribable yearning. At first, he thinks this yearning is Lust, personified as brown girls, but when he unmasks the mistake, he decides to flee his homeland and perceived oppressor, the Landlord, in search of the far-off Island.

Along the way he meets Mr. Enlightenment, who personifies nineteenth-century rationalism. He invites John to join him on his travels to Claptrap, but John decides to continue his search for the Island. In the cities of Thrill and Eschropolis (meaning an ugly city in Greek), John meets personifications of romantic love, the modern literary movement, and Freudianism. He thinks he finds the Island through aesthetic experience, but seeing his error, he abandons the cities. Eventually, he is captured by the giant called Spirit of the Age. The character is drawn as a spirit whose gaze makes everything transparent. So when the giant looks at John, everyone

---

8. Lewis, *Miracles*, 134, note 1.

9. Lewis, *Miracles*, 134, note 1.

including John can see his insides, that is, his bowels, stomach, lungs, and all his internal organs. The giant tries to convince him that he is only material, but Reason, personified as a gallant woman knight, comes to the rescue. Fearing Reason, the giant tries to send her away, but she agrees to leave only after the giant answers three riddles, upon which the giant wagers his life. Unable to answer her riddles, the giant is slain by Reason, who then leads John to the Grand Canyon of sin and unbelief.

As John tries to figure out how to cross, the church, personified as Mother Kirk, comes and explains the reason for the canyon (which is the Sin of Adam) and that she is the only one who can get individuals across the chasm. John thanks her but decides to take the long way around. As he goes North, he meets three pale men personified as Mr. Neo-Angular, Mr. Neo-Classical, and Mr. Humanist who are served by a creature named Drudge.[10] These men are unable to help John as they talk of things they do not understand. John proceeds farther North to a valley filled with caves inhabited by trolls and ruled by a giant named Savage. These serve as models for Marxism and Fascism. Turning back and going South along the road, he meets Mr. Broad who represents a "modernizing religion which is friends with the World and goes on no pilgrimages."

John eventually reaches the house of Wisdom, who teaches him what is lacking from notable philosophies of the twentieth century such as Idealist philosophy, materialism, and Hegelianism. Continuing along the canyon, John runs into a Man from whom he learns he must accept Grace or die. John had wondered if he could live by Philosophy or pantheistic beliefs, but after accepting Grace he feels obligated to acknowledge the existence of the Landlord. He hadn't wanted to admit this, for he wanted to call his soul his own.

Moving on, John discovers a hermit named History. History tells him that not everyone has as clear visions of the Islands as he does, but that all people receive similar pictures. Some don't have the benefit of Mother Kirk but the Landlord stirs up pictures and sweet desires to lead them to her. Still accompanied by Reason, John wishes to travel alone, but Reason refuses to leave, leading him to Mother Kirk, who instructs John to dive into a pool of water. John says that he doesn't know how to dive, but learns that diving is simply the art of ceasing to struggle. After diving, John finds the Island,

---

10. It is hard to miss in Mr. Neo-Angular, Lewis's antipathy to T. S. Eliot and the Anglo-Catholic movement to which Eliot converted in 1927.

only to discover that it is but the other side of the mountains he had known in Puritania.

Crossing the chasm with Mother Kirk's help, John encounters Guide, who tells him "the way to go on is to go back." The Regress portion of the title becomes evident as John journeys back home. However, as he heads East again, he discovers that the country looks very different on the return journey; it is the same land, yet different, for he has been transformed, and that makes all the difference. He now sees everything in a new light and that the road he took is a knife's edge between Heaven and Hell. In the end, it is not a place we seek (the Island), but a Person (the Landlord). Even the Church is fallible and may crumble and fail. However, the Church's influence "never quite crumbles: for as often as men become Pagans again, the Landlord again sends them pictures and stirs up sweet desires and so leads them back to Mother Kirk even as he led the actual Pagans long ago. There is, indeed, no other way."[11]

When *The Pilgrim's Regress* was published in 1933, the book caused anger and controversy because of its broadsides against High Anglicanism and the Broad Church approach to Christianity. While the book's title implies the calling of those spiritually redeemed to return to society in service and ministry, the path is that of "mere Christianity," not of dogmatic or strident Christianity. In suggesting that the spiritual path involves a regress, Lewis seemed to be indicating that he would not enter Christianity by a new path, but by the old one, that paved by paganism and myth.

For Lewis, conscience and desire (spiritual longing) work together to create a whole person. Desire "does not always take the form of an Island . . . The Landlord sends pictures of many different kinds. What is universal is not the particular picture, but the arrival of some message, not perfectly intelligible, which wakes this desire and sets men longing for something East or West of the world; something possessed, if at all, not in the act of desiring it . . . something that tends inevitably to be confused with common or even with vile satisfaction lying close at hand, yet which is able, if a person faithfully lives through the dialectic of its successive births and deaths, to lead us at least where true joys are to be found."[12] As for the shapes in which this desire comes, sometimes it comes as an image, sometimes as an image telling a story. While all images are fallible, debunking them is not the cure.

11. Lewis, *Pilgrim's Regress*, 105.

12. Lewis, *Pilgrim's Regress*, 108–9.

THE GOAL OF ALL SPIRITUAL QUESTS

As is evident, Bunyan's allegory exemplifies the one-way quest, while Lewis's allegory exemplifies the two-way quest, the version most natural and common in mythological literature. All quests are characterized by beginnings and endings, but in in one-way quests, the seeker does not begin at home, but rather hopes to end there. However, in two-way quests, the hero's journey involves a departure and a return.

While the linear quest expresses the progressive nature of history, it also depicts the dualistic struggle between good and evil and the ultimate role of morality in that struggle. On the cosmic scale, such a plot is portrayed in Milton's *Paradise Lost*, wherein the scope of evil is confined to a directed sequence of crises, beginning with the war in Heaven and ending with the apocalyptic close of history. Bunyan's interpretation is that of Milton.

Lewis's *Pilgrim's Regress* is more complex, for it integrates the one- and two-way quest, acknowledging two distinct journeys. The framing journey is one-way, for the pilgrim John is responding to a call from beyond the world, a calling couched in the mystery of desire or longing for which no earthly object proves to be adequate. Like Christian's call, this call draws us beyond the world. However, Lewis's second quest describes the convert's regress (or return) from the world's edge to the human community for fellowship and ongoing growth as well as for witness and service. This is a circuitous journey that is both a progression from adolescent rebellion toward acceptance of moral choice and discipline and a regression from contemporary secularism toward a more holistic and responsible Christianity those distorted versions represented by Puritania and Mr. Broad (liberal religion). The notion of a circular journey served Lewis well, for it is a pattern he develops further in his space trilogy and in the *Chronicles of Narnia*.

For Bunyan's pilgrim, conversion comes near the beginning of his one-way quest and the River of Death defines the transition into the next world. For Lewis's pilgrim, conversion does not come until the traveler passes through the spiritual death and rebirth defined by death's river at the world's edge, and his specifically Christian pilgrimage begins, rather than ends, at this point. John's regress, then, is the analogue to Christian's progress. The first quest calls beyond the world, whereas the second directs John back to what he has left behind.

In Bunyan and Lewis we have two very different versions of the spiritual journey. Which model should we follow? As we discover, using scripture as our guide, as is the case with both Bunyan and Lewis, is in-conclusive, for both models are biblical. Bunyan was deeply influenced by the biblical pilgrimage of Abraham from Ur to Canaan and by the jour-ney of the Israelite slaves from Egypt to the Promised Land, both one-way quests. Lewis, on the other hand, was influenced by Israel's journey from the Babylonian Exile back to Judah and by the inclusive visions of the New Jerusalem in Revelation 21 and 22, symbolizing the church's return to God's primeval Garden, now a city, its gates never shut (21:25) and the leaves of its Tree of Life now a balm "for the healing of the nations" (22:2).

If there will be a new heaven and a new earth, as the book of Revela-tion indicates, if God's kingdom will one day fully manifest itself on earth, as Matthew indicates, and if there will be a future resurrection, as 1 Cor-inthians 15 declares, then Christians must be concerned not only about heavenly things but also about earthly things—for all creation shall one day be redeemed (Rom 8:19–20). No one should be more concerned about caring for the earth and matters of global import than Christians, since they are evidently God's concern as well. God not only made creation, God loves all of creation, and is already in the process of redeeming it. It is an impoverished vision of the Gospel "that cares for the souls of the unsaved but not their bodies or minds, that cares for heaven but not the conditions on earth, that cares for spiritual things but not also material things."[13]

How, then, do we read scripture? Does history end with rapture to a heaven far away (Luke 12:33; John 14:2–3; 2 Cor 5:1; 1 Thess 4:17; Heb 11:13–16), or does it continue with a new heaven and a new earth (Isa 65:17; Rev 21:1), with the realization that earth is the house of God (Gen 28:17; Jer 22:34), with heaven come down to earth (Rev 21:2), and with God and Christ making their home with us here on earth (John 14:23; Rev 21:3)?[14]

The paradox of the traveler's two quests are set forth well in Lewis's *Surprised by Joy*: "I had hoped that the heart of reality might be of such a kind that we can best symbolize it as a place; instead, I found it to be a Person."[15]

---

13. Witherington, *John's Wisdom*, 113.

14. Contrary to ideas about the "rapture" of the church from earth, there is no "rap-ture" in Revelation. Instead, it is God who is "raptured" to earth to live with us. At the end of Revelation, humans are not in heaven; there is no longer need for dualistic thinking, because God dwells on earth; and where God is, there is heaven.

15. Lewis, *Surprised by Joy*, 230.

QUESTIONS FOR DISCUSSION AND REFLECTION

1. Assess the meaning of the author's statement, "the goal of life's journey is not perfection but wholeness."

2. Assess the meaning of W. B. Yeats's line, "Nothing can be sole or whole that has not been rent."

3. Define the term "allegory." In your estimation, what did C. S. Lewis mean when he stated that "all good allegory exists not to hide but to reveal"?

4. In your mind, need there be conflict between science and the arts, or between science and religion? Explain your answer.

5. As far as possible, explain the perennial popularity of Bunyan's *Pilgrim's Progress*.

6. In your estimation, how did Bunyan's theology, particularly his eschatology, influence *Pilgrim's Progress*?

7. Despite its obvious Christian perspective, can you detect themes in *Pilgrim's Progress* that might be of value to secular non-Christians? Explain your answer.

8. The idea of questing or journeying is central to Bunyan's *Pilgrim's Progress* and Lewis's *Pilgrim's Regress*. In your own words, explain what allegorical writers mean when they depict life as a spiritual journey.

9. Explain the difference between *logos* and *mythos* as ways of knowing, and how *mythos* is better able to probe humanity's deepest needs and emotions.

10. Explain what Lewis and his fellow Inklings meant by understanding Christianity as "Perfect Myth and Perfect Fact."

11. In *Pilgrim's Regress*, what did Lewis mean by the word "regress"?

12. Explain the role of "longing" in Bunyan and Lewis.

13. Explain and assess Lewis's meaning of "progressive revelation."

14. In your estimation, what is the primary insight gained from this chapter? Explain your answer.

Chapter 9

OVER THE RAINBOW

ONE OF YESTERYEAR'S MOST BELOVED tales is *The Wizard of Oz*, known and remembered primarily in film format. The book, published in 1900 as *The Wonderful Wizard of Oz*, was written by L. Frank Baum and later adapted as a popular Broadway musical in 1902. However, it was the 1939 musical film adaptation, produced in Technicolor by Metro Goldwyn Mayer, which became commercially successful. The movie version, considered one of the greatest films of all time, starred Judy Garland as Dorothy, alongside Ray Bolger, Jack Haley, Bert Lahr, Frank Morgan, and Margaret Hamilton as Scarecrow, Tin Man, Cowardly Lion, the Wizard, and the Wicked Witch of the West.

The book's initial success, together with that of the Broadway musical adaptation, led Baum to write thirteen additional Oz sequels to the original story. The book has become an established part of multiple cultures throughout the world, having been translated or adapted into over fifty languages, at times modified to local customs and perspectives. In one of the Jewish versions, the book's Land of Oz was rendered in Hebrew as *Eretz Uz* ("land of Uz"), the new title the same as the original Hebrew homeland of the biblical Job. For Hebrew readers, this choice of terms added a layer of biblical connections absent from the English original.

Characterized by its use of Technicolor (the brilliant three-color process widely used during Hollywood's Golden Age of cinema), fantasy storytelling, musical score, and memorable characters, the film was nominated for six Academy Awards, including Best Picture, which it lost to *Gone with the Wind*. It did win in two categories, including Best Original Song for "Over the Rainbow" and Best Original Score. The lyrics were written by Edgar "Yip" Harburg and the songs composed by Harold Arlen. The musical score and incidental music were composed by Herbert Stothart.

While the 1939 release was sufficiently popular at the box office, it failed to make a profit for MGM until the 1949 re-release. The 1956 television broadcast premiere reintroduced the film to the public, an event shown annually on American television from 1959 to 1998 and then several times a year beginning in 1999. According to the U.S. Library of Congress, *The Wizard of Oz* is the most seen film in movie history. In 1989, it was selected by the Library of Congress as one of the top twenty-five films for preservation in the National Film Registry for being "culturally, historically, or aesthetically significant."

In 1974, the story inspired "The Wiz," a Tony Award-winning musical featuring Diana Ross as Dorothy and an all-black cast and set in the context of modern African-American culture, exchanging New York City for Kansas. In 2003, the high grossing musical *Wicked* opened on Broadway to great acclaim. Due to its popularity, *Wicked* has led productions in cities across the United States and around the world. Based on the 1995 Gregory Maguire novel *Wicked: The Life and Times of the Wicked Witch of the West*, the musical tells the backstory of the Wizard of Oz and what happened before Dorothy arrived in the Land of Oz

The Wizard of Oz chronicles the adventures of a young teenaged farm girl named Dorothy who lives in a farmhouse in Kansas with Uncle Henry, Aunt Em, and her dog, Toto. Dorothy is an orphaned girl of indeterminate age, and Aunt Em and Uncle Henry are impoverished but loving people acquainted with hardship. Despite her own adversities, Dorothy can make others laugh. Toto, in turn, also makes Dorothy laugh. The farmhouse is a small cabin, unanchored to the land, with only a storm shelter crudely dug in the yard nearby.

In the film's prologue, Dorothy returns home with Toto, fearful that Toto will be taken from her by Almira, her socialite neighbor, who has falsely accused Toto of biting her, and is bent on revenge, threatening to give Toto to the dogcatcher. However, the adults pay Dorothy little attention, for all are busy with farm chores. Longing for respect, freedom, and fairness, Dorothy sings "Somewhere over the Rainbow." When Almira comes to the farmhouse to take Toto, Dorothy runs away from home, but only temporarily, for she misses home and her Aunt Em. As a cyclone approaches,

Dorothy is preoccupied with Toto, and by the time she catches him, she is unable to reach the storm cellar. Dorothy and Toto find temporary shelter in the house before the cyclone carries it away to the magical Land of Oz, located somewhere over the rainbow.

When the house finally lands, it falls upon the Wicked Witch of the East, instantly killing her. Dorothy discovers that she is in a beautiful land inhabited by short, strangely dressed creatures called Munchkins, who are grateful to Dorothy for having killed the Wicked Witch of the East, thus freeing them from her control. The Witch of the North gives Dorothy the slippers of the dead witch and advises her to go to the Emerald City to see the Great Wizard of Oz, who might help her return to Kansas. The witch sends Dorothy off along the yellow brick road with a magical kiss to protect her from harm.

On the long journey to the Emerald City, Dorothy and Toto are joined by Scarecrow, who wishes he had brains, Tin Woodman, who longs for a heart, and Cowardly Lion, who seeks courage. They face many trials along the way, but they overcome them all, often because of Scarecrow's good sense, Tin Woodman's kindness, and the bravery of Cowardly Lion.

Having to adapt Baum's book to film, the screenwriters did an amazing job. Cutting material to fit the timeframe was essential. However, in the process, they gave some characters dual roles, introducing individuals into the prologue such as Professor Marvel, the carnival fortune teller; Almira Gulch, Dorothy's mean neighbor; and the three farmhands, reusing them in the Oz section as the Wizard of Oz, the Wicked Witch of the West, and Dorothy's three traveling companions.

Upon reaching the Emerald City, the Guardian of the Gates provides them green-lensed glasses and leads them to the Palace where, to their dismay, the Wizard tells them that no favors will be granted until they bring the broomstick of the Wicked Witch of the West. The companions embark on their next journey, heading to the land of the Winkies, ruled by the Wicked Witch of the West. The witch summons her Winged Monkeys, who apprehend Dorothy's traveling companions and bring Dorothy and Toto to the witch, who enslaves Dorothy.

The witch wants Dorothy's shoes, which she knows carry powerful magic. She contrives to take Dorothy's life, so she can grab the shoes. In the process, the witch tries to set Scarecrow afire, and Dorothy reacts by throwing a bucket of water at him, but she misses, hitting the witch instead, who then melts away. Dorothy and her companions return with the broomstick to Oz, where they are kept waiting by the Wizard. When they are finally admitted into his presence, he seems reluctant to grant their wishes. Toto knocks over a screen, revealing that the Wizard is merely a phony ventriloquist. However, he convinces Scarecrow he has brains; he pins a metal on Cowardly Lion, making him a member of the Legion of Courage, and he provides Tin Woodman a token heart. He finds a hot-air balloon to carry them out of the Land of Oz, but the balloon flies away without Dorothy and Toto.

At that point Glinda, the Good Witch of the South, appears, telling Dorothy to click her slippers three times, which she does, repeating "There's no place like home!" Thus, Dorothy and Toto return to the farm in Kansas, awakening as from a reverie.

The Wizard of Oz is generally read as a child's tale, with the predominant theme of self-sufficiency. Scarecrow, Tin Woodman, and Cowardly Lion, Dorothy's traveling companions in Oz, all seek external magic to give them qualities they already possess but fail to recognize. Dorothy, the main character, represents the best of what is valued in the American character: she is kind, shows spunk, is levelheaded, honest, and willing to face the unknown with courage.

In 1964, historian Henry Littlefield identified political undertones in Baum's book, characterizing *Wizard* as a thinly veiled allegory of the Populist movement, an effort that grew from a grassroots farmers' fraternity known as The Grange. It might seem far-fetched that a child's tale might deal with the politics of the 1890s, specifically relating to the debate over whether America should hold on to the gold standard for currency or start converting to silver as well.

Interestingly, Baum was a political reporter for part of his life, and was a temporary resident of South Dakota. This means he observed the rise of the Populist movement among Midwest farmers, and their formation of the People's Party to address a variety of issues in the country. In the last twenty years of the nineteenth century, American farmers took an economic beating as the result of harsh weather and crop devastations caused by swarms of locusts. These contributed to the rise of Populism, as farmers blamed their misfortunes on banks, railroads, and nature.

According to Littlefield, Scarecrow represents those farmers. In the book, Scarecrow thinks he lacks a brain. This indictment, Littlefield contends, parallels the view that Easterners in the country had of Midwestern farmers as being uneducated, irrational, and ignorant. Against that characterization, the Scarecrow character demonstrates a good deal of common sense on his journey to Emerald City, and a great deal of resilience, proving he is far less ignorant than others might think.

Tin Woodman is said to represent the dehumanized and mistreated factory worker whose self-worth has been eroded by outside forces. Covered with rust when Dorothy and Scarecrow first encounter him, he represents the suffering of myriads of factory workers at the height of the second industrial revolution, many unemployed during the 1890s recession. According to Littlefield, Cowardly Lion represents William Jennings Bryan, the hero of the Populist movement at the time. As support for his view, Littlefield notes that Bryan was called a lion by the press. He was also a strong supporter of the "Free Silver Movement" and advocated moving away from a gold standard.

The Emerald City and the Royal Palace of Oz represent Washington, D.C. and the White House, the seats of American political power. The Wizard represents President William McKinley, president of the U.S. from 1897 until his assassination in 1901. In the story, the wizard is a charlatan who has convinced those around him that he wields great power, something he truly lacks.

The Wicked Witches are said to represent the major financial/political interests that hold sway over American politics. When Dorothy's house falls on the Wicked Witch of the East, this is a reference to destroying Wall Street's power. Her sister, the Wicked Witch of the West, symbolizes the financial elite who live in the western region of the country, including railroad magnates and bankers. In Baum's story, Dorothy's slippers are made of silver, representing the silver standard. In the film version, the slippers are ruby red, changed to take advantage of three-color Technicolor.

Littlefield concludes his analysis by noting that the themes of fiscal and political struggle are so prevalent in *Wizard* that it must have been intentional on Baum's part. On the other hand, Baum was not a Populist, and there seems to be no reason why he would encode its message into his book. Littlefield was a high school teacher, and the piece he eventually published originated as a teaching aid in one of his classes. He had been exposed to a political and social interpretation through a reworked stage version, written for a different audience. Of course, it is always easy to complicate a tale, but much more challenging to simplify one. If one starts out looking for veiled and hidden meanings, it shouldn't be surprising to find them. If one has to put on green-tinted glasses and squint to find a veiled message, it might be there.

On the other hand, if we familiarize ourselves with Baum's life and literary purpose, his intent becomes clear. Born into a wealthy upstate New York family, Baum developed a love of writing and everything theatrical early on. He became involved in numerous projects, both successful and unsuccessful throughout his life, none quite as successful as *The Wonderful Wizard of Oz*. A writer by avocation, Baum was primarily a businessperson. Following the publication of *Wizard*, others adapted his book for the stage, making it a show for adults, complete with political references and parodies.

Such adaptation, however, was far from Baum's mind. Unlike C. S. Lewis, Baum never wrote an essay on writing for children, but at one point Baum noted that he never wrote of romance love, since he believed such love beyond a child's comprehension. We can assume, therefore, that Baum felt there to be a stark difference between stories written for children and those written for adults. We may also assume that he was writing a children's story (he says he is), that it contained a moral (he says it does), and that the moral is for children (as he says at the end of the story).

While it is impossible to prove Baum's political intent, if any, it is instructive to consider his symbolism from a spiritual point of view. Did Baum intend to create a spiritual allegory? While the possibility exists, Baum was arguably cynical with regard to the ability of the young mind to process adult-level ethical and spiritual concepts. Unlike Lewis, Baum would argue that adults must write at the level of a child, meaning that ethical and spiritual concepts should be clearly set out and explained, if used at all, and greatly simplified. Simplification, however, is a good thing, not only for children, but also for adults. When trying to understand complex spiritual concepts, it serves better to deconstruct than to construct. Sometimes things are not as simple as they look—they are simpler! In his effort at creating a simple allegory for young readers, Baum inadvertently created a profound understanding of love, courage, and intellect, and thereby an insightful understanding of the spiritual journey.

HEADING HOME

One way to read Baum's book or to watch the film version is through the concept of finding home. Reading the story thus, we discover that Dorothy's character is a universal representation of four journeys or quests of life:

1. *Leaving home.* The tornado that takes Dorothy from Kansas to the Land of Oz represents the journey through adolescence, which uproots children from their security and naïveté.

2. *Finding stability.* The journey to Emerald City represents early adulthood and the "first half of life," a necessary period of spiritual formation when we determine our values and boundaries, choose lifelong companions, and focusing on a career.

3. *Navigating midlife.* The journey to the Land of the Winkies and the experiences with the Wicked Witch of the West represent the crises, detours, and frustrations of life.

4. *Returning home.* The journey back to Kansas represents the spiritual transformation to the "second half of life," awakening to one's second naïveté.

The fourth journey is an amazing resolution of life's quest, for through it each of the characters find homes—that is, places of meaning and purpose, but also of unending insight and transformation—as well as resolution to their individual journeys. This is not to say that their journeys have ended, for the end of every journey is the beginning of another. In this phase, each character emerges from his or her journey transformed and ready for the next episode of self-discovery. The seed has taken root and become a seedling, taking root and ready to open into full flower, continuing the process of life.

To this point, each character has been looking for a home. At the start, all are orphans, wounded, forgotten, and seemingly alone in the world. At the start of the fourth journey, each has a home to return to, loving and beloved friends to be made, and a new purpose to accomplish. At this point Baum explains the moral he crafted into his tale. Dorothy always had the power to return home. Had she known the power of the slippers—and through them discovered her deeper inner magic[1]—she could simply

---

1. When C. S. Lewis spoke of "the deeper magic from before the beginning of time," he was neither referring to humanity's inherent spirituality nor to the "image of God" within humans, but rather to a set of spiritual laws placed into Narnia at the time of its

have returned home.[2] However, she would not have experienced the quest that transformed her, and would have returned, unchanged, the same incomplete person she had been before. She might have been aware of some magic—some spiritual quality—available to others, but ignorant of its true nature, depth, and power, much less the proper ways of using it. She might have followed endless detours, forever trying to capture a weak replica or reflection of spirituality through meaningless rituals and valueless trinkets and charms, but she would never have returned home. Only by taking the journey—leaving home, finding stability, and navigating midlife—would she discover the full splendor of spirituality, and more importantly, how to use it properly.

The "magic" is hers, now, by right, and would forever be a part of her. Having glimpsed the "kingdom of God," as Jesus called it, and having been transformed into "kingdom" people, we realize what the apostle Paul meant when he noted that salvation is not external—that is, it is not achieved by relying on sacraments, priests, and churches—but rather is internal, for "one believes with the heart and so is justified, and one confesses with the mouth and so is saved" (Rom 10:10).

It is that simple. Once a child learns to walk, she no longer needs a walker for support; once she learns to eat, she no longer needs to be fed; once she learn to ride a bicycle, she no longer needs a tricycle. Once she learns how to walk, however, she still must learn how to dance. Earlier experiences will allow her to use the same magic, even more effectively, and she will know that she must take more journeys to reach her destination.

However, what is a dance unless it is shared with others? What is walking if we walk alone? Artistry is best appreciated with others, and walks are more satisfying when taken with friends and lovers. As Dorothy discovers, had it not been for disruptive journeys, neither she nor her companions would have found their potential or their home. In the end, the Wizard would never have realized he was more than a humbug, and the citizens of Emerald City would never have benefitted from Scarecrow's gentle wisdom and simple intelligence. Freed from the curtained façade of illusions he used to hide his inability and self-doubt, the Wizard, too, begins his journey, recognizing that home is not a place but a quality within. Once the Wizard is healed, so are his land and his people. None of this would have

---

creation, laws regarding cause and effect and the law of substitutionary atonement.

2. To be clear; the "deeper magic" is not in the slippers. Dorothy always had the magic, but she didn't know it.

happened had Dorothy not taken her journey and learned to use the magic in her slippers.

When Dorothy embarks on her second and third journeys, her question is, "where do I find the magic to return home." That, however, is not the right question. The proper question, she discovers, is the question of all spiritual quests, "whom do the slippers serve?" It isn't until she undertakes her fourth quest that she will learn the question one must ask in order to live spiritually, that is, fully and compassionately.

THE FOURTH QUEST

What happened to Dorothy, we wonder, when she had grown up, when her aunt and uncle were gone, and she was left, as we all eventually are, to find her way home? Did she visit the spot nearby where Toto was buried, remembering a special moment when he made her laugh, or perhaps, that heart-wrenching day she spent cradling him in her arms, waiting until death took him away? Did she fall into a waking dream, remembering joys and sorrows shared, voices and laughter and lips kissing away tears?

This is what makes a place home, she must have thought. Enjoying companions when we have them, bidding them farewell and moving on when we must; that's the way things go. However, nothing can be the same again. All our endings are beginnings; all beginnings are born in endings. Dorothy found her way home from Oz. Could she find home again? Will she need the slippers again, or are they simply a contrivance, like the devices the Wizard gave to the others, to represent their own faith, hope, and love?

Slippers . . . shoes . . . spirituality! All are vehicles, for they take us on quests. Shoes get us where we are going, and slippers bring us home again. In the beginning, slippers represent the journey. When the Wizard sends Dorothy and her companions to destroy the witch, and is revealed a fraud, the travelers encounter Glinda, whose knowledge of the slippers' magic takes Dorothy home. However, the story doesn't end there, for, as Baum intended, the journey becomes an unending quest.

In the story, all characters undergo radical transformation. Scarecrow, the most intelligent of the group, finally obtains the confidence to use his intelligence wisely. The Wizard gave him confidence, but Scarecrow obtains wisdom though experience—by taking the journey. Tin Man, the most loving and gentle from the outset, obtains confidence and wisdom to use his heart properly. Again, the Wizard gave him confidence, but he gains wisdom through his journey. Lion was always brave; he simply mistakes bravado for courage, and prudence and temperance for cowardice. However, he is the most courageous of the companions, needing only confidence and wisdom; qualities gained through his journey. The Wizard, too, eventually comes to admit his phoniness; even his Emerald City is an illusion, created by requiring others to wear tinted glasses. However, he has love and wisdom, but, like the others, never knows the gifts he has until forced to take his journey of self-discovery.

What of Dorothy? She is filled with innocent love and kindness from the beginning, but she matures in love along the way, displaying charitable love throughout. All along, Dorothy had a heart, courage, and a brain. What could she possibly have needed by way of spiritual transformation?

Dorothy is an orphan. Perhaps this feature best explains her transformation. For most children of her age, "home" is where parents are. Home is where you belong, and the orphaned Dorothy must certainly have been injured spiritually. For a child, parents represent security, comfort, and eternity. To a child, parents are immortal. The loss of a parent by an adult is a wound; the loss of a parent by a child is an amputation. It calls into question everything sacred and stable, even the very nature of "home."

Dorothy's search for a way home is more than a search for a place; it is a quest for meaning and spiritual wholeness. When Dorothy returns to Kansas, she has found all that the spiritual idea of home entails. She has learned, among other things, to love more deeply and purely, including herself. She has learned that home is where you love and find love, that home is within. Home is where you belong, whether it's in Kansas or just south of Munchkinland. Spirituality will take her there, wherever it may be, because finding home requires a journey, or many journeys.

In the book and, apparently in the movie, Dorothy loses the slippers on the way home. Of course! She no longer needs them. Real magic only works when needed, not when summoned. Dorothy has become the magic now; and the magic Dorothy embodies is more real and more powerful than any charm, amulet, or enchantment the wizards of life might offer.

Despite transformed companions, Dorothy's transformation is the greatest. Dorothy the small and meek has become Dorothy the great and powerful, a transformation due not to the Wizard's stagecraft but to the power of wisdom and love nurtured through experience. In the end, Dorothy has found home, not in a farmhouse, but as a place we inhabit when we can never return home again.

Dorothy probably turned the key in the door many years later and smiled as she thought of the slippers. Then, with an even deeper smile, she remembers the joys and fears of those years and turns, clicking the heels of her tattered shoes, whispering softly, "there's no place like home." As she does, she begins trusting that the old magic—her own spirituality—will take her wherever she loves and is loved, wherever she belongs at that moment in time . . . home!

QUESTIONS FOR DISCUSSION AND REFLECTION

1. Insofar as possible, explain the perennial popularity of *The Wizard of Oz*.

2. In your estimation, is *The Wizard of Oz* an allegory? If so, what does it allegorize?

3. In your experience, what scene or episode from *Wizard* is most memorable? Explain your answer.

4. Explain and assess the meaning of the statement that Dorothy's companions "all seek external magic to give them qualities they already possess but fail to recognize."

5. The character of Dorothy in *Wizard* is attractive and exemplary. Which of her qualities do you find most compelling? Explain your answer.

6. If *Wizard of Oz* is a child's tale, why, in your estimation, do adults find it so alluring?

7. Explain and assess Henry Littlefield's characterization of *Wizard* as "a thinly veiled allegory of the Populist movement" in late nineteenth-century American society.

8. Explain and assess the author's characterization of *Wizard* as a spiritual allegory.

9. Assess the merits of the author's attempt to explain the universality of Dorothy's character through the lens of four journeys or quests of life.

10. In allegories such as Bunyan's, Lewis's, and Baum's, is it appropriate to equate the metaphor of "journey" with that of spiritual questing, such as occurs in the "first" and "second" halves of life? Explain your answer.

11. Explain and assess the meaning of the author's statement, "the end of every journey is the beginning of another."

12. In your estimation, what is the meaning of the statement, "once a child learns to walk, s/he still must learn how to dance"?

13. Explain and assess the author's use of "home" as an extended metaphor for the spiritual journey.

14. In your estimation, what is the primary insight gained from this chapter? Explain your answer.

Chapter 10

The Power of Music

What would life be like without music? It is hard to imagine. Due to inventions such as the radio, the phonograph, and television, and through the use of tapes, CDs, and music apps, modern consumers can experience the widest variety of music on demand. With expanding technology, including the Internet and smart phones, music of every type is now available on outlets such as Pandora, Spotify, YouTube, and Sirius.

Music—like romance—is the language of the soul. Music allows us to express ourselves, and in so doing makes us feel alive. Analyzed scientifically, music consists of wave vibrations that can shatter glass and change the ripples in water. If music can affect objects soft and hard with its vibration, it can certainly influence human beings, our bodies consisting of about 60 percent water, with some organs, such as our heart and brain composed of 73 percent water and our lungs of 83 percent water.

Because of its influence on humans around the world, music is said to be a "universal language," enjoyed regardless of nationality, culture, and social class. In addition, music has an effect on human brains and emotions that is profound, different yet more comprehensive than that of words and other forms of communication. Music is therapeutic because it can change our mood, calming our nerves and helping us relax, thus enhancing our body's healing ability. However, music with a strong beat can stimulate brain waves, improving concentration and preparing us for action.

Music is the language of the soul because it can express our feelings and emotions at a visceral level, often beyond our ability to state verbally.

Music resonates with our personality in unique ways. The type of music a person likes says a great deal about that person. While there are aesthetic standards in the music industry, each of us differs in the music we like or prefer, a preference that can change depending on our mood or emotional condition. However, some music affect us profoundly, stimulating our inner being. Such music we might call sacred, although to distinguish between sacred and secular music definitely varies, not only between individuals, but also between cultures, religions, and even races, genders, and social classes.

THE NATURE OF MUSIC

There are few people who do not react to music to some degree. The power of music is diverse, and people respond in different ways. To some, music is mainly an instinctive sound to which they dance or move their bodies. Others listen for its message, or take an intellectual approach to its form and construction, appreciating its formal patterns or originality. The effect of music, however, is not singular but comprehensive. Above all, people listen to music or perform musically because it is a psychosomatic experience that, as well as promoting harmony and wellbeing, produces inner joy and satisfaction. This integrative power stems from deep within the human soul. As the noted composer Ludwig van Beethoven remarked, "Music is a higher revelation than all wisdom and philosophy." Noting music's aesthetic and impractical nature, the evolutionary biologist Charles Darwin felt music must be ranked among the most mysterious qualities within human nature. Composer Robert Schumann, aware of music's universal appeal, believed that listening to the masterworks of different ages and places would cure humans of vanity and selfishness.

While it is easy for students of music to classify music into genres or types, such as vocal or instrumental, popular or classical, secular or religious, rhythmic or expressive, rock or folk, blues or jazz, country or hip-hop, techno or funk, and so on, or by culture or nationality, ultimately, there is only good music and bad. By bad music I mean music that does not have honesty, integrity, and essence of genius, qualities good music shares with healthy spirituality. For me, good music includes classical, opera, jazz, folk, American popular song, Big Band, country, and gospel, some elements within these having greater appeal than others do. Beauty, of course, is in the ear as well as the eye of the beholder, and the appreciation of a piece of music depends to some extent on the listener's culture and upbringing. To some people raised in the West, for example, the music of Asia is mysterious and possibly difficult to appreciate, primarily because its idiom is unfamiliar. Happily, once the context is understood and the preconceptions about musical conventions are set aside, it becomes more accessible. Even without such understanding, all music has the power to exert an effect on our emotions.

While we in the Western world are blessed with a variety of musical forms and types, each kind of music offers something to, and requires something of, the listener. Popular music is primarily a source of entertainment and relaxation. It also has important sociological significance as an expression of culture at a given time. Even when the best popular music of any age is of high quality and substance, the very aspects that render music "popular" tend to make it short-lived. Many popular songs, for example, soon sound dated, and their appreciation by later generations often involves nostalgic or purely aesthetic considerations.

Some kinds of music are functional, that is, they serve a particular purpose or elicit a specific response. For example, it is easier to exercise, dance, march, or perform a rhythmic task if music sets the pace. The background music in a film intensifies emotional reactions while providing a sense of continuity between scenes. Music in a religious service may express a message or simply enhance the spirit of worship.

On the other hand, art music does not necessarily serve any functional purpose, but may simply express something the composer had in mind and thought worth sharing. The famous nineteenth-century writer and art critic John Ruskin, defined art as "the expression of one soul talking to another," and most composers of serious or artistic music have tried to communicate to their listening audience something of their experience, their personality, their mind, or indeed their soul. Ultimately, however, we do not have to analyze music to discover its power; we simply need to go into our own souls, for that is where music emanates, thrives, and belongs. Good music, like spirituality, is harmonious, and when it introduces dissonance, its resolution always results in surprising possibilities and unexpected newness.

THE ORIGIN OF MUSIC

To understand music and its role in life generally, we must ask about its origin. This takes us back tens of thousands of years, to the time when prehistoric humans began to speak. While there may have been primitive language, these were not languages we now use, whereby words represent actions, objects, and sensations. Original communication was surely more elementary, with nonverbal sounds such as shouting, grunting, and cooing, or changing one's breath to change the character of these sounds, playing a role in expressing sentiments and ideas.

By using dynamics, such as raising or lowering the tone or volume of one's voice, more specific and complex ideas could be expressed. By changing pitch, or in the act of modulating the voice to shorten or prolong a tone, or by creating a melodic line that crossed a range of tones, vocal music began.

Ancient peoples also lived in constant contact with nature. Their survival depended on learning the sounds of nature. The cry of a wolf, the roar of a lion, the screech of an own, the hiss or rattle of a snake, or the sounds of an approaching storm, these are some of the sounds to be observed in nature. The songs of birds, however, serve another purpose, for they awakened in humans the possibility that music could exist. Each bird, with its unique sounds and songs, turned humans into listeners of languages that had no words but were remarkably expressive and differentiated. Some birds repeat the same sounds, others improvise and create variations on their original themes. A walk in the woods may let you hear one bird singing a song, or two singing a duet; or there might be a call and response, with a bird in one tree having a dialogue with another; or it might be a forest full of birds singing at once.

Nature also provided humans with rocks to hit, reeds to blow, animal skins to stretch and pound, metal or animal parts to pluck, animal horns to blow, or wood to carve into instruments. Accompanied by song and dance, instruments contributed to tribal solidarity and individual wellbeing. Archaeologists have found whistles dated to over 40,000 BCE, and cave paintings from about 18,000 BCE that depict musicians.

The earliest compositions were probably songs. While some such songs consisted of only a repeated syllable, focusing on sounds such as "ah" or "la," other songs contained words, making sound and meaning equally important. These songs would be sung by individuals or groups. The same applies to instrumental music, which could have been played individually or in combination. It is hard to say what most of this ancient music sounded like, because none was written or recorded. Charles Darwin was convinced that musical notes and rhythm were first used for the sake of charming the opposite sex, an idea not lost to modern lovers. However, we can be sure that early music was profoundly spiritual, for it had a unitive function, bonding people to one another, to nature, and to the deity within and beyond life on earth.

The story of music, like that of religion, begins with the story of humanity. Our earliest human ancestors were animistic, conscious that nature was spirit-infused. Their life was holistic, for they viewed the natural, social, and spiritual dimensions as profoundly integrated. Music, an integral part of their religious sensibility, represented primitive attempts to establish harmony with the powers in and beyond nature, powers they sensed directing human life. In this regard, spirituality for them (and for us) meant direct relationship between themselves and the deeper realm around and within them.

When primitive humans struck a piece of rock or skin, or blew into an old bone or hollow reed, they probably thought that what they heard was the voice of the object. They would have assumed that by awakening the "voice" of the object, they could propitiate the unseen nature of which their life was a part. Likewise, when they felt moved to sing or dance, they were giving voice or motion to the spirit within, thus becoming one with the spiritual powers animating their lives.

By 3000 BCE, the Sumerians, an ancient society living in the fertile crescent of Mesopotamia, had assembled a range of musical instruments including lyres, harps, and reed pipes, which may have been played as an ensemble. We also know from written records that they practiced antiphonal singing or chanting in their temples. It is clear that their music was a sophisticated part of their culture, and that it had religious and ceremonial significance. The five-tone or pentatonic scale was first developed in China about the same time The religious function of music continued in ancient civilizations, including Egypt, India, Israel, Greece, Persia, and Japan. In ancient Rome, music was a rich and constant presence, including public entertainment and cultic life.

During the first millennium CE, there seems to have been little innovation in Western music, with the exception of the Gregorian chant used in church worship. Initially, such church music involved reshaping the older Roman chant, in which melodies were sung to the accompaniment of a sustained note on a stringed instrument. Associated initially with Pope Gregory I (590–604), who ordered the codifying and collection of the plainsong used in the Roman church, under Charlemagne (742–814) the Gregorian chant became widely used all over Europe. The chant's system of eight tones, directly related to the eight church modes, was for unaccompanied voice only, for according to some early church leaders, any form of musical instrument was a tool of the devil. Even Augustine, educated in Greco-Roman philosophy but the victim of adolescent passion, expressed concern over the seductive "peril of pleasure" created by beautiful singing.

However, in the ninth century, Benedictine influence fostered the advancement of music in Europe, and by the late tenth century, organ music was introduced into churches, not yet as accompaniment to singing, but rather for calling people to worship. Religious songs were also sung outside the church, especially on long journeys such as to the crusades and on pilgrimages.

The Middle Ages saw the birth of polyphony, a new form of music based on two or more parts. Polyphony made possible the mass, the chief musical ritual of the Roman Catholic Church. This period also saw the birth of a secular musical tradition, alongside the liturgical. Performers known as troubadours, typically wandering musicians, based their popular melodies on poems of courtly love. They made creative use of new musical instruments to accompany their lyrics, written mostly in the vernacular languages rather than in Latin, the liturgical language of the church. In Germany, the late Middle Ages was the heyday of the Minnesinger, the German equivalent of the French troubadour. In addition to troubadours, another professional class of entertainers was the minstrel, of more lowly birth. All these singers were both poets and composers, for at this time very few sang other people's music.

In the twelfth and thirteenth centuries, Paris was the musical center of the Western world, and its university was one of the first to teach music. A century or two later, Italy, the cradle of the Renaissance, developed a flourishing musical culture. While Giovanni Bellini was painting his incomparable madonnas, Italians were composing madrigals, a mostly secular polyphonic form using two to as many as eight vocal parts. During the humanistic Renaissance, beauty in art and craft was a highly valued element of life.

Italian and English musicians had highly artistic standards. Performances were constant and lively, and for the first time notated music was published. New instruments were created in abundance, including organs, harpsichords, cornetti, shawms (forerunners of the oboe), sackbuts (early trombones), viols (cousins of the modern violin, cello, and viola), flutes, lutes, and dozens of others. By the late sixteenth century, any person of rank or pretension was expected to have musical proficiency. Most were excellent sight-readers. The reign of Elizabeth I (1558–1603) was a golden age for the arts, and music thrived in the home, at church, and in the theatre. Shakespeare used song prolifically in his plays. Across Europe, the sixteenth century was a time of high musical creativity. During this time, conflicts between polyphony and melody grew. At the end of the sixteenth century, a new art form arose, combining drama and song. The invention of opera signaled the birth of the Baroque era.

The age of classical music, which began developing in the 1720s, made radical departures from counterpoint and Baroque forms. In stark contrast to Baroque polyphony, its keynote was homophony, a single melody supported by progressions of chords (harmony) in accompaniment. Modern music was promoted by Enlightenment thinkers such as Jean-Jacques Rousseau, who opted for melody. The Enlightenment spurred on a new spirit of classical secularism that made a gigantic leap forward in 1709 with the invention of the pianoforte, antecedent of the modern piano. By the 1740s, the modern orchestra was developing, and by 1824, the deaf Beethoven faced a weeping audience after conducting his Ninth Symphony, whose finale, a musical setting of Schiller's *Ode to Joy*, proclaimed brotherhood and freedom. These two moments mark, respectively, the end of the polyphonic era and the high point of tonal homophony.

Despite fulfilling the classical ideal, Beethoven became the spiritual father of musical Romanticism, the music of his middle and late years so suffused with expressive and elemental power that it haunted the nineteenth century. The first generation of full-fledged Romantic composers is represented by composers such as Schubert, Berlioz, Mendelssohn, Schumann, Chopin, Liszt, Verdi, and Wagner, an amazing harvest of genius all born within a decade and a half of one another. The generation of Richard Strauss and Gustav Mahler, born in the 1860s, furnished Romanticism its last rites. In Russia, Romantic art music developed more slowly than in other countries, as Russia had no Classical tradition. When it did arrive, it belonged almost exclusively to that subset of Romanticism that merged with the nationalistic spirit.

The late nineteenth century, in turn, led to Modernism, a term commonly used for composers living into the twentieth century. Modernist composers reacted not so much against rigid forms as against the tonal system. No composer was more aware than Franz List that he was working in an exhausted musical vocabulary. Liszt was the first to realize that the major and minor key tonal system would eventually collapse, and by the mid-1870s he was writing piano pieces that were tonally ambiguous. Nobody wanted to listen to these pieces, however, and most thought the great virtuoso had gone mad. At the time of his death in 1886, he was the most radical composer in the world.

Liszt would be followed by creative Modernist composers such as Claude Debussy, Maurice Ravel, Ralph Vaughan Williams, Alexander Scriabin, Charles Ives, Sergei Rachmaninoff, Béla Bartók, Sergei Prokofiev, George Gershwin, Aaron Copland, Dmitri Shostakovich, and others. Nevertheless, for the twentieth-century musical public, none was more inventive than the Russian-born Igor Stravinsky, who composed in nearly every genre, inventing new rhythms and a vast array of textures, juxtaposing idioms, creating unique harmonic combinations, and even shocking the musical establishment through serialism.

WHAT MAKES MUSIC SACRED?

Having distinguished good music from bad, and liturgical from secular, we need to ask what makes music sacred. The answer, if one exists, is surely debatable, for while there is clearly a difference between good and bad music, or liturgical and secular, the terms "sacred" and "spiritual" are highly subjective. To answer the question, three general approaches may be taken.

1. *A particularistic religious approach.* This approach may be said to take a traditional view of spirituality, namely, that relegates the religious almost exclusively to such times, place, and situations that are considered indisputably holy, making of the sacred something occasional and unique by nature. This view would include as sacred most music set to liturgy, and would certainly include musical works (or moments) of undisputed universal transcendence and ineffability.

2. *A reductionist religious approach.* This second and quite opposite approach desacralizes supposedly sacred or spiritual qualities in music, reducing or subordinating them to the purely secular.

3. *A holistic religious approach.* This approach is undergirded by the theological possibility that all times, places, and situations are potentially sacred. Supportive texts from scripture include the refrain from the first account of creation in Genesis 1, where the narrator speaks for God by way of response to the various acts of creation: "And God saw that it was good." Two passages from the Psalms also speak of the transparency of all creation to God's lordship and to the worship of God: "The earth is the Lord's and the fullness thereof, the world and those who dwell therein" (24:1) and "the heavens are telling the glory of God" (19:1).

As LeRoi Jones notes, this third, mystical approach is found commonly in primal perspectives, from native American to native African: "Before the Renaissance, art [in the West] could find its way into the lives of almost all people because all art issued from the Church, and the Church was at the very center of Western man's life. But the discarding of the religious attitude for the 'enlightened' concepts of the Renaissance also created the schism between what was art and what was life. It was, and is, inconceivable in the African culture to make a separation between music, dancing, song, the artifact, and a man's life or his worship of his gods."[1]

While I take a holistic approach to sacredness and spirituality, there are certainly distinctive forms of music, which, when enhanced by certain inward disciplines and commitments such as emptiness, humility, and purity of heart, have the capacity to transform the human spirit, thereby lifting the listener or seeker from the ordinary and mundane to higher levels of awareness and experience. This is what Zen Buddhism calls "satori," or sudden flashes of insight.

Here I am reminded of a quality of religiosity mentioned by Fred Streng, Charles Lloyd, and Jay Allen in their text, *Ways of Being Religious*, namely, that "religious" persons see themselves as only potentially human. They are not content with the way things are, with the status quo, but they long for change. It is this attitude of dissatisfaction with the status quo, this understanding that one's life is under threat, coupled with a commitment to a lifelong journey towards "ultimate transformation," that characterizes persons as authentically "religious." There is something appealing about viewing spirituality from this dynamic perspective, but I also find something lacking, for this view can become reductionistic, viewing the holy, the

---

1. Jones, *Blues People*, 29.

sacred, and the spiritual as abnormal rather than normal, sporadic rather than continuous.

JAZZ: AMERICA'S MUSIC

Life is filled with profound memories, some happy and exhilarating, others sad and even tragic, but apart from the experiences that cause such memories, life would be trivial and devoid of meaning. Most of us can remember in vivid terms the specific circumstances of our lives when we heard of certain historic events. Those of us who have been around awhile may recall events such as the attack on Pearl Harbor, the explosion of the first atomic bomb over Hiroshima; the first lunar landing; the assassinations of John F. Kennedy, Robert Kennedy, and Martin Luther King Jr.; the terrorist attacks on September 11, 2001, and most recently, the January 6, 2021 assault on the U.S. Capitol.

Of life's happy memories, one of the sweetest is surely the universal experience we call our "first love," a moment of emotional infatuation or physical intimacy we treasure forever. Many music lovers can recall with comparable vividness their discovery of certain musicians, a first hearing of a song or musical performance, or an introduction to a specific musical genre such as classical, rock, soul, or jazz.

For me, such memories include the first hearing of Rachmaninoff's "Third Piano Concerto," recorded live at New York City's Carnegie Hall in 1958 by the twenty-three-year-old pianist Van Cliburn shortly after his stunning victory at the First International Tchaikovsky Piano Competition in Moscow at the height of the Cold War; the clarinet glissando at the start of George Gershwin's "Rhapsody in Blue"; the arresting quality of voice exhibited by a youthful Barbra Streisand at the gripping climax to her rendition of "Happy Days are Here Again"; my first exposure to the Beatles when they appeared on the Ed Sullivan show in 1964; and attending a live performance by the Cuban-born Paquito D'Rivera, whose skill and energy on clarinet and alto sax galvanized my passion for jazz. Each of these unique musical experiences has combined to form my musical treasury of "first loves."

Ken Burns recalls that when he began his PBS television series on jazz, he had perhaps two jazz records in his large music collection. "Today," he states, "I can't find all the others . . . I listen to jazz all the time . . . I play it day and night, in the car, as I go to bed, as I write now, its sophisticated rhythms and elegant lines simply medicine for me."[2]

My own experience with jazz was not that different. Prior to my "discovery" of jazz some thirty years ago, when I purchased a single jazz album at a used-record sale, I knew very little about jazz, having only a few albums in my record collection that were related to jazz, including some bossa nova albums recorded by Stan Getz and one by Brazilian vocalist Astrud Gilberto. One cold Saturday morning I was among the first to line up outside the WQED studios of Pittsburgh, Pennsylvania's classical music station. The CD era had rendered phonograph players obsolete, so patrons of the classical station had donated their old LPs for purchase by nostalgic record collectors. Hoping to find albums by popular groups from the 1950s, '60s, and '70s, I felt fortunate to locate some records by the Beatles and Elton John. Later, after most of the customers had departed, I made my way to the jazz section, an area that had seen a great deal of traffic earlier in the day. Though the remaining albums were in poor condition, one album caught my attention, probably more for the modernistic painting by Joan Miró on its cover than for its musical content. Titled *Time Further Out*, the recording was by the Dave Brubeck Quartet.

That night I found myself enthralled as I listened to the album, particularly to those tracks written in odd time signatures. Having listened to music—classical, popular, sacred—all my life and having performed publicly on piano and guitar, I was nevertheless transfixed. That experience was an awakening, the start of a love affair with jazz that resulted in a musical collection that has grown to hundreds of albums, tapes, and CDs. Eventually I enrolled in courses on jazz and began taking lessons on the clarinet and saxophone. The purchase of that old jazz album affected my musical tastes forever. Hardly a day has gone by since that I have not listened to jazz, talked with others about it, analyzed it, or done research on the subject.

My induction into the jazz fraternity, I've since discovered, has been replicated many times. Jimmy McPartland, a founding member of the group of Chicago youngsters known since the 1920s as the Austin High Gang, recalls how in 1922 he and a few of his schoolmates first became interested in jazz:

Every day after school, Frank Teschemacher and Bud Freeman, Jim Lannigan, my brother Dick, myself, and a few others used to go to a little place called the Spoon and Straw. It was just an ice-cream parlor where

2. Ward and Burns, *Jazz, A History*, x.

you'd get a malted milk, soda, shakes, and all that stuff. But they had a Victrola there, and we used to sit around listening to the bunch of records laid on the table . . . This went along for two or three months; we'd go in there every day, and one day they had some new Gennett records on the table, and we put them on. They were by the New Orleans Rhythm Kings, and I believe the first tune we played was "Farewell Blues." Boy, when we heard that—I'll tell you we went out of our minds. Everybody flipped. It was wonderful . . . We stayed there from about three in the afternoon until eight at night, just listening to those records one after another, over and over again. Right then and there we decided we would get a band and try to play like these guys.[3]

Another such convert, jazz critic Gene Lees, recalled his discovery of jazz pianist Bill Evans, which occurred in 1959, shortly after he joined the jazz periodical *Down Beat*: "In the office, I noticed among a stack of records awaiting assignment for review a gold-covered Riverside album titled *Everybody Digs Bill Evans*, bearing the signed endorsements of Miles Davis, Cannonball Adderley, Ahmad Jamal, and others of like stature. I took the album home and, sometime after dinner, probably about nine o'clock, put it on the phonograph. At 4 A.M. I was still listening, though by now I had it memorized."[4]

Jazz music, the only art form created by Americans, reminds us that the genius of America is improvisation, that America's unique experiment is a profound intersection of freedom and creativity, for better and for worse. A good beat, a contagious rhythm, an emotional ballad, creative improvisation: jazz has it all. This chapter, like the stories above, is written to encourage readers to appreciate jazz, to treasure each day and to open to daily moments of discovery, awakening, and renewal, helping them to reconnect with musical "first loves."

An enduring expression of America's promise and genius, jazz functions as a prism through which much of American history can be told— and felt. Tragic, bawdy, creative, and rhythmic, jazz music is fascinating, compelling, and honest. It keeps things real, and so it necessarily becomes a story about race and prejudice and class conflict, suggesting in powerful ways that those who represent the underneathness of society might actually be at the center of history.

3. Shapiro and Hentoff, *Hear Me Talkin'*, 118–19.
4. Gottlieb, *Reading Jazz*, 419.

It is fair to say that no one can study American culture, whether religious or secular, without appreciating the role of jazz. Jazz has been described as "America's music," and though it is no longer exclusively so, its influence in American culture has been pervasive. Rock, funk, soul, rap, show music, movie scores, television shows, and modern concert music all contain elements drawn from jazz. Jazz has inspired creativity in other art forms as well, including dance, choreography, literature, and painting. In the words of Quincy Jones, a central figure in late twentieth-century jazz and popular music: "I can only hope that one day America will recognize what the rest of the world already has, that our indigenous music, jazz, is the heart and soul of all popular music."[5]

WHAT IS JAZZ?

The influence of jazz, like its presence, is pervasive. Rock, funk, soul, rap, show music, movie music, television music, modern concert music, all contain elements drawn from jazz. There is something so compelling about this music that it can be said to define the human being in the twentieth century. Indeed, it is almost fair to say that jazz is the foundation on which modern popular music has been built. So much so, in fact, that by the late 1980s Afro-American musical styles had become the most popular in the world, among all races in every geographic region.

The roots of jazz, its history, indeed its primal nature, display inclusivity and openness that beckon performer and audience alike to participate in a ritual reminiscent of the call and response characteristic of the "holiness" worship traditions. The relationship to West African dance ceremonies and the practices of African-American churches that descended from them is obvious. There is a palpable spirituality to this music which reminds us that all music, when it addresses humanity's needs, hopes, and fears, is spiritual and hence, therapeutic. So what is this music that has had such a consistent commitment from its participants and such powerful initial responses on its hearers?

It has been said that jazz, in a half-century, recapitulated the history of four centuries of European history, moving from the heterophonic polyphony of the early New Orleans style, through the big-band romanticism of the 1930s, to the chromaticism of bop and the free-form experiments after 1960. This analysis underscores jazz's penchant for rapid change, a

5. Hasse, *Jazz*, iv.

tendency documented in the bohemian lifestyles of musicians like Charlie Parker as well as in the stylistic restlessness evidenced in the musical experimentation of Miles Davis and John Coltrane.

There is no generally accepted definition of the word "jazz," nor is it known where the word came from or what it originally meant. To some extent, jazz likes to consider itself a mystery, so much so that when Louis Armstrong was asked what jazz was, he is said to have responded, "If you gotta ask, you'll never know." The story, though apocryphal, illustrates an attitude universal to jazz musicians and listeners alike, that at the heart of this music lies something inexplicable that can be felt but not explained.[6] This doesn't mean, however, that jazz cannot be analyzed or described, for jazz texts try to do just that.

In his popular *Jazz Styles*, James Gridley provides the following categorization:

1. For many people, music need only *be associated with the jazz tradition* to be called jazz. For example, music might be called jazz because it has a bluesy flavor, or because it uses instruments associated with jazz, such as saxophones or drums, or because it has "jazzy rhythms" or displays manipulations of pitch and tone quality that are associated with jazz, such as blue notes, scoops, or smears.

2. For others, a jazz performance is one that *projects a jazz swing feeling*. According to this view, jazz is a feeling more than anything else, a way of playing music more than the type of music being played.

3. A third group views jazz as a type of music that *requires improvisation* (this perspective, though essential to most jazz, fails to distinguish from other kinds of music that also employ improvisation, such as pop, rock, and the music of India and Africa).

4. The most common definition seems to be one that *requires both improvisation and swing* in the jazz sense.[7]

When a performance exhibits these qualities, in a manner deemed inspired, then you have jazz at its best. Dizzy Gillespie got to the heart of the matter when he described jazz in the following manner: "Improvisation is the meat of jazz. Rhythm is the bone." When a performance exhibits these qualities, in a manner deemed inspired, then you have jazz at its best.

6. Collier, *Making of Jazz*, 4.
7. Gridley, *Jazz Styles*, 6–7.

Though the jazz tradition cannot be confined to any one of these views, the four perspectives, taken together, seem to provide an adequate starting point for any understanding of jazz. And it is a holistic approach that points to jazz's unique appeal, for throughout its history jazz has never been monolithic. During the 1960s and '70s, the term "fusion" arose to characterize attempts by jazz musicians of the time to mix musical idioms, but it is clear that jazz was eclectic from its origins, when it blended folk music, popular music, and light classical music that were current around the start of the twentieth century, especially in New Orleans. The common presupposition that jazz is a combination of African rhythms and European harmonies, though simplistic and some-what inaccurate, nevertheless underscores jazz's syncretistic and restless nature. Jazz's many styles, which include ragtime, Dixieland, blues, swing, bebop, cool, progressive, third stream, avant-garde, jazz-rock, and free jazz, all represent amalgams and fusions, a shifting balance between the free, improvisatory, and spontaneous aspects of the music, often seen as African or "black," and the more formal, arranged elements, sometimes viewed as European or "white." Jazz has continually crossed and recrossed an imaginary line between these opposites, always being drawn back when it strayed too far in either direction.

During the 1950s and '60s African-Americans began to build on a paradigm shift in consciousness that emerged after World War II; they started thinking differently about themselves, their place in American society, and the methods for bringing about change. "Black is beautiful" emerged as a powerful slogan, soul food became popular, and Afros were in style. But more importantly, African-Americans assumed leadership of the emerging civil rights movement. Blacks, of course, saw jazz as their contribution to American culture. If black was beautiful, why not play jazz in a black way? By way of response, a number of jazz styles emerged during the 1950s, though the majority, including some of the "cool" styles that persisted, differed only slightly from bebop. The underlying difference, however, was the conscious attempt by these players to build upon the African-American folk music tradition out of which jazz had grown. It was to their roots, primarily the gospel churches and the blues, that this second generation of bop players went in search of inspiration. As this new music developed, it came to be called "funk" or "soul" music, but a third term, "hard bop," seemed the most technically accurate.

Jazz music represents, for the first time in a uniquely American synthesis, a union of body and soul, mind and spirit, carnal knowledge and eternal truth. Pittsburgh's popular jazz host, Tony Mowad, exhorts his audience spiritually through his signature sign-off: "Keep a bit of love in your heart and a taste of jazz in your soul."

Ultimately, jazz is more than mere music. For jazz would not exist apart from people: performers, composers, arrangers, producers, critics, authors, and finally, listeners. Jazz is the story of extraordinary human beings, "protean geniuses—black and white, male and female, addicts and orphans, prostitutes and pimps, sons of privilege and of despair—who . . . took enormous risks, shouldered unimaginable responsibility, and are able to do what the rest of us can only dream of: create art on the spot."[8]

QUESTIONS FOR DISCUSSION AND REFLECTION

1. In your estimation, why is music described as "the language of the soul"?

2. If you were to list your favorite categories of music, what would they be? As you reflect on your choices, to what extent are they due to upbringing and peer influence, and which are due purely to your own nature and personality?

3. What type of music typically meets your "spiritual" needs? Explain your answer.

4. After reading this chapter, what did you learn about the origin of music?

5. In your estimation, what was it about the Renaissance that led to such a creative explosion in the arts?

6. In your estimation, what makes classical music distinctive, and what was it about the Enlightenment that led to the age of classical music?

7. Compare and contrast the essential elements of Romantic and Modernist music.

8. After reading this chapter, what did you learn about what makes music sacred?

9. Do you have a musical "first love," an emotional musical experience that bonded you with a particular musician, a musical style, or a musical genre? Explain your answer.

8. Ward and Burns, *Jazz: A History*, ix.

10. After reading this chapter, what did you learn about jazz music?

11. In your estimation, why is jazz called "America's music"?

12. In your estimation, what is the primary insight gained from this chapter? Explain your answer.

Chapter 11

Jazz Icons

By its very nature this music, stylistically, ethnically, and culturally diverse, represents a cohesive vision that holds significant promise for the new millennium. For over one hundred years, jazz and its antecedents have provided a paradigm of an idealized democratic culture that encourages maximum creative participation by an individual within a group.

Readers interested in the stories of individual jazz personalities are encouraged to examine my 2011 volume *Blue Notes*. That book contains profiles of 365 jazz personalities (including performers, composers, arrangers, lyricists, bandleaders, producers, critics, authors, educators, recording engineers, record producers, and publishers), one for each calendar day of the year. In this chapter, I focus on four performers—Louis Armstrong, Ella Fitzgerald, Duke Ellington, and John Coltrane—who helped define the music while embodying its relentless search for newness.

LOUIS ARMSTRONG: "FATHER OF JAZZ"

When one looks at Louis Armstrong's (1901–1971) background and upbringing, it is obvious that the cards were stacked against him. He was born into poverty, schooled in drudgery, and raised in ignorance. He could not read music and did not even study music until he was thirteen. Yet within months he was the leader of his school band; four years later he was cornetist with the leading jazz band in New Orleans. Four years after that, at the age of twenty-one, his peers acknowledged him to be the best jazz musician alive.

A brief look at Armstrong's background and upbringing indicates that he overcame great odds. His father, William Armstrong, was a factory worker who abandoned the family soon after the boy's birth. Armstrong's mother Mayann, only fifteen at the time of his birth, went to work in a nearby red-light district, leaving Louis in the care of his paternal grandmother. (It should be remembered that in the New Orleans subculture in which Louis lived, prostitution was looked upon as an almost normal way of making a living; Armstrong's first wife, Daisy, was a prostitute.) Once in school, Armstrong joined his mother, taking whatever odd jobs he could find in the Crescent City's poorest neighborhood, a violent and vice-ridden district known as "the Battlefield." Louis wore little more than rags and ate the cheapest of food, occasionally scavenging in garbage cans.

His mother, loving but irresponsible, frequently left Louis and his younger sister to the kindness of strangers for days at a time. Around the age of seven he became acquainted with an immigrant Jewish family from Russia named Karnofsky, who fed him, taught him songs, put him to work, and provided him with his first instrument, a tin horn. Because of that kindness, Armstrong retained a special affection for Jews, wearing a Star of David all his life. Despite the kindness of the Karnofskys, Louis dropped out of school at the age of eleven and joined a street-corner quartet, singing for pennies. Music fascinated him, but it couldn't keep him out of trouble.

The pivotal event of his formative years occurred on New Year's Eve, 1912. Armstrong was living with his mother at the time, for his parents had separated long before. By this time there was a constant series of what Louis called his "stepfathers" coming and going through the family apartment. The young adolescent got hold of a .38 caliber pistol belonging to his current "stepfather" and joined the traditional holiday revelry by firing the gun off in the street. A policeman arrested him (probably not so much to punish him as to save him from an environment of delinquency) and remanded him to the Colored Waifs' Home. There he sang in a vocal group before joining the brass band. He started on tambourine but soon, because of his sense of timing, was promoted to drums. A short time later he switched to the alto horn, a band instrument like the cornet, only pitched lower. Armstrong displayed such natural ability on that horn that his bandmaster took him under his wing and made him the institution's bugler. He eventually taught him the cornet and promoted him leader of the band.

At the age of fifteen, Louis was released from the institution, where-upon he formed his own band. At the same time he started hanging around the cabaret where a band led by trombonist Kid Ory was playing. This band featured Joe "King" Oliver on cornet. Oliver took a liking to the young man and taught him some tricks of the trade. Oliver occasionally invited Armstrong to substitute for him, and when Oliver went north to Chicago in 1918, Ory hired Armstrong as the replacement. Though Louis was only seventeen, he claimed to have been born on July 4, 1900 and therefore to be eighteen, old enough to work in a cabaret. At this time Ory's band was quite possibly the best jazz band in New Orleans, which made Armstrong the leading cornetist around.

When Oliver boarded the train for Chicago, Armstrong was at the station to say farewell. The two wouldn't see each other for four years, but when Oliver called in 1922 and urged Armstrong to join him in what had become Chicago's hottest ensemble, it signaled the start of something new, the ascendancy of the virtuoso soloist and a decade that would be known as the Jazz Age. As the plump, friendly young man soon to be called "Satch-mo" (a reference to his mouth being as large as a satchel – a small suitcase) stepped from the train in Chicago's South Side carrying little more than a cornet case, few would have guessed that a musical revolution was packed inside that case.

Louis Armstrong is often called the "father of jazz," and for good rea-son. A true musical genius, he was one of the first and greatest soloists in jazz history. Together with Duke Ellington, Count Basie, Billie Holiday, Charlie Parker, Miles Davis, and John Coltrane, he clearly ranks among the elite of jazz geniuses. His command of the trumpet was arguably greater than that of any preceding jazz trumpeter on record. His enormous brassy tone and remarkable range, together with his superb sense of pacing and ability to build dramatic tension, made him one of the foremost musical architects in jazz history. His graceful syncopation of selected rhythmic figures, as though he were playing behind the beat, produced the swing feeling so essential to jazz.

During a period when collective improvisation predominated, Arm-strong stressed solo improvisation, and while most improvisers were con-tent simply to embellish or paraphrase a tune's melody, he frequently broke away from the melody, improvising original, melody-like lines that were compatible with the tune's chord progressions. This became the predomi-nant approach for improvisation in the next fifty years of jazz history. Rare, perhaps even nonexistent, is the jazz musician who does not owe a great debt to Louis Armstrong.

Louis Armstrong is considered the most important and influential musician in jazz history, equally influential as a singer and as an instrumentalist. Although he is often identified as a trumpet player more than a singer, his singing and trumpet playing are twin manifestations of a single artistic urge. Over the years countless admirers imitated Armstrong's unique singing style; he popularized scat singing and his phrasing affected virtually every singer to emerge after 1930, including Bing Crosby, Ella Fitzgerald, Billie Holiday, and Frank Sinatra.[1] As an instrumentalist, Armstrong changed jazz from an ensemble-oriented folk music into an art form that emphasized inventive solo improvisations.

By 1930 Armstrong was a star, with imitators all around him, but his business life had come to a temporary impasse. In 1935 he encountered a powerful, often ruthless Mafia operator named Joe Glaser, who would handle Armstrong's fortunes for thirty-five years. From this point, at the expense of his career as a jazz musician, he began to concentrate on his role as a popular entertainer. Under Glaser's guidance, he became the first black to appear regularly in feature-length films and to have a sponsored radio show; by the late 1930s he was a nationwide star. In 1947, after working with a big band, he formed the All-Stars, an immensely successful sextet. Playing Dixieland and swing standards along with a variety of comedy numbers, Armstrong began a schedule of nonstop traveling that lasted until his death.

During the 1950s and '60s Louis had major hits in "Blueberry Hill," "Mack the Knife," and "Hello Dolly," the latter followed by a gold-selling album of the same name. It won him a Grammy for best vocal performance. This pop success was repeated internationally four years later with "What a Wonderful World," which did not gain much attention in the U.S. until 1987, when it was used in the film *Good Morning, Vietnam*, after which it became a Top 40 hit. By the mid-1950s "Satchmo" was one of the best-known entertainers in the world. He appeared in almost fifty popular films and traveled internationally, often in the capacity of "Ambassador of Jazz" for the U.S. State Department. When he died in 1971, no jazz musician could approach him in popularity.

---

1. Bogdanov et al., *Guide to Jazz*, 37.

ELLA FITZGERALD: THE "FIRST LADY" OF SONG

Considered by many to be the most outstanding non-operatic singer of the twentieth century, Ella Fitzgerald (1917–1996) was arguably the finest female jazz singer of all time (though some would surely vote for Billie Holiday or Sarah Vaughan). Blessed with a beautiful voice, Ella could outswing anyone and had near-flawless technique. Despite having a small and somewhat girlish voice, she offset those qualities by near-perfect elocution and an extremely wide range (of three octaves) that she commanded with a remarkable agility and an unfailing sense of swing. Her mastery of swing eighth notes and perfect timing of syncopations enabled her to give performances that rivaled those of the best jazz instrumentalists in their virtuosity, particularly in her improvised scat solos, for which she was justly famous. Singing in tune, with an exquisite articulation, her overall manner achieved great presence and warmth. Her combination of spirit and ease imparted a bright touch even to ballads, as though she were never really sad. A youthful quality always pervaded her work, even when she was in her seventies. Her fans loved her because she was a survivor, weathering the decades and getting better with time.

Ella's life was always about moving on. One would never guess from her joyous singing that her early days were terribly bleak. Her parents never married, and her stepfather abused her. In 1911, when Ella was two, the family left Virginia for New York City, joining the great African-American migration northward, fleeing racism and poverty. She ended up in Yonkers, a few miles north of Harlem, at the high point of what we now call the Harlem Renaissance, a high mixture of culture, musical theatre, and literary talent concentrated in a small area of just a few blocks. Ella took it all in, ready to join the Swing Era. Music and dance were paramount in Harlem, a further escape from poverty and racism. If you were black, your life was ruled by social restrictions and racial prejudice. Everyone in New York listened to popular music on the radio, including the teenaged Ella, who was struck by Louis Armstrong's scat singing and later developed it further.

When her mother died in 1932, she dropped out of high school, and two years later, she was living on the streets of Harlem. This was the Great Depression, and half of all African-Americans were unemployed. On November 21, 1934, she got her big break. Overweight, awkward, and dressed in secondhand clothes, she decided to compete in an amateur show at the Apollo Theater in Harlem. Thinking she would dance, she changed her mind during the competition, turning instead to song. Singing in the style of her idol, Connee Boswell, she won the contest. She returned to the streets, entered other amateur events, and won again at a Harlem Opera House concert. Meanwhile, bandleader Chick Webb was looking for a female vocalist that could help him reach the huge white audience that Benny Goodman and others now commanded. When his male singer, Charles Linton, brought Fitzgerald, Webb was appalled by her size and appearance. However, it soon became apparent that she had an extraordinary voice, so Webb decided to give her a chance. It was the best decision he ever made.

Starting in 1935, Ella began recording with Webb's orchestra and by 1937 the majority of the band's selections featured her voice. Her upbringing and lack of glamor could be seen as a liability, but ultimately she won audiences not only with her God-given talent and strong work ethic, but also with her innocence, humor, and humility. That year she won first place as the best female vocalist poll in the country's leading jazz magazines, an honor she achieved for eighteen consecutive years. Soon every band wanted her, and she started cutting records, singing in nightclubs and ballrooms across the country. The following spring she and Webb recorded an old nursery rhyme, "A-Tisket, A-Tasket," which became Webb's biggest hit. After Webb died in 1939, Ella fronted the orchestra until 1941, when she disbanded the group and went solo. Her subsequent recordings for Decca produced numerous hits.

With her voice, Ella made it seem as if anything was possible. That, of course, is the mystery of artistry. With Ella, visible first impressions were deceiving, because their welled within her an inexhaustible font of creativity.

When a new form of music erupted during World War II, Ella embraced the bop revolution, holding her own with innovative stylists such as Dizzy Gillespie and Charlie Parker, using her voice to improvise with the best bebop instrumentality. Ella began doing something vocally that had never been done before—at least not at that level—creating sounds with her voice that rivaled the most innovative saxophonists and trumpeters of the era. Such singing was empowering, not only to Ella as a musician, but as a woman in a man's world. She stretched the boundaries of what was musically possible, not only because of her rhythmic and harmonic ability, but because she heard internally sounds others did not hear. In that regard, she took spirituality to its creative limits.

Around 1946, while she toured with Gillespie's big band, she adopted bop as part of her style and started including exciting scat-filled romps in her sets. Though she did not invent it, Fitzgerald was scat singing's best-known practitioner. Among the modern scat singers who followed, almost all cite her work as their first inspiration. Contained within her scat devices were stock phrases from late swing and early bop improvisers. On some recordings she functions as a horn, using nonsense syllables exclusively.

When Ella sang popular tunes, she incorporated chords and phrasing from many songs into her scat singing, but always within the same chord structures. Such ability cannot be taught; it is pure genius. In a memorable concert in Berlin in 1960, Ella exploded with a five-minute scat version of "How High the Moon," quoting from more than forty symphonies, nursery rhymes, folk tunes, novelty songs, show hits—a joyous torrent of invention—ending the scat with segments of "A-Tisket, A-Tasket" and a version of "Smoke Gets In Your Eyes," substituting "sweat" for "smoke" as perspiration flowed down her face.

Despite her scat singing, Fitzgerald gets high marks from listeners who like a singer to stick to the melody as written. Some of the greatest pop tune composers were eager to have her perform their songs because her readings were so true to their original intent. Thus in addition to her exalted position in jazz, she also had a large following among pop music listeners. Many consider her creative peak to be the 1950s and '60s, yet she was still giving remarkable performances during the 1970s and '80s.

In 1955 she signed with Norman Grantz's Verve label and over the next few years she recorded her seminal "songbook" albums, dedicated to the works of George Gershwin, Harold Arlen, Johnny Mercer, Jerome Kern, Cole Porter, Irving Berlin, and Duke Ellington. Although those were not her most jazz-oriented projects, these magnificent albums did a great deal for her career and established Fitzgerald among the supreme interpreters of the classic American popular song repertory. By the time of her death, she was a household name and one of the world's undisputed musical treasures.

DUKE ELLINGTON: MASTER PAINTER

For many musicians and listeners, Edward Kennedy (Duke) Ellington (1899–1974) stands at the very top of musical achievement in the United States. He is without doubt one of the most significant figures in jazz history, not only as a performer or even as musician, but also as consummate artist. There is simply no explanation for his musical genius. By the mid-to late 1930s, around the time that swing bandleaders such as Goodman and

Basie were establishing themselves around New York, Ellington was already an international star whose home base was Harlem's Cotton Club. Ellington was the first jazz bandleader to be considered a modern composer, comparable to Ravel, Dibelius, and Stravinsky. When Stravinsky visited New York in the early 1930s, he told reporters that the first thing he wanted to do was go to Harlem to see Ellington at the Cotton Club. The combination of two aspects of Ellington's life, his nomination for a Pulitzer Prize and the fact that he celebrated his seventieth birthday at the White House, could hardly have occurred in the life of any other jazz figure. This sort of attention came to Ellington, in part because he was a composer, but to a greater extent because of the kind of person he was.

Born in Washington, D.C. to a middle-class family, he grew up in a secure and happy home, and from the start was a natural leader. The story concerning the origin of his nickname is marvelous. Coming down in the morning, he would stop at the foot of the stairs and order the adults present to "stand over there." Then he would announce, in grand fashion, "This is the great, the grand, the magnificent Duke Ellington." He would bow and request applause before rushing off to school. The nickname "Duke" seems actually to have been granted later, more for his natty clothes and appearance than for his talent or instinct for leadership, though all were evident from his youth.

As a boy, Ellington was interested in painting, but as he grew up he began to realize that there were social advantages to playing the piano, not to mention financial benefits. Like many other aspiring pianists of his generation, Ellington listened to the ragtime and barrelhouse piano players of the era, teaching himself to play by slowing down the roll on the family pianola and placing his fingers on the depressed keys. By his late teens he was playing professionally, sometimes with bands of his own. When it came time to go to college, he passed up an art fellowship and chose a music career instead.

Ellington's first visit to New York came in 1922, where he worked briefly with Wilbur Sweatman, whose claim to fame came from playing three clarinets at once. A year later he returned to New York, this time as part of the Washingtonians, a five-piece group that included Sonny Greer, who would be Ellington's drummer for thirty years. For six months in New York the Washingtonians starved. Ellington may not have been overly exaggerating when he said the group sometimes split a hot dog five ways. They raised money by playing at rent parties, a phenomenon of the time used by people to raise rent money for their apartments. On such occasions, renters provided food, drink, and entertainment, for which they charged admission. Musicians didn't always get paid, but they could eat and drink for free. It was at such parties that Ellington first met and competed with pianists James P. Johnson, Willie "The Lion" Smith, and Fats Waller, who though five years younger than Ellington, taught him some things about jazz piano.

As an aspiring composer, Ellington sought out Will Marion Cook, a renowned composer and conductor, hoping to match his success. One summer day, as they rode home together in a taxi, Cook urged Ellington to acquire a formal education at a conservatory. Ellington balked, replying that the academies were not teaching what he wanted to learn. In that case, Cook told him, "First . . . find the logical way, and when you find it, avoid it, and let your inner self break through and guide you. Don't try to be anybody else but yourself."[2] Ellington followed that advice throughout his career.

In 1927 Ellington began a three-year engagement as bandleader at Harlem's Cotton Club. With its glamorous revues and erotic dancing shows, no nightspot offered more thrills. Ellington fully understood the absurdity of much that went on at the Cotton Club. But the club also provided him with a priceless training ground, teaching him how to produce on deadline and how to showcase talented people. And while the "jungle music" tag would follow him for a time, neither distant Africa nor the perverse version of it that helped lure whites to Harlem was ever his source of inspiration. For that, he would always draw upon what he called "the everyday life and customs of the Negro." Unlike most other bandleaders, "Ellington wasn't interested primarily in establishing a good beat for dancing; he wanted to explore his musical imagination. Memories, sound colors, moods, emotions—these were his focal points . . . With musical insight and sensitivity, Ellington composed pieces with his players in mind . . . and in so doing, lifted individuality within his band to an artistic zenith."[3]

As a pianist, Ellington was not a virtuoso, although as a performer on his chosen instrument—the orchestra—he was unequaled. The secret of his success was that he understood something about jazz that few leader-composers understood. He knew that in jazz it is the musician, not the instrument or the bandleaders, that makes the music. While other leaders looked for musicians who fit a common predetermined pattern, Ellington

2. Ward and Burns, *Jazz: A History*, 99.
3. Hasse, *Jazz: The First Century*, 62.

constantly sought out musicians who could give his imagination something new to work on and who made his band sound different from any other. He made his musicians sound good not only in performances but also on records. He constantly experimented with sound. It is no accident that Ellington records sound better than almost any other jazz of his era.

The arrival in the band of two musicians from the New Orleans tradition was the catalyst that turned the band toward jazz. The first was trumpeter James "Bubber" Miley, who came to jazz upon hearing King Oliver's Creole Jazz Band in Chicago in 1921. Miley taught his effects to trombonist Joe "Tricky Sam" Nanton, and the two created a sound later dubbed "the Ellington effect." The second major influence on the band was soprano saxophonist Sidney Bechet, who entered the band around the same time as Miley. He feuded with Miley and several other members of the band and quit shortly thereafter. However, during his short stay, he too taught the band how jazz was to be played. In 1924 Bechet was possibly the finest jazz player alive, a fact acknowledged by the famous Ellington quote: "Of all musicians, Bechet to me was the very epitome of jazz." Not only was Bechet the band's jazz foundation, he also had a direct effect on Johnny Hodges, who worked with Bechet in Boston and New York before joining Ellington. Hodges went on to become the premier soloist in Ellington's band and the finest alto saxophonist in jazz before Charlie Parker.

Ellington's contributions as bandleader were legendary. Not only did he lead one of the earliest jazz-oriented big bands, but his group proved to be one of the most stable and durable in jazz history, beginning in 1923 and lasting until his death in 1974. Some of Ellington's musicians remained with him for twenty or thirty years at a stretch. His musicians had strong, unique styles of their own, and together they made up an all-star unit. Despite the contributions made by its musicians, the Ellington band was essentially the creation of the master himself. None of his players ever had significant careers apart from him; it was he who found out what they could do and then made them do it, and his ability to do this was crucial to his accomplishment. Above all, musicians liked to play for Ellington because he made them sound better than anybody else did.

Of the hundreds of records made by his bands over the years, two that had an immediate impact when they were issued were the early *Black and Tan Fantasy*," recorded in several versions in 1927, and "*Ko-Ko*," considered by many critics to be his finest accomplishment, made in 1940. These and dozens more like them are at the core of the Ellington repertoire; alive with fire and color, they constitute one of the great works of music created in the twentieth century.

Despite his significance as bandleader and jazz pianist, Ellington's greatest musical contribution stems from his being the single most creative and prolific composer-arranger in jazz history. He wrote over two thousand compositions as well as an enormous number of arrangements. His best known songs include "*I'm Beginning to See the Light*," "*Solitude*," "*Moon Indigo*," and "*Don't Get Around Much Anymore*." Many of his tunes were composed in collaboration with his sidemen. From 1939 until 1967 he worked closely with pianist-composer-arranger Billy Strayhorn. The two collaborated so closely and their styles were so similar that at times even the composers themselves could not identify their specific contributions. Nevertheless, of their famous tunes, "*Satin Doll*" is thought to be Strayhorn's, as well as "*Take the 'A' Train*," which replaced "*East St. Louis Toodle-o*" as the band's theme. Musicians are especially fond of Strayhorn ballads "*Chelsea Bridge*" and "*Lush Life*," the latter of which he wrote while still in high school, long before he joined Ellington.

In addition to writing hundreds of three-minute instrumentals (three minutes being the standard length of one side of a 78 rpm record), Ellington also composed extended works such as "*Creole Rhapsody*," considered by the English as the first true jazz "composition." Other longer pieces include "*Diminuendo in Blue*" and "*Crescendo in Blue*," as well as his most respected work in this category, "*Black, Brown, and Beige*," a fifty minute-long composition.

A distinguishing mark of Ellington's music is his exploration of "moods." His music was filled with color, close harmony, and command of dissonance. His mastery of melody ranks him as possibly the finest composer of short melody in twentieth-century America. Perhaps his greatest skill, however, was his ability to find and develop the instrumentalists who were able to produce the sounds he desired. His music often featured some of his outstanding soloists, to whom Ellington left lots of room to improvise.

As a public figure, Ellington was the ideal leader, a tall, handsome, suave, and elegant individual who seemed to control the band telepathically. Offstage he was charming, not only with women, but also with other artists. "As a teenager I saw him as a God figure," quipped dancer Alvin Ailey, who later choreographed many of Ellington's works.

What is perhaps most enduring, and instructive about the story of Ellington is the matter of character. Despite aloofness and an arrogance that grew as he aged, Ellington was a mature, completed personality. That fact has immense importance, for he was a late starter, an artist who grew slowly, a step at a time. He did not begin to do any important work in jazz until he was twenty-eight, an age at which Louis Armstrong was creating his most enduring masterpieces, and at which cornetist Bix Beiderbecke was already finished. If Ellington had died as early as Beiderbecke, he would live in jazz history only as an obscure pianist who had once led a band containing Johnny Hodges. Had he died at the age of thirty-four, as Charlie Parker did, he would have been remembered as the leader of a fine band. Had he died at the age of thirty-nine, as Fats Waller did, his most famous records never would have been made, and he would have gone down as an important jazz composer, but certainly not, as he is considered by some critics, the equal of Armstrong and Parker. He lived a full life, yet he did not get involved with drugs. He learned to control his eating and drinking, managed his business affairs well, kept order in his band, and went on studying and learning and letting his art slowly mature. Beiderbecke, Armstrong, and Parker possessed far more raw talent than Ellington, but Ellington had taste, intelligence, and a nature that allowed him to select sound artistic goals and move toward them consistently. There are no long, fallow periods in Ellington's life, and few false starts. In 1926 Beiderbecke was five years younger than Ellington, but nearly ten years ahead in artistry. It is stunning to think what he could have achieved had he had Ellington's character. However, it was Ellington who had the character, and it counted for more than talent.[4]

JOHN COLTRANE: THE JAZZ MESSIAH

The history of jazz is filled with the names of musical personalities who have been extravagantly admired: Armstrong, Bechet, Beiderbecke, Davis, Ellington, Fitzgerald, Getz, Goodman, Hawkins, Hodges, Monk, Parker, Sinatra, Tatum, Young, but no jazz musician has ever received the extreme adulation visited upon John Coltrane (1926–1967). Not merely loved or even idolized, he came to be revered as a saint, as a mystical figure on a spiritual level with the founders of the world's great religions (there is a church in San Francisco founded in his name). As a musician, saxophonist John Coltrane is considered among the top ten most important figures in jazz

4. This paragraph is taken nearly verbatim from James Lincoln Collier's ending to his chapter on Ellington, *Making of Jazz*, 257. It stands as an honest and lasting tribute to "the only jazz musician to become a public figure as an artist."

history. Whereas some traditionalists feel that jazz history ended with Coltrane, many modernists feel it only just started with him. Coltrane exerted that kind of effect on his listeners. Not everyone liked his music; indeed, some hated it. But among those impressed by it, few remained impassive.

Despite a relatively brief career, Coltrane was among the most important, and most controversial, figures in jazz. No single performer has come along to dominate the succeeding decades as he dominated jazz during the 1960s. He leaped to fame during the mid-1950s while playing in the Miles Davis quintet. By this time he had developed an individualistic style, consisting of choppy, staccato pieces and filled with odd, often unrelated figures. It contained what has been described as a searching quality, and it was this searching that is perhaps the most salient characteristic of his life and work. He sought for truth by rummaging endlessly among religions, hoping to find a final answer, a word to illumine his path. During the final decade of his life there was a constant experimentation with new musical forms, systems, and theories. This restlessness, this hope of finding finality, began to personify John Coltrane, and to attract followers.

A contemporary of Miles Davis, Coltrane was a late bloomer. He was born and raised in North Carolina, the son of a successful tailor who died when John was but twelve. Shortly after that his maternal grandfather, a charismatic preacher highly regarded by the local populace, also died. These two deaths, occurring at the start of Coltrane's adolescence, undoubtedly made a mark on what was already a somewhat withdrawn personality. In 1941, after the start of World War II, his mother moved to Philadelphia, where there was high paying war work. Coltrane stayed behind to finish high school, and then moved to Philadelphia. He began to study alto saxophone at a small music conservatory, then was drafted into the U. S. Navy and sent to Hawaii, where he played in a navy band, mainly as clarinetist.

Upon his discharge he returned to Philadelphia, resuming his musical studies while performing with local bands. He made his first professional recordings with Dizzy Gillespie's big band in 1949 and continued with Gillespie in New York until 1951, when he moved back to Philadelphia. By now he was determined to make a significant mark on music. He was not simply ambitious, as Miles had been, or intent on being the best, like Hawkins, or pleased with acclaim, like Armstrong. Coltrane was a driven man, impelled by the intense desire to become a major figure. And he was willing to work hard to achieve his goal.

Upon returning to Philadelphia, he enrolled once again in a music conservatory, this time studying both saxophone and music theory, the latter with Dennis Sandole, who was particularly interested in theories of bitonality (the use of two keys at once, a feature that had long been a part of European concert music) and the use of scales as a basis for composition and improvisation. These features intrigued Coltrane and became essential to his playing and compositional style in the late 1950s and '60s. To hone his virtuosity, Coltrane spent countless hours obsessively practicing Nicolas Sloninsky's *Thesaurus of Scales and Melodic Patterns*, a vast storehouse of modes and scales that could be used as a basis for improvisation.

Two aspects of his character were now well developed. The first was his shyness. After a gig he often retired to his room to practice alone rather than go out with the guys. In a business filled with flamboyant personalities and oversized egos, Coltrane was quiet and agreeable, with a need to be liked. The other defining aspect of his personality was a compulsive behavior, displayed through his work ethic as well as through oral addictions. Coltrane loved sweets: candy bars, Cokes, and his favorite, sweet potato pie. Though he smoked and drank heavily, it was the addiction to sweets that proved most detrimental to his health.

In 1955, he got a call from Miles Davis. By this time, Coltrane had developed an individualistic style, consisting of a vigorous approach and a huge, dark tone that was rough-textured and biting. The entire range of his sound was full of searing intensity. He leaped to fame while playing in the quintet with Miles, Red Garland, Paul Chambers, and Philly Joe Jones, for the group recorded prolifically. He stayed with the band from 1955 to 1957, and it was with this group that he earned the nickname "Trane." The name, it seems, was more than just a pun on his last name. It also symbolized freedom and change. For African-Americans, the word "train" conveyed the hopes and longings of a people who dreamed of a way to get away from the land of their slavery. The old blues people had written hundreds of tunes to titles like "*Train Blues*" and "*Train Whistle Blues*." The word also indicated the coming of modern times and the possibility of going somewhere and experiencing new things.

As saxophonist with the Davis quintet, a band rapidly becoming the leading group in jazz, Coltrane began to attract a good deal of attention. By now he should have been recording on his own, but emotional problems plagued him. He was drinking heavily; he tried breaking his drug habit, only to take it up again. In 1957 he was asked to leave the Davis band, not on account of the drugs, for there was plenty of that in the band, but for their effects on his playing.

Sometime in 1957, the pivotal event in his life occurred. During a stay at home, Coltrane, by now addicted to alcohol and heroin, made the decision to fast on water alone and not emerge from his room until he was free of his addiction. After several days, the experiment proved successful. In the process, he experienced a spiritual awakening, which had immediate consequences on his life and music. His emotional life now in order, Coltrane was prepared to make his mark. *A Love Supreme*, the 1964 recording that made him a public figure, symbolized the enduring presence of his earlier liberation. This work became his quintessential personal statement, the recording that underscored his preeminence in the 1960s.

Biographers often speak of this event as a religious conversion, for from that time on Coltrane became more and more intrigued by religion, especially Eastern religions. His emotional life now in order, Coltrane was prepared to make his mark. He recorded the first of many albums under his own name. He also recorded and performed with Thelonious Monk. A live engagement with Monk at the Five Spot, a club that in 1956 had given pianist Cecil Taylor his first exposure and that in 1959 would launch the free-jazz movement with its booking of Ornette Coleman, brought Coltrane before a knowledgeable audience and furthered his musical education. Coltrane considered Monk to be a musical architect of the highest rank. The two worked together closely, as Monk provided answers to Coltrane's musical questions. Thelonious was an eccentric player, whose spare style and approach to rhythm was almost the direct opposite of Coltrane's playing. Though they shared a fondness for irregularity, Trane's approach at this time exhibited what came to be called his "sheets-of-sound" style, meaning that the notes poured out so fast that they could not be heard individually, only as a continuous stream. The approach underscored Coltrane's desire to transcend beyond fixed pitch to a level of pure emotion.

By 1957 Coltrane was playing with remarkable speed and agility, as much as any other saxophonist in jazz history. At times he played at speeds approaching a thousand notes a minute. This fluency, which inspired hundreds of saxophonists to exceedingly high levels of instrumental proficiency, did not come easily to Coltrane. It was achieved only through an obsessive devotion to technical mastery. Saxophonist Lee Konitz once remarked that Coltrane must have practiced eight to ten hours a day to play the way he did. In 1957 Coltrane signed a recording contract with Prestige;

his reputation was such that other record companies, including Atlantic, were ready to sign him whenever he became available. Thus in his thirties, at an age when most jazz musicians had already done their best work, Coltrane finally arrived. In 1960, following a European tour with Davis, he went on his own. Because Coltrane's development was slow, his fans were able to follow the unfolding of his career more closely than with other musicians. Four stages of his career can be delineated rather clearly: his early days as a hard bopper; the sheets-of-sound period; the modal period, and the free-jazz period before his death.

Coltrane's pre-1960s style showed an infatuation with rapidly changing chords. By the late 1950s, he started employing a system whereby he regularly used four chords to replace each chord in the progression. His first important record, *Giant Steps*, was cut in late 1959 and was the first album over which Coltrane had control. Each of the compositions was his, but it was the title track that caused a fuss. Though performed in the hard bop style, what gave the piece interest was the chord progression, which was based on an alternating pattern of a minor third up, then a fifth down— hence the title, "*Giant Steps*." For musicians, the excitement lay in the fact that the chord changes came steadily, every two beats. Taken at the tempo Coltrane selected, the relentless harmonic exploration was a killer exercise in improvising at a rapid clip to an unusual set of chords. To this day, the tune continues to provide the ultimate challenge for many jazz musicians.

If "*Giant Steps*" looked backward, there were other tracks on the record that prefigured the future, particularly in their fascination with modes. Coltrane had been aware of modes and other types of scalar playing for some time, going back to Slonimsky's *Thesaurus* and his studies with Dennis Sandole in Philadelphia. In addition, Coltrane's interest in religions had led him to the study of Eastern music, particularly Indian music, with its heavy reliance on modes. Earlier, he had explored modes while performing with Davis on *Kind of Blue*, the first record dedicated to modal exploration.

One of Coltrane's most famous modal performances can be heard in the title track from the album *My Favorite Things*, based on the popular Rodgers and Hammerstein show, *The Sound of Music*. The tune, in waltz time, contains very simple chord changes and relatively long passages, giving it something of a modal character. As the rhythm section played to a purely modal form, Coltrane improvised, sticking close to the notes implied by the modes, which in turn were suggested by the melody itself. The result was a highly approachable piece of music. It proved to be one of

Coltrane's best sellers, with fifty thousand copies sold in its first year alone. When the album was released in 1961, the title track became a blockbuster on jazz radio, despite its nearly fourteen-minute length. With the album's success, Coltrane became the most respected figure in jazz.

Another reason for the album's success is that it featured Coltrane on the soprano saxophone. Up to this point, with the exception of Sidney Bechet (who died in 1959) and Steve Lacy (only narrowly known in the late 1950s), the instrument had been largely ignored in jazz. But Coltrane changed all that. He had been listening to Bechet for some time, and through his association with Monk he had become aware of the work of Lacy, who had played soprano with Monk. In 1959 Coltrane purchased a soprano. He liked its smooth, dulcet sound and its higher range. It seemed the perfect instrument to convey the sound he sought for *"My Favorite Things."* In this performance, Coltrane combined his customary robust style with a haunting eastern wail, creating a voluptuous sound that was appealing, modern, and novel. The piece took on a life of its own, with some forty-five versions recorded between 1960 and 1967. The Atlantic version of 1960, however, remains the classic. Recorded when Coltrane was still finding his way, it is an enduring delight, opulent, erotic, emotionally generous, and technically flawless. This album, the debut of Coltrane's quartet, featured McCoy Tyner on piano and Elvin Jones on drums. The third member of the classic Coltrane quartet, bassist Jimmy Garrison, joined in 1961. Together they constituted one of the most important groups in jazz history. Indeed, some historians consider the quartet the most influential of all jazz combos.

Given Coltrane's character, it was inevitable that he became interested in free jazz. Keep in mind that Coltrane was determined to stamp himself with greatness. He could not allow a revolutionary current to pass without comment. He became interested in the music of Ornette Coleman, the most prominent figure in the free jazz movement, and this led to an album called *Avant-Garde,* which Coltrane recorded in 1960 with Coleman's band. Although Coltrane became committed to free jazz during the early 1960s, the recording that made him a public figure, *A Love Supreme,* was not in that vein. The album, recorded in 1964, symbolized the enduring presence of Coltrane's 1957 conversion and liberation from addiction.

As the title suggests, *A Love Supreme* was Coltrane's beatitude to God. Spiritual values now meant a great deal to him, and they were featured in sections titled *"Acknowledgement," "Resolution," "Pursuance,"* and *"Psalm."* The work, an autobiographical four-part suite and canticle, became Coltrane's quintessential personal statement, the recording that underscored his pre-eminence in the 1960s. His enormous influence at this point was undeniable. According to jazz historian Gary Giddins, "an expanding coterie of musicians looked to him as a leader, and a generation of listeners depended on him as a shepherd for a music that was hurtling into no-man's-land."[5] Ironically, at the very moment critics were cheering *A Love Supreme* and followers were affirming its message, Coltrane was in the studio with ten other free spirits recording *Ascension*, a forty-minute free-jazz marathon described by Giddins as "the single most vexatious work in jazz history."[6]

Whatever one thinks of Coltrane and his music, his personality and artistic pilgrimage epitomized the enigmatic, restless 1960s. A "jazz messiah" to some, an "anti-jazz" figure to others, Coltrane was followed because he excited the senses and kept his audience in a state of apprehension, awaiting each transforming step with pleasurable foreboding. Coltrane altered the face of jazz, not by forcing a comprehensive retooling of the music, as Armstrong and Parker had done, but by instigating a reimagining of possibilities for those who were to follow. Each of his style periods caused musicians to experiment with the techniques he popularized. Jazz saxophonists adjusted their styles to accommodate the changes he brought about in their instrument. The urgency of his attack struck a chord with rock musicians, who constructed improvised solos on pedal points, a technique that Coltrane helped popularize. Conservatory saxophonists, also affected, began exploring the harmonics and overtones he perfected.

Coltrane was gravely ill for perhaps a year before dying of liver cancer in the summer of 1967, and when he died, jazz suffered as well. Coltrane's followers were uncertain as to his future direction, for surely it would have been the next frontier for jazz. For thousands of fans around the world, Coltrane was an ethical and cultural leader, an exemplary guide, and the embodiment of the 1960s.

Though far from being a saint, Coltrane was no mere mortal. He was a driven man, for whom music was more than a career, a pastime, or even an aesthetic. For him music was therapeutic, a philosophical and spiritual means for working out his personal problems. In his later live performances his audience regularly discovered a palpable spirituality that took on the aura of religious experience. For those many followers who venerated him

---

5. Giddins, *Visions of Jazz*, 486.
6. Giddins, *Visions of Jazz*, 487.

as more than an artist, he was a worthy spiritual model. As a wounded artist, he became a healer of sorts.

Of course, the music remains. In the end, we are left with the artifacts of a brilliant career, of a journey into music's darker realm, available to anyone willing to set aside certain preconceptions about art and music. There is much about Coltrane we can never know. But we do know that he was, with Parker and Armstrong, one of the great formative influences in jazz. His encouragement of other, lesser-known musicians more "modern" than himself set an exemplary standard of selflessness, openness, and diversity. Perhaps this is why no single performer has come along to dominate the succeeding decades as Coltrane, "The Last Giant," dominated the 1960s.

Leo Tolstoy once wrote: "In order to influence people, the artist must be constantly searching, so that his work is a quest. If he has discovered everything and instructs people or deliberately sets out to entertain them, he has no influence on them. Only when he is searching for the way forward, do the spectator and the listener become one with him in his quest." John Coltrane became such an artist, sharing everything he had, including his pilgrimage, with his audience.

QUESTIONS FOR DISCUSSION AND REFLECTION

1. In your own words, explain how jazz music provides a paradigm not only of African-American culture, but also of an idealized democratic society.

2. In your estimation, why is Louis Armstrong called the "father of jazz"?

3. After reading this chapter, what aspect of Armstrong's personal story do you find most memorable? Explain your answer.

4. After reading this chapter, what aspect of Armstrong's character do you find most compelling? Explain your answer.

5. After reading this chapter, what aspect of Ella Fitzgerald's personal story do you find most memorable? Explain your answer.

6. After reading this chapter, what aspect of Fitzgerald's character do you find most compelling? Explain your answer.

7. After reading this chapter, what aspect of Duke Ellington's personal story do you find most memorable? Explain your answer.

8. After reading this chapter, what aspect of Ellington's character do you find most compelling? Explain your answer.

9. After reading this chapter, what aspect of John Coltrane's personal story do you find most memorable? Explain your answer.

10. After reading this chapter, what aspect of Coltrane's character do you find most compelling? Explain your answer.

11. In your estimation, what is it about these four jazz icons that illustrates for you the connection between the arts (in this case, music) and spirituality? Of these four, which do you find most attractive (either personally or musically)? Explain your answer.

12. In your estimation, what is the primary insight gained from this chapter? Explain your answer.

Chapter 12

THE POWER OF THEATRE

THEATRE IS A COLLABORATIVE ART form that combines words, voice, movement, and visual elements to express meaning. Theatre uses live performers to present the experience of a real or imagined event before a live audience in a specific place, often a stage. Modern theatre includes performance of plays and musical theatre, encompassing not only live improvised and scripted work, but also dramatic forms such as film, television, and other electronic media. The art forms of ballet and opera are also part of the theatrical world, and were influential to the development of musical theatre.[1]

THEATRE AND SPIRITUALITY

When Shakespeare wrote the phrase, "the play's the thing," what did he mean? In his time, there was no public media, certainly nothing like we have today. Theatre, designed to entertain, also served other functions, including communication. Intended for the general public, theatre was also an entertaining way to get the attention of the ruling authorities.

The theatre served as public forum, and drama was essential to its message. Drama is essential to religious liturgy as well, central to worship and to the perpetuation of religious values, beliefs, and social morality.

1. In this chapter and elsewhere, I spell the word "theatre" with the traditional British spelling to distinguish theatre from the movie theater, the stage versus the screen, the production versus the building. American English now acknowledges the traditional spelling as a way of honoring the difference between the two art forms.

When we attend a religious event such as a service or worship, what do we expect? We expect to be inspired and educated, but also to be entertained. When the latter element is missing, worship becomes dull and perfunctory. To be effective, worship must be holistic: the music must be stirring, the scripture lessons inspiring, the prayers edifying, and the preaching challenging. When all four work together, we depart wanting more, for we have been "moved," lifted from the mundane to the realm of the Spirit. When these factors coalesce, we are entertained, though much more has happened. The same is true of musical theatre. It is entertainment, but so much more! Theatre is aliveness, and that is the starting point of authentic spirituality.

Worship involves music, song, drama, even dance, all components of musical theatre. Taken together, the elements of worship are called "liturgy," from the Greek word *litourgia*, meaning "public worship," or more literally, "service/work of the people." Early Christian worship took place in house churches, that is, in peoples' homes, the order of worship including readings from scripture, prayer, preaching, and singing, a pattern modeled after synagogue worship. The service closed with a distinctly Christian addition, the breaking of bread (the Lord's Supper or Eucharist), the central mystery at the heart of Christianity (see Acts 2:42).

By the fourth century, when Christianity was established as the official religion of the Roman empire, institutional Christianity had developed significantly, including elaborate rituals, ornate clerical vestments, hierarchical priestly patterns, worship based on sacraments, the use of elaborate music, ornamental altarpieces, and pulpit furnishings such as paraments (used to highlight liturgical seasons and festival days). Worship, no longer confined to small spaces such as houses or burial chambers, now took place in elaborate basilicas. As church architecture and organization expanded, so liturgy expanded to fill the enlarged space allotted to it. Building on pagan rituals such as sacrifices, festivals, and processions, Christian liturgy began to take on the characteristics of such public worship, including open-air processions, pilgrimages, elaborate rituals (such as bowing and genuflecting), rich garments, and the use of musical chants.

In high church liturgy, sets, costumes, dramatic roles, celebration, procession, chants, songs, rituals, and pageantry (all originally secular in function and significance) became consecrated and ordained for sacred use—the profane transposed into the pious, the pagan into the devout, the theatrical becoming the liturgical. In "The Circus Animals Desertion," one of the last poems W. B. Yeats wrote before his death, he reflects on his past and current writing, his sentiments supremely captured in the last three lines from that poem: "Now that my ladder's gone / I must lie down where all the ladders start / In the fowl rag-and-bone shop of the heart."

This pattern of using the common and ordinary to illustrate the extraordinary goes back to Jesus, whose teaching was based on parables, themselves radically profane stories. There are no gods, demons, angels, miracles, or time before time in Jesus' parables, only people like us: Palestinian landlords traveling and renting their fields, stewards and workers, sowers and fishers, parents and children, husbands and wives, eating and drinking; in a word, ordinary people doing ordinary things. The paradox in these narratives of normalcy is not that they point to mundane situations, but to God's kingdom, to the eternal in the temporal. The paradox is that the extraordinary is like the ordinary. This is what things on earth look like, what they become, when people of faith look at life with nondualistic eyes: "God saw everything that he had made, and indeed, it was very good" (Gen 1:31).

Notice, however, that when the gospels speak of God's kingdom, they do not tell us what the kingdom *is*, only what it is *like*. When Jesus speaks of God's kingdom, he speaks metaphorically. Only analogy is used, only images, because analogy saves us from abstraction. While it is possible to derive dogma (concepts, doctrines, and beliefs) from individual parables, this is not what Jesus intended. The parables of Jesus make a whole, constituting what French hermeneutical philosopher Paul Ricoeur called "a network of intersignification."[2] There is more in the parables taken together than in any conceptual system about God's presence and purpose for the cosmos.

For example, the parable of the Good Samaritan (Luke 10: 29–37) has often been interpreted as though it were an allegory intended to teach the plan of salvation. According to Augustine and many after him, the man "going down from Jerusalem to Jericho" refers to Adam, who fell from blessedness into mortal sin. The robbers are the devil and his angels; the priest and the Levite, who saw him and passed by, stand for the law and the prophets of the Old Testament, which are unable to save the sinner. The Good Samaritan, who rescues the traveler, is Christ, who takes him to the church. The two denarii that the Samaritan gives to the innkeeper are the promises of this life and of that which is to come. Finally, the promise of the Samaritan to return teaches the Second Coming of Christ.

2. Reagan and Stewart, *Philosophy of Paul Ricoeur*, 242.

Other commentators, perceiving the parable's literary context, note that the parable teaches, not the plan of salvation, but the moral lesson "what's mine is yours, and we will share." Of course, when parables are isolated, not only from their literary context—which reflects the gospel writer's intention more than that of Jesus—but from one another, it is easy to extract from them static, frozen dogma rather than holistic spirituality. Take, for instance, the three parables in Luke 15. Taken alone, the parable of the lost sheep (15:3–7) can be seen as teaching the doctrine of universal salvation; the parable of the lost coin (15:8–10), the doctrine of predestination; and the parable of the prodigal son (15:11–32), the concept of individual salvation and a theology of free will.

If we read the gospel parables carefully, we will notice that they are not intended to be read literally. They obviously teach, but not in ordinary ways. Rather, they resort to paradox, hyperbole, and antithetical formulations. Their initial intent is not to orient but to disorient, and only after that, to reorient. Taken individually, it is easy to transpose the parables into moral fables or trivial platitudes. In isolation, these parables say nothing directly about the kingdom of God, but together they provide clues to Jesus' intent. Jesus' parables are eschatological at their core, for they teach that when God's kingdom breaks into human lives and situations, it results in shocking patterns of behavior, where all prejudices die and new ways of life emerge. As a sage, Jesus did not simply instruct, but more importantly, his purpose was to move listeners to action or decision, something he accomplished by persuasion and never by coercion.

It is when they are taken together that the parables become revelatory, allowing us to "think through" rather than simply to "think about." Taken together, they say more than any rational theology can declare. To listen to the parables of Jesus is to let one's imagination be opened to new possibilities. If we look at these poetic dramas as addressed first to our imagination rather than to our will, we will not be tempted to reduce them to mere moralizing allegories. The word "poetic" means creative, and it is their poetic power, not their didactic message, that parables open us to creativity.

The same can be said of theatre. There really is no such thing as "theatre" in the singular, for it is a holistic endeavor. Music, poetry, prose, theatre; these four parts of what we broadly refer to as the arts are interconnected. Viewed individually or particularistically, theatre's power is limited and its impact partial, but taken holistically, as a composite art form, theatre is transformative, even revelatory.

But so are all of the arts, and even the line dividing art and science is ambiguous, for music incorporates language and form, but also mathematical elements and interpretive performance. Poetry is a musical art, employing meter and sound structures along with language to communicate an image or concept, to give form to the formless, and to communicate that which words taken alone cannot communicate. Prose often crosses over into poetry, especially when expressed in the stream of consciousness, evoking images and sensations that initially seem impossible to communicate in prose.

Each art form contains echoes and resonates aspects of the other arts. The musician or composer weaves language into his scores. The poet weaves music into her words. The prose writer weaves poetry into her images. Playwrights, producers, score writers, lyricists and directors weave many things together to reflect life and form in ways that could not be so well expressed in any single medium.

Theatre draws together the arts and sciences, removing barriers to incorporate all of the arts and sciences, everything that can help communicate the full range of sensation, emotion, and communication. Theatre is a most eclectic medium, for when words are insufficient to communicate ideas or emotions, then lighting, scenery, orchestration, and an unlimited repertoire of artistic tools and tricks are available to enhance the performance. Theatre combines all the arts—visual, physical, musical, poetic, and prosaic—an endless and unlimited range of sensory inputs that create a sensory whole, giving form to emotion and progressive action.

Bob Fosse gave expression to the raw power of the art of dance as a form of communication and expression. In his productions, dance was no mere spectacle or visual entertainment, but an expression of the otherwise inexpressible. When an idea or emotion was too powerful for words, he resorted to song; if an idea or emotion was too powerful to express in song, it had to be danced. As Gwen Verdon once observed, his seemingly effortless, organic and sensual movements were, in fact, precisely choreographed "to the third joint of the little finger."[3] Such is the language of the soul, the instrument being the body. Using simple sets and props and impossibly perfect feats of body isolation, Fosse turned dance into a symphony of motion, a ritual act of spiritual evocation.

---

3. Bob Fosse's distinctive style of choreography won him eight Tony Awards. He is the only person ever to have won Oscar, Emmy, and Tony Awards in the same years (1973).

Theatre is the only medium where other forms and means of expression are available to express the forms and ideas being communicated. Everything from costume design and makeup to props, lighting, and stage setting work are used to complement the dialogue, song, and dance elements. Theatre at its best is a spiritual experience, as we will observe in two of musical theatre's best exemplars: Bob Fosse's *Cabaret* and Stephen Sondheim's *Into the Woods*.

THE MEANING AND MESSAGE OF *CABARET*

Cabaret is a 1966 musical produced and directed by Harold Prince, with music by John Kander, lyrics by Fred Ebb, and book by Joe Masteroff. The musical was based on John van Druten's 1951 play *I Am a Camera*, which was adapted from the semi-autobiographical novel *Goodbye to Berlin* (1939) by Anglo-American writer Christopher Isherwood. Despite its billing as a musical, a spectator's comment after an opening-night production says it best: "*Cabaret* is more than a musical!"

The show focuses on the hedonistic nightlife at the seedy Kit Kat Klub, and revolves around American writer Clifford ("Cliff") Bradshaw's relations with English cabaret performer Sally Bowles (the 1972 film version renames Bradshaw as Brian Roberts and portrays him as English and Bowles as American). The stage version includes a subplot regarding the doomed romance between German boarding house owner Fräulein Schneider and her elderly suitor Herr Schultz, a Jewish fruit vendor.

It has become a custom to see an innovative Broadway musical as a trendsetter, especially since the time of *Show Boat* (1927). As the world changes, so do the best of Broadway musicals. *Cabaret*, writes Stacy Wolf, "is meant to unsettle." Most aspects of the show can be read in two opposing directions, the result of long-standing Broadway conventions that have encouraged double readings. Set in 1931 Berlin during the final days of the Weimar Republic as the Nazis are ascending to power, the musical provides a symbolic edge that tips the show into the realm of fascinating metaphor. *Cabaret* is set in sleazy, raucous, nervous pre-World War II Berlin, a venue defined by the German cabaret world.

This was Prince's first experiment with a concept musical—a show in which the story is secondary to a central message or metaphor. With its seedy characters, luridly placed against the scene of a declining Weimar Republic and a rising Nazi party, the show's dark material seemed to threaten the standard model of the musical, establishing it as antimusical. The show was understood to be a cautionary tale or parable, and its method of expression said to consist of analogies, parallels, and metaphors rather than direct statements.

Cabaret is actually a metatheatrical musical, a rare balancing act that is both entertaining and instructive, one that makes music, dance, dialogue, and décor part of the action rather than passing fancies. The Kit Kat Klub is both cabaret setting and symbolic microcosm, and the performances are all incorporated within a single contaminated world on the verge of extinction. *Cabaret*'s function is both a celebration of the club's festive escape from reality and a platform for social protest. From the first incarnation of the musical to the Bob Fosse 1972 film version and subsequent stage productions that have taken the liberty of carrying Berlin decadence as far as modern theatre and social tastes allow, *Cabaret* uses sex as a way of indicating what is happening politically in the Germany of that era.

The original Broadway production was a huge success; it ran for three years (1,165 performances) and won eight Tony Awards. The theatrical version inspired numerous subsequent productions in New York and London as well as the popular 1972 version, directed by Fosse and starring Liza Minnelli, Michael York, and Joel Grey as the Emcee. The film, known for its distinctive choreography, was nominated for ten Academy Awards and won eight. More adventurous than the stage show with the seedier side of Berlin, the film clearly portrays the male lead's bisexuality and emphasizes sexuality more erotically and explicitly.

Every production of *Cabaret* has modified the original score, with songs being changed, cut, or added. The 1972 film version added several songs, including the hit song "Maybe This Time," previously written by Kander and Ebb for the unproduced musical *Golden Gate*. In the final scene of the 1993 London revival, the Emcee removes his outer clothes to reveal a striped suit of the type worn by internees in concentration camps; on it was pinned a yellow badge (identifying Jews), a red star (marking Communists and socialists), and a pink triangle (denoting homosexuals).

Prince's staging was unusual; as the audience filled the theater, the curtain was already up, revealing a stage containing only a large mirror tilted downward to reflect the audience, making those in attendance peer into the darkness within their own souls, becoming voyeurs of their own public lives. The film version followed suit, opening with an image resolving itself ever so slowly into a distorting mirror: viewers see reflections of people seated at tables, a waiter passing, a woman dressed in red, and finally a man's face—rouged, heavily made up—fills the mirror, and then he starts to sing "Welcome" in three languages. The Master of Ceremonies is a leering, flamboyant figure who embodies decadent culture, and the club itself serves as a metaphor for the ominous social and political developments in late Weimar Germany.

Outside the club, an Aryan boy in a Nazi youth uniform starts to sing a song in a beer garden—a patriotic anthem to the Fatherland that slowly descends into a darker, Nazi-inspired marching song, becoming the strident "Tomorrow Belongs to Me." He initially sings a cappella, before others join in. In the original stage show, the song was sung as a quartet by a group of waiters inside the club, with the Emcee joining in the last line. In Act 2, the cabaret girls—along with the Emcee in drag—perform a kick line routine that eventually becomes a goose-step. This is followed by a song-and-dance routine in which the Emcee performs with a woman in a gorilla suit, insinuating that Germans view Jewish girls as gorillas ("If You Could See Her").

At its core, *Cabaret* is a devastating critique of apathy, and a clever yet terrifying look at totalitarianism. The horror grows as too many characters stay locked in denial or self-interest. At the end, an unrepentant Sally returns to the cabaret singing that life is a cabaret, signifying her decision to live in carefree ignorance and freedom. Will the audience do likewise?

When the film version was released in 1972, the decadence of Berlin and the rise of the Nazis reminded audiences of America's role in the Vietnam War. *Cabaret* forced current audiences to ponder more generally the marks of society in decay. In the stage version, Harold Prince focused on Cliff Bradshaw, whereas the film version shifted the focus to Sally Bowles and her romance with Cliff (renamed Brian Roberts). Despite Sally's efforts to act as a femme fatale, she seeks true love amidst encroaching ruin. Inside the cabaret, she is independent, strong, and seductive, an entertainer fascinated by the decadence of Berlin embodied by the Emcee.

In the musical number "Money," she satirizes capitalism, yet she is indicting herself, for she, too, considers money supreme. In the song, a duet sung with the Emcee, the two approach each other with eyes wide open. As they repeat the word "money" the music gets progressively louder. Their faces are so close they almost kiss, yet they narrow their eyes, repeating the word "money" in an ecstatic trance: money and sex define their character. While Sally tries to portray the independent American woman, she is actually a woman in bondage to decadence, no longer a femme fatale but a tragic figure, living self-destructively. At the end, the stage of the Kit Kat Klub has become her home, the only place where she is needed and accepted, but only if she continues to wear her mask, fooling herself as well as others. She has decided to live a fantasy, not in reality.

At the conclusion of the show, Sally is in the spotlight, blinded by the light yet capitulating to Nazi darkness. In the number "Cabaret," she recommends that people disengage from the pain of life and live only for momentary pleasure, as she herself does. Offstage, Sally represents the "flapper," the single American girl of the 1920s but also a staple of the 1960s and early '70s, who denies the values of her parents' era in her promiscuity and folly. Sally is a person who challenges patriarchy, and who is self-reliant even in having an abortion. At one point, however, her mask is torn away, and her innocence and fragility are revealed when her father stands her up. On this occasion, her vulnerability is evident, for her mask of invincibility no longer works. She is human and needy after all.

Cabaret is considered the first "concept" musical to portray society in decay, criticizing a society that creates art only for its own sake. In this regard, Sally is no artist, for she seems to perform only for her own pleasure, without social conscience. While *Cabaret* offers a strong artistic voice opposed to totalitarianism, it also offers self-criticism of the entertainment industry, when it becomes obsessed with money and fame as an escape from reality. The tradition of theatre as a forum where artists can speak truth to power, criticizing uncontested power and authority through satire, must be encouraged and supported.

That, too, is the role of spirituality. When society becomes a wasteland, it must come under criticism, not just for its victims, which invariably include everyone, but also for those in positions of privilege and authority, living, like Sally Bowles, in denial.

THE MEANING AND MESSAGE OF *INTO THE WOODS*

Into the Woods, with music and lyrics by Stephen Sondheim and book by James Lapine, debuted as a musical in San Diego in 1986 and premiered on Broadway in 1987, where it won several Tony Awards in a year dominated by *Phantom of the Opera*. A Disney film adaptation, directed by Rob Marshall, was released in 2014, receiving three nominations at the Academy Awards. The musical has since been produced many times, including a

1988 national tour, London and Broadway revivals, and in 2012 as part of New York City's outdoor *Shakespeare in the Park* series. The stage production starred Bernadette Peters as the witch, a role performed admirably in the film version by Meryl Streep. The show takes iconic characters such as Little Red Riding Hood, Jack and the Beanstalk, Rapunzel, and Cinderella and intertwines their fates with a baker and his wife, whose longing to have a child sends them on a quest to reverse a witch's curse.

Ultimate credit for the show's ingenious integration of screenwriting with music and lyrics goes to Sondheim, whose vision and genius brings unity to a bewildering diversity of characters and themes. The plot intertwines characters and themes of numerous fairy tales with the lives of multiple families in a village with a deep woods at its heart—a heart of darkness, danger, and destiny. According to Lapine and Sondheim, the musical was inspired by Bruno Bettelheim's 1976 book, *The Uses of Enchantment*, subtitled "The Meaning and Importance of Fairy Tales."

In *Into the Woods*, Sondheim develops themes and characters through text, music, and fairy tale motifs. In order to comprehend this show, it is important to understand the structure and elements found in traditional fairy tales. The fairy tale was originally an oral art form. Each story was communally authored and survived through repetition. The fairy tale was originally intended for an adult audience, although many such these tales have been adapted for children in modern times. The setting of a fairy tale is often described as "Once upon a time, in a kingdom far, far away." Thus, the setting seems timeless, vaguely medieval. Often the setting is extreme, either harsh or utopian, reflecting nostalgia for a simpler past time.

Characters in fairy tales have defining characteristics. Like the setting, they are distinct. They are either good or evil, admirable or hateful. Typically, the characters in trouble end up content, their enemies vanquished, and their troubles overcome. In fairy tales, goodness is defined by the situation, not by the characters' actions; good characters are considered good no matter what they do. Physical appearance often defines character: wicked witches are ugly, good princesses are beautiful, and noble princes are handsome. In addition, heroes are often children, poor, or foolish, whereas villains have high social status, great size and strength, or great knowledge. Furthermore, heroes are often isolated or forced to act alone.

Various themes are central to fairy tale plots, such as social reversals, where powerless underdogs change places with the characters who exerted power over them. This is evident in the case of Cinderella, where the stepfamily becomes Cinderella's servants after she marries the prince. Another theme is the rite of passage, such as the passage from childhood to adulthood. This idea is central to the story of Little Red Riding Hood. Other common themes include escaping mighty and evil enemies, accomplishing monumental tasks, and of course, providing happy endings. In the plot of a fairy tale, action is more important than character development; consequently, conflicts are quickly established and events move swiftly to their conclusion.

While fairy tales are written to entertain, that is only secondary to their primary purpose, which is to illustrate a moral in a memorable way. What sets fairy tales apart from other literature is that magic or some kind of enchantment is required. In fairy tales, magic is a vehicle to a universal truth, sparking something in our hearts and imagination that has a lasting impact. The stories and characters transcend the details of the magical world to teach us about love, values, virtues, vices, the difference between right and wrong, and what things are worth fighting for. They make heroes out of children and ordinary people, and show how good conquers evil.

Into the Woods takes iconic characters such as Cinderella, Little Red Riding Hood, Jack and the Beanstalk, and Rapunzel and blends their themes and plots to create a new and composite storyline. To understand the role these characters play in the show, we must become familiar with the themes in the original tales. For example, the story of Cinderella teaches the morals of kindness toward all, forgiving others for doing wrong, and never letting bad things ruin your heart. The themes of this story are good versus evil and the reversal of fortunes. Little Red Riding Hood teaches the importance of obeying parents, being cautious with strangers, and relying on one's instinctual warning system regarding danger, truth, and falsehood. In this story, good and evil are portrayed by light and darkness. The theme of good and evil is also central to Jack and the Beanstalk; Jack embodies good, and the giant embodies evil. In this tale, good triumphs over evil, and readers are taught to take advantage of life's opportunities. The moral of Rapunzel is that parents cannot secure their children from evil. The tale places ultimate value on the right of freedom and warns of the dangers of control and possessiveness.

Before we examine *Into the Woods*'s meaning and message, it is helpful to provide a brief synopsis. At the beginning, various characters are introduced, each with a wish: a baker and his wife wish to have a child; Cinderella wishes to go to the king's festival, Little Red Riding Hood wishes for bread and sweets to bring to her grandmother's house; and Jack wishes his cow would give milk. The baker and his wife are visited by the neighborhood witch, who reveals to them that she placed a curse on their family. She explains that they are infertile because of a spell she placed on the baker's father many years ago. She tells them that when the baker's mother was pregnant, she craved vegetables, so the baker's father stole them from the witch's garden. He stole supposedly normal beans that turned out to be magic. Because she had lost the beans, the witch's mother turned her ugly and in return, the witch stole their daughter Rapunzel,[4] and placed the spell. The witch has raised Rapunzel in a tall tower accessible only by climbing Rapunzel's long hair. The only way to lift the spell is to find four ingredients in the woods—Jack's cow (a cow as white as milk), Red Riding Hood's cape (a cape as red as blood), Rapunzel's hair (hair as yellow as corn), and Cinderella's slipper (a slipper as pure as gold)—and bring them to her in three days, prior to midnight.

The principal characters all begin their journey into the woods: Jack to sell his beloved cow, Cinderella to her mother's grave, Little Red to her grandmother's house, and the baker to find the four ingredients. In the woods we find Little Red, who is trying to visit her grandmother; the wolf, who loves tasty little girls and persuades Little Red to take a longer path and admire the beauty; Rapunzel, locked in her doorless tower; and two princes chasing after their loves. The baker, clutching six beans he found in his father's jacket, meets Jack, and convinces him that the beans are magic. Jack accepts five beans said to be worth one pound apiece, and bids Milky White a tearful farewell.

Meanwhile, the first prince spies Rapunzel and plans to meet her. The baker, in pursuit of the red cape, slays the wolf and rescues Little Red and her grandmother. In return, Little Red gives him her cape. Jack's mother, disgusted that Jack has traded the cow for five worthless beans, tosses them aside, where they grow into an enormous stalk that reaches into the heavens. Cinderella, who has received a gown and golden slippers from her mother's spirit after wishing she could live in the palace, flees the festival, pursued by a second prince, and the baker's wife hides her. By the end of the first act, everyone has gotten their wish and we expect they will live happily ever after. Cinderella has her prince; Red Riding Hood has killed

---

4. A careful reading of the play suggests the likelihood that the baker's father had been unfaithful to his wife and had seduced the witch, meaning that Rapunzel is actually the witch's biological daughter.

her wolf; Jack has chopped down the beanstalk, killing the giant; Rapunzel has gotten her prince and been rescued from the tower; the baker's wife is pregnant; and the witch has regained her beauty and youth. However, the characters fail to notice a second beanstalk climbing skyward.

In the second act, everyone still has wishes. The baker and his wife face new frustrations with their infant son; Jack misses the kingdom in the sky; Cinderella is bored with life in the palace; Rapunzel has been taken from her tower, only to find herself imprisoned in a swamp;[5] and Cinderella's prince has developed wandering eyes and is back on the chase. Now the main characters find the consequences of their actions haunting them in disastrous ways. After the death of the giant, the giant's wife decides to avenge her spouse and kill his murderer. Jack's mother intervenes, only to die in the process. The baker's wife is seduced by Cinderella's prince, only to be crushed by the marauding giantess. The giant destroys the village, and the royal family flees for their lives.

By the end, only four characters are left to overcome their common adversary: the baker and his child; Cinderella and her birds;[6] Jack and his treasures (the golden egg and harp); and Red Riding Hood, now dressed in a wolf skin cape. United, they set out on a common Grail quest—to defeat a giant and save their kingdom. Pooling their meager resources, the four "Davids" defeat their "Goliath," and they become a family, together raising their child. They achieve victory, but only by making sacrifices. In the woods, the characters learn that they cannot live only for themselves; they must bear responsibility to others. The survivors band together, and the spirit of the baker's wife comforts her mourning husband, encouraging him to tell their child their story. The baker begins the tale, while the remaining characters, dead and alive, offer a final lesson: "Careful the things you say: Children will listen."

Only when love meets courage and resourcefulness can the giant be slain. Cinderella's mother's final advice to her, "are you sure that what you wish is what you want?" is one of the broad themes of the story. Having wished for her prince, she found him in the woods, among giants, witches,

---

5. The film version of the story has Rapunzel rescued by the second prince, who has been blinded by the witch's treachery but restored to sight by Rapunzel's tears.

6. Because Cinderella is left to fend for herself, the birds often come to the rescue. The giant's rampage had left her mother's grave ruined, symbolizing that "mother cannot guide you, now you're on your own." Her birds are her inner magic, personal to her and thus inalienable. They come from within, reflecting her inner purity and strength. In the end, her birds become part of the solution to the problem of the giant.

and wolves. But the purity of her heart becomes her liberation, and that of her fellow travelers as well. Our giants aren't defeated by brute force, nor by compromise and capitulation—but by the four natural virtues (prudence, justice, temperance, and fortitude) working in tandem. Wishes don't end in fulfillment; they often have unforeseen consequences, but a bean can begin an adventure.

Like ancient fairy tales, *Into the Woods* has much to tell us about life, its ongoing theme being, "be careful what you wish for." In this respect, audience members, like the characters in the story, must learn to distinguish between temporal wishes (which are linked to changing external circumstances) and lifelong longing (which comes from one's inner core). As is true of all art, there are many ways to interpret or analyze this show. It can be heard, read, or seen as a tale about childhood and growing up, with specific guidance for parents and children. As a morality tale, *Into the Woods* has much to say about actions and their consequences, including advice about strangers, placing limits on wants and desires, learning how to be adaptable, being loyal and courageous, accepting personal limitations, and finding good friends and lifelong companions.

In addition to these lessons, we can interpret *Into the Woods* as a quest for identity, the first act illustrating first-half-of life quests, and the second act, second-half-of-life quests. In this case, the first and second halves of life do not refer to biological or chronological halves of life, but rather to two spiritual journeys, two distinct ways of thinking and living. While the second journey represents the culmination of one's faith journey, it is largely unknown today, even by people we consider deeply religious, for most individuals and institutions are stymied in the preoccupations of the first half of life: establishing identity, creating boundary markers, and seeking security. The first-half-of-life task, while essential, is not the full journey. Furthermore, one cannot walk the second journey with first-journey tools. One needs a new toolkit.

Evidence suggests that in addition to the first-half-of-life task, there is another great undertaking to human life. The first task is to build a strong "container" or identity; the second is to find the contents that the container is meant to hold.[7] The first task—surviving successfully—is obvious, one we take for granted as the purpose of life. We all want to complete successfully the task that life first hands us: establishing an identity, a home, a career, relationships, friends, community, and security, all foundational for getting

7. Rohr, *Falling Upward*, xiii.

started in life. Many cultures throughout history, most empires in antiquity, and the majority of individuals in the modern period have focused on first-half-of-life tasks, primarily because it is all they have time for, but also for lack of vision.

Most of us are never told that we can set out from the known and the familiar to take on a further journey. Our institutions, including our churches, are almost entirely configured to encourage, support, reward, and validate the tasks of the first half of life. Shocking and disappointing as it may be, we struggle more to survive than to thrive, focusing on "getting through" or on getting ahead rather than on finding out what is at the top or was already at the bottom. As wilderness guide Bill Plotkin puts it, many of us learn to do our "survival dance," but we never get to our actual "sacred dance." The first half of life, then, involves a quest for identity; the second half involves a quest for meaning and purpose.

How can you know you are entering the second half of life? The following road markers are quite reliable: when you experience new urges

- sense a new vision
- are ready to let go of old securities
- are ready to risk giving up the patterns of the past for the promise of the future
- are as focused on the "inner" life as on the outer dimension of life.

While individuals can describe their experience of the second journey and even serve as mentors, they cannot define or outline the journey for others. This is due both to the uniqueness of the journey and to a subtle factor, known by generations of mystics and spiritual masters but elusive to many of our contemporaries: One does not choose this second journey; rather it chooses you. It finds you by means of your soul, your personal center and true home, the source of your true belonging.

In the opening number of *Into the Woods*, Sondheim develops small musical motifs that function much like an overture in an opera. In particular, the opening words "I wish" are set to the interval of a rising major second, a musical unit that is repeated and developed throughout the show, much as the storyline explores the consequences of "wishing" and self-interest. Wishing and self-interest are clearly first-half-of-life themes.

The show introduces the principal characters as wishing for things important to beginning stages of life: Cinderella wishes to attend the king's festival; Jack wishes his cow would give milk; the baker and his wife wish to have a child; Jack's mother wishes to be wealthy; Little Red Riding Hood wishes for bread and sweets; the ugly old witch wishes to regain her beauty and youth; Rapunzel wishes to leave her tower; the two princes wish to find true love; and the giants in the sky want to be left alone. All are trapped in first-half-of-life worlds. When Little Red enters the woods, she proclaims, "Into the woods! I must begin my journey." The journey is not only a fairy tale motif, but also a quest motif. In the beginning, Little Red demonstrates her innocence by telling the baker and his wife, "The path is straight, I know it well." The path represents both the path to her grandmother's house as well as her path in life. Little Red has not yet been confronted with any life-altering decisions; therefore, her life's path is without forks or bends.

In a later scene, paralleling the opening sequence when the characters reveal their wishes, Jack's mother sarcastically states, "I wish my son were not a fool; I wish my house was not a mess; I wish the cow was full of milk; I wish the walls were full of gold—I wish a lot of things . . ." adding, "We have to live; I don't care how." According to her definition of right versus wrong, she feels it is right and necessary to do whatever she can to survive; she is not yet concerned with the consequences, and not yet engaged responsibly with her first half of life.

As Scene 1 draws to a close, the characters gather and prepare for their journey "into the woods." The baker, his wife, and Cinderella explain, "The path is straight, I know it well, but who can tell?" Like Little Red earlier, these characters also have not faced life-altering decisions, so their definition of right, like the path, is straight. To them, losing the way is equivalent to losing the right path and, therefore, constitutes their definition of wrong. In Rapunzel's case, the witch has deprived her of opportunity by closing all her doors. This action does not guarantee her safety or security, but rather prompts her rebellion. It is not long before Rapunzel begins contradicting her mother's claims of perfection. She wishes her mother "would cut her nails . . . didn't have those pointy teeth." Both Rapunzel and Little Red have limited frames of reference because their mothers have tried to control their experiences. Cinderella, too, has no real interest in the prince. Essentially, she just wants to go to the ball to get away from her life at home.

Repeatedly throughout the first act, Sondheim introduces coming-of-age songs. In "Agony," the two princes sing of their newfound love interests. They have to overcome their hidden fears in order to obtain lasting love. In "It Takes Two," the baker admits it takes two to produce a child, admitting that he needs his wife's help to gather the items they need to reverse the curse. It is in the woods that the wife begins to discover the merits of her husband, admitting that right and wrong don't matter in the woods. In "Giants in the Sky," we learns of Jack's coming-of-age, a theme paralleled in Little Red's song, "I Know Things Now." The final song of the first act begins with triumphant music that reflects the characters' pride at having gone into the woods and survived their journey. The song ends with the company listing their reasons for going into the woods. The list given includes, "to lift the spell," "to loose the longing," "to have the child," "to wed the prince," "to get the money," "to save the house," "to kill the wolf," "to find the father," "to conquer the kingdom," and "to go to the festival." The characters remain oblivious to the growing beanstalk. They do not expect the story to continue.

In the second act, we learn that happiness doesn't last forever. The baker, his wife, and Little Red "enter from another part of the woods," ready to take another journey. The group is lost because "now there is no path." During Act 1, the path symbolized a character's definition of right or wrong. Some paths were straight; others were curved. Now there are no paths. Consequently, the characters must strive to redefine right and wrong in this unfamiliar place. They must tell a story that hasn't been told before. They are confused by this task and feel that "the path has strayed from them." In one of her songs, the witch explains that children can only grow from something you love to something you lose. She did not know how to let go of Rapunzel and allow her to become a woman. Act 2 does not follow the same rules as Act 1; there are no rules now because the characters have not remained within the confines of their first-half-of-life stories. It is up to them to make their own rules. Some live, some die, but all change.

In "The Last Midnight," the witch warns that time is running out, so if the characters are going to escape their predicament, this is the moment. In "Told a Little Lie," she reminds the characters to reexamine their morals or to revise their definition of right versus wrong. Throughout the show, the word "nice" is used by the characters in reference to themselves, as they realize that they don't always have to be good to be right. In Act 2, the witch continues her accusations with "You're so nice. You're not good, you're not bad, you're just nice." Essentially, she feels that although they are now nice, they have lost sight of the good and the bad. As a result of the strictures of their first-half-of-life mindset, their moral growth has come to a halt. They are "just nice," and nothing more. The witch then describes herself, admitting, "I'm not good, I'm not nice, I'm just right." The witch is claiming omniscience, ultimate authority on right versus wrong in life.

While it is easy to dismiss the witch, her role in this story is central. The true narrator, she also serves as teacher, tour guide, and mentor, launching others into their journey. She may not be good, but she isn't always bad. She is the witch—no more and no less. Like each of us, she is more complex than she appears. Like each of us, she's not good and not bad, but a mixture. In the end, the witch is right about one thing: blame solves nothing, and simply diverts energy and attention from finding a solution. In her own perverse way, she is downright good, for she is willing to accept blame, if it stops the cycle of blame and leads to a reasonable discussion of solution.

In the first half of life, one needs external authority figures, occasionally yielding to their autocratic whims. In the second half of life, things are different, and authority come from within, something Cinderella and the baker understand, when they declare, "witches can be right, giants can be good. You decide what's right. You decide what's good."

In the stage version, as the final music starts, the characters recite their morals, and give us glimpses into have they have changed throughout the show. Jack's mother admits, "The slotted spoon can catch the potato," showing that Jack is smarter than she originally thought. The baker's father also has newfound appreciation for his son, saying "Every knot was once straight rope," implying that though his son is not yet ready for the responsibility he faces, he will somehow rise to the occasion. Finally, Little Red's Granny reprises the opportunity theme by saying, "The knife that is sharp today may be dull by tomorrow." The characters' morals demonstrate their growth throughout the show. When the baker questions how he can be a father "with no one to mother my child," his wife appears and tells him, "Just calm the child . . . Tell him what you know." The audience knows that the wife is dead, but as she explains it, "No one leaves for good." The baker will always have memories of his wife. It is these memories that give him the courage to whisper to his son, "Once upon a time. . . ." As the baker tells his story, the company sings, "Children Will Listen."

In the final moments of the stage show, the company gathers onstage to remind us that we must listen; we can't just act, we have to think. The company, we discover, has learned to think for themselves, an ability they did not have at the beginning of the show. We see the growth of the characters again when they tells us that we too must go into the woods, "you have to every now and then." Now they realize that they cannot stay the same. Life is dynamic, not static. The way is dark, and the light dim; now they must rely on each other. Strongly nondualist, *Into the Woods* is not a morality play and hence, not a fairy tale for children. Rather, it is a fairy tale for grownups, a second-half-of-life fairy tale.

Into the woods, then out of the woods, and "happy ever after." That is the theme, that is the message. The show ends the way it started, reminding us that life is circular and the chance for growth never ends. Cinderella declares, "I wish . . . ," followed by the same chord that functioned to awaken the characters at the beginning of the show. The chord announces their awakening to the second half of life. The woods have become a metaphor for life, including the challenges, dreams, hopes, illusions, temptations, failures, and accidents of both halves. Along the way, we learn when to follow and when to lead; when to talk and when to listen; when to act, and when to pause; when to stay on the path, and when to stray.

Into the Woods, a group of fairy tales masterfully brought together on stage by Lapine and Sondheim, creates from individual themes grander themes that serve as an extended metaphor for our lives. Like Jesus' parables, fairy tales are intended to reflect on life lessons as experienced by everyday people. When they were written, princes, bakers, wood choppers, peasants, and step sisters were among the commonplace people the reader would be familiar with in everyday life. Witches, giants, elves, and fairies weren't entirely commonplace, granted, but in bygone eras, they weren't entirely consigned to fantasy, either. In his *Folk and Fairy Tales of the Irish Peasantry*, William Butler Yeats relates encountering an old woman in the west of Ireland who related some of her favorite folk tales. Yeats asked whether, in the modern industrial age, she still believed in the fairies. "Of course not!" she replied curtly, "but they're still there" she added, after a pause. Fairy tales clearly employ fantasy. Talking cats dressed as cavaliers, wolves seducing girls in the forest, self-playing harps, and geese laying golden eggs weren't necessarily realistic in antiquity, but, when combined with the theatrical device of temporary suspension of disbelief, they worked effectively.

In many ways, fairy tales partake in the same devices commonly associated with mythological stories and legends. J. R. R. Tolkien blanched at having his stories called allegories. They were, he explained, histories; fantasy histories, surely, but written in the style of history. Fairy tales also are presented as histories: "Once upon a time..." they often begin. Yet they are also fantasies, parabolic in nature. Overall, they place recognizable characters in recognizable situations solving problems and emerging transformed. Fairy tales, like allegories, are transformation stories. *Into the Woods* is a transformation story.

While there is a great deal of dialogue in *Into the Woods*, together with an abundance of drama and music, there is little dance. There is no Fosse to choreograph, but there is a Sondheim, and his contribution is stunningly integrative. While on the surface, dance seems to be missing, somehow the entire show is dance. This is so because life is dance. In the first half of life, we learn our "survival dance"; in the second half, our "sacred dance." This theme is brilliantly captured in the modern folk hymn "Lord of the Dance." In the lyrics to the Shaker tune, words written by English songwriter Sydney Carter in 1963, we hear Jesus beckoning us to the spirituality of the dance,

The underlying theme of theatre, as of spirituality and life, is "aliveness." In his 2019 interfaith Chautauqua lecture on the nature of God, Rabbi Rami Shapiro, one of America's foremost teachers of perennial spirituality, likened God to grace, by which he meant not simply discernable moments of blessing, but "the whole of life." While people often limit "grace" to goodness, Shapiro views grace as "the whole thing, the stuff we like and the stuff we don't like. And because grace is the whole thing, then God is the whole thing. We want a God who is good, as we define good . . . I am suggesting God isn't good. God is God! God is Reality. God is the aliveness that happens."[8]

This is what the arts provide to spirituality, for where the secular and sacred coalesce; where the trivial, mundane, and transitory meet eternity; there is aliveness. A form of scripture, the arts contribute to the metanarrative we call spirituality, together feeding the human spirit's endless "longing for belonging."

QUESTIONS FOR DISCUSSION AND REFLECTION

1. After reading this chapter, what similarities and dissimilarities do you find in theatre and religious liturgy?

2. In your estimation, how can musical theatre enhance our understanding and practice of spirituality?

---

8. This paragraph is taken from my book *Walking on Water*, 51.

3. Explain and assess the meaning of W. B. Yeats's insight that all his artistic and existential ladders start "in the foul rag-and-bone shop of the heart."

4. In your estimation, how does Jesus' use of parables illustrate the connection between theatre and spirituality?

5. Explain and assess the validity of the author's statement that "it is when they are taken together that the parables of Jesus become revelatory." How does this idea illustrate the connection between the arts and spirituality?

6. After reading this chapter, what did you learn about the meaning and message of *Cabaret*?

7. In your estimation, does Sally Bowles's character typify "antispirituality," or is she only an unredeemed artist? In your estimation, does Sally display any "redeeming" qualities? Explain your answer.

8. After reading this chapter, what did you learn about the meaning and message of fairy tales?

9. After reading this chapter, what does *Into the Woods* teach about first- and second-half-of-life tasks and quests?

10. In your estimation, what does the witch mean when she accuses the other principal characters of being neither good nor bad, but "just nice"?

11. After reading this chapter, what did you learn about the meaning and message of *Into the Woods*?

12. Explain and assess the meaning of the author's statement, "life is dance."

13. In your estimation, what is the primary insight gained from this chapter? Explain your answer.

EPILOGUE

THE DISCOVERIES OF MODERN PHYSICS have revolutionized our thinking of reality. So astounding and counterintuitive that they almost defy belief, baffling theories such as quantum mechanics and general relativity must be correct, if solely because many of today's key technologies wouldn't work without them. For example, mass is not the amount of matter in an object, as we normally think. It is actually much stranger than that.

In 2012, scientists confirmed the detection of the long-sought Higgs boson, also known by its nickname the "God particle." The Higgs boson had long been thought the key to resolving the origin of mass. The Higgs boson is associated with a field known as the Higgs field, theorized to pervade the universe. According to theorist Peter Higgs, an energy field permeates the universe, giving mass to a certain class of particles. Those particles that don't interact with the field, such as photons, have no mass.

Such is the case with spirituality. People that focus solely on material and physical things are separated from spirituality. Likewise, people that focus exclusively on spiritual things, to the neglect of the body, are incomplete. Spirit needs matter, and matter longs for spirit. Together, they are whole; apart, they are fragmented. Humans are social animals. We don't need science or religion to tell us that, because we know it instinctively—we look to make friends even in our youngest years, and we feel safer and happier when we are connected to others. In fact, neuroscientific research shows that our desire for social connection is as biologically based as our need for food and sleep. The human brain is literally wired for social connection, a need technology currently achieves through electronic devices such as radio, television, and particularly social media. Today, more than one hundred websites and apps are available to help meet social needs, something formerly met almost exclusively by religious, educational, recreational, and entertainment resources such as available at churches, lecture halls, musical venues, arenas, ballparks, nightclubs, and theaters, for these were places where people felt connected and somehow whole.

In *Walking on Water*, my earlier study on metaphor and myth, I argued that "reducing mythology to theology is a violation of intent." [1] This, of course, is what institutional Christianity has done with the Bible. Thinking theologically, traditional religious authorities regularly turn poetry into narrative, historicizing symbol and literalizing metaphor. In mature spirituality, however, doctrine is interpreted poetically, and theology is interpreted metaphorically. This is what biblical literalists and theological fundamentalists miss. The role of healthy spirituality is not to theologize, meaning its intent is not to lead people toward doctrine or belief, but rather to deepen theology to the level of mythology. Mature spirituality is less about knowing then about unknowing, more about deconstructive than about construction. Knowing is central to formation, but unknowing leads to transformation. As learning is central to theology, so unlearning is central to spirituality.

For the past six hundred years, Christian formation has focused on the head—on belief and theology—only occasionally speaking of the heart, the seat of emotion and allegiance. Growing spiritually involves growing outward as well as inward, downward as well as upward. While spiritual formation promotes affirmation of all that is wholesome, good, and beautiful, spiritual transformation promotes integration with all that is wholesome, good, and beautiful. Such integration turns "believers" into "lovers," to what Jesus called "kingdom people."

As I concluded in *Walking on Water*, we walk on water by becoming the water.[2] By so doing, we still remain ourselves—that is, waves—yet, more than waves, we become the sea itself. That's incarnational! If we understand the biblical story of Jesus "walking on water" literally, such understanding is superficial. Rather, we must learn to "wade in water," that is, to get wet, going deep with our spirituality, even diving into the water with Jesus. Walking on water is not, as we might think, about staying on the surface of things, but rather about going deep into the ordinary aspects of our life and finding gold. It is not about attaining exotic moods or about practicing indiscriminate "blind" faith, but about "living into a new way of thinking." Getting wet, getting dirty, is spirituality at work. All else is theory.

---

1. Vande Kappelle, *Walking on Water*, 114.
2. Vande Kappelle, *Walking on Water*, 164.

SPIRITUAL GROWTH

Spirituality thrives in newness and change. True to its nature, spirituality cannot allow us to remain unchanged. Dynamic rather than static, spirituality's "deep magic" produces spiritual growth, a truth intuitively grasped by creative artists. The dynamism of spirituality is evident in musical theatre, in the poems of Emily Dickinson and the jazz legacy of John Coltrane, and it characterized the writings of C. S. Lewis.

Lewis's *Chronicles of Narnia* describe the spirituality of change, both in Narnia and in those who enter Narnia. One of the motifs of *The Lion, the Witch, and the Wardrobe* is that of renewal and growth: spring comes to long-frozen Narnia, and all come alive again. Further, the seeming accident by which the Pevensie children enter Narnia grows into a larger divine plan, and the magic at work becomes progressively deeper. Growth is also central to the idea of Narnia's creation in *The Magician's Nephew*, and in the remaining books in the series; travels and shifts in location are frequent. The continual element of surprise, of being abruptly shifted from one world to another, reinforces the themes of growth, change, and renewal. The fact that Lewis's readers can never anticipate what is going to happen next, never familiar enough with the ground rules of Narnia to form suppositions from them, gives a strange contingency to the narrative. Peculiar to Lewis's fantasy literature is the sense that boundaries are indistinct, unpredictable, even unknowable. No place is impermeable, for all seems possible in this liminal world.

Evident at Narnia are certain kinds of growth that have little to do with time and belong to deeper spirituality. There is, for example, the idea of something significant being made of something insignificant—the haphazard choice of a ring sets in motion a power that culminates in the making of Narnia; a lion's song calls forth light and life from death and darkness; the broken-off piece of a lamppost the witch uses as a weapon against Aslan grows into a lantern to light the way into Narnia for its later human saviors; the swelling sound of a tiny bell reverses an ancient curse and restores a dormant empress; a cabdriver and his wife become the first king and queen of Narnia; dumb animals become rational Talking Beasts; the power of one apple retrieved in obedience becomes a tree to preserve Narnia. Disproportion is at the heart of Christianity as well, whether for good or ill.

In the *Chronicles of Narnia* C. S. Lewis describes the place he calls "New Narnia" in terms of both continuity and transformation. In *The Last Battle*, the characters find themselves in a new Narnia, citizens of a transformed society. This New Narnia is not an escape from old Narnia but rather an entry more deeply into the very same place. New Narnia has the same hills and the same houses as their hometown, but everything is more radiant. New Narnia is a "deeper country; every rock and flower and blade of grass looked like it meant more." New Narnia is "world within world," where "no good thing is destroyed."

TRUTH TELLING

Recently, former U.S. Vice President Mike Pence was greeted by a pro-Trump rally with hissing and booing. Trying to speak over a disgruntled minority, who apparently defined him by partisan standards, Pence responded by baring his soul, informing the audience that he was a Christian, a conservative, and a Republican, in that order. While labeling others or oneself is not generally helpful, since self-awareness changes over time, sometimes situations require taking a stand. Mike Pence took a stand, and if I were forced to name my top three descriptors, they would be human (a global citizen), panentheist, and nondualist, in that order. What such terms mean, of course, changes frequently. If asked to define your current identity in three words, how would you respond?

In the Bible, spirituality is truth telling. However, the Bible communicates its truth not superficially, such as through facts or formulas, but profoundly, through story and myth. Think of "creation" in the Old Testament and "incarnation" in the New. Such teaching is not meant to be rational nor informative. In other words, these accounts do not use fact or science to convey truth, but rather metaphor and poetry to convey meaning.

When Jesus was concerned with meaning and spirituality, he resorted to parabolic teaching; when Paul was concerned with meaning and spirituality, he resorted to allegory (see Gal 4:21–31). Why? Because they both knew that spiritual truth is best understood imaginatively. If I can summarize the message of this book, it would be that human creativity, as displayed through the arts, is an effective way to experience and express our spirituality, helping us overcome life's dualistic dilemma.

Those who are unaware, theorize and theologize;

Those who are aware, actualize and realize.

Those who are unaware, criticize;

Those who are aware, harmonize.

As noted earlier, creation and incarnation are ongoing, signs that all things flow from a common origin toward a common goal. Spiritually speaking, that's the role of creative and performing arts such as poetry, allegory, music, drama, dance, and theatre. When they become "thin places," they connect us with the ultimate ground of our Being. Awakening to this awareness is evidence of the life-giving spirituality around us and within us. When we wade in this water, we are fully alive, and this aliveness becomes a "thin place," connecting us to divinity.

BIBLIOGRAPHY

Adey, Lionel. *C. S. Lewis: Writer, Dreamer, and Mentor*. Grand Rapids, MI: Eerdmans, 1998.

Allison, Jr., Dale C. *The Luminous Dusk: Finding God in the Deep, Still Places*. Grand Rapids, MI: Eerdmans, 2006.

Armstrong, Karen. *The Case for God*. New York: Anchor, 2010.

———. *A Short History of Myth*. New York: Canongate, 2005.

———. *Visions of God: Four Medieval Mystics and Their Writing*s. New York: Bantam, 1994.

Bogdanov, Vladimir, et al. *All Music Guide to Jazz*. 4th ed. San Francisco: Backbeat, 2002.

Borg, Marcus J., and N. T. Wright. *The Meaning of Jesus: Two Visions*. San Francisco: HarperSanFrancisco, 1999.

Bourgeault, Cynthia. *The Heart of Centering Prayer: Nondual Christianity in Theory and Practice*. Boulder, CO: Shamhala, 2016.

———. *The Holy Trinity and the Law of Three*. Boston, Shambhala, 2013.

Campbell, Joseph. *The Hero's Journey: Joseph Campbell on His Life and Work*. Edited by Phil Cousineau. Novato, CA: New World Library, 2003.

———. *The Inner Reaches of Outer Space: Metaphor as Myth and as Religion*. Novato, CA: New World Library, 2002.

———. *The Power of Myth: with Bill Moyers*. New York: Doubleday, 1988.

———. *Romance of the Grail: The Magic and Mystery of Arthurian Myth*. Novato, CA: New World Library, 2015.

———. *Thou Art That: Transforming Religious Metaphor*. Novato, CA: New World Library, 2001.

Carr, Ian, et al. *Jazz: The Rough Guide*. 2nd ed. London: Rough Guides, 2000.

Chesterton, G. K. *The Everlasting Man*. San Francisco: Ignatius, 1993.

Collier, James Lincoln. *The Making of Jazz*. New York: Delta, 1978.

Collmer, Robert G. *Bunyan in Our Time*. Kent, OH: Kent State University Press, 1989.

Dante Alighieri. *The Divine Comedy*. Translated by Dorothy L. Sayers. London: Penguin, 1949.

Delio, Ilia. *The Unbearable Wholeness of Being: God, Evolution, and the Power of Love*. Maryknoll, NY: Orbis, 2013.

Dieleman, Karen. *Religious Imaginaries: The Liturgical and Poetic Practices of Elizabeth Barrett Browning, Christina Rossetti, and Adelaide Procter*. Athens, OH: Ohio University Press, 2012.

Dowd, Michael. *Thank God for Evolution*. New York: Viking, 2007.

Dunn, Stephen, and Anne Lonergan, *Befriending the Earth*. Mystic, CT: Twenty-Third Publications, 1991.

Eliot, T. S. *The Three Voices of Poetry*. New York: Cambridge University Press, 1954.

———. *The Use of Poetry and the Use of Criticism*. New York: Barnes & Noble, 1933.

Fox, Matthew. *Creation Spirituality*. San Francisco: HarperSanFrancisco, 1991.

———. *Original Blessing*. Santa Fe, NM: Bear & Co., 1983.

Franklin, R. W. *The Poems of Emily Dickinson*. Cambridge, MA: The Belknap Press of Harvard University Press, 1998.

Freedman, Linda. *Emily Dickinson and the Religious Imagination*. Cambridge: Cambridge University Press, 2011.

Freshwater, Mark Edwards. *C. S. Lewis and the Truth of Myth*. Lanham, MD: University Press of America, 1988.

Gardner, Helen. *The Art of T. S. Eliot*. New York: Dutton, 1950.

Giddins, Gary. *Visions of Jazz*. New York: Oxford, 1998.

Gottlieb, Robert. *Reading Jazz*. New York: Vintage Books, 1996.

Gridley, James. *Jazz Styles*. 4th ed. Englewood Cliffs, NJ: Prentice Hall, 1991.

Habeggar, Alfred. *My Wars Are Laid Away in Books: The Life of Emily Dickinson*. New York: Random House, 2001.

Hasse, John Edward. *Jazz: The First Century*. New York: William Morrow, 2000.

Haught, John F. *Deeper Than Darwin: The Prospect for Religion in the Age of Evolution*. Boulder, CO: Westview, 2003.

———. *God After Darwin: A Theology of Evolution*. Boulder, CO: Westview, 2000.

———. *The Promise of Nature: Ecology and Cosmic Purpose*. Mahwah, NJ: Paulist, 1993.

Hentoff, Nat. *The Jazz Life*. New York: Da Capo Press, 1975.

Hollis, James. *Finding Meaning in the Second Half of Life: How to Finally, Really Grow Up*. New York: Gotham, 2006.

———. *The Middle Passage: From Misery to Meaning in Midlife*. Toronto: Inner City Books, 1993.

Holmes, Urban T. *The History of Christian Spirituality*. New York: Seabury, 1980.

Johnson, Greg. *Emily Dickinson: Perception and the Poet's Quest*. Tuscaloosa, AL: The University of Alabama Press, 1985.

Jones, LeRoi. *Blues People*. New York, William Morrow, 1963.

Keeble, N. H. *John Bunyan, The Pilgrim's Progress*. New York: Oxford University Press, 1984.

Kelley, Phillip, et al. *The Browning Correspondence*. 27 vols. Winfield, KSS: Wedgestone, 1984–2020.

Kernfeld, Barry. *The New Grove Dictionary of Jazz*. 2nd ed. 3 vols. New York: Macmillan, 2002.

Kirchner, Bill. *The Oxford Companion to Jazz*. New York: Oxford, 2000.

Lapine, James and Stephen Sondheim. *Into the Woods*. New York: Theatre Communications Group, 1987.

Lewis, C. S. *The Abolition of Man*. New York: Macmillan, 1947.

———. *The Allegory of Love: A Study in Medieval Tradition*. Oxford: Oxford University Press, 1938.

———. *Essays on Theology and Ethics*. Grand Rapids, MI: Eerdmans, 1970.

———. *God in the Dock*. Grand Rapids, MI: Eerdmans, 1970.

———. *Mere Christianity*. New York: Macmillan, 1960.

———. *Miracles: A Preliminary Study*. New York: Macmillan, 1960.

———. *Of Other Worlds: Essays and Stories.* Edited by Walter Hooper. New York: Harcourt, Brace, 1966.

———. *The Pilgrim's Regress: An Allegorical Apology for Christianity, Reason, and Romanticism.* Online: http://www.sanizdat.gc.ca.

———. *Surprised by Joy.* New York: Harcourt Brace, 1955.

Lindskoog, Kathryn. *Finding the Landlord: A Guide to C. S. Lewis's "Pilgrim's Regress."* Chicago: Cornerstone, 1995.

McCully, George. "Multiversity and University." *The Journal of Higher Education* 44 (1973) 514–31.

McIntosh, James, *Nimble Believing: Dickinson and the Unknown.* Ann Arbor, MI: University of Michigan Press, 2000.

McLaren, Brian. *Everything Must Change: Jesus, Global Crises, and a Revolution of Hope.* Nashville: Thomas Nelson, 2007.

———. *Faith After Doubt: Why Your Beliefs Stopped Working and What to Do About It.* New York: St. Martin's, 2021.

———. *Naked Spirituality: A Life with God in 12 Simple Words.* New York: HarperOne, 2011.

Plotkin, Bill. *Nature and the Human Soul: Cultivating Wholeness and Community in a Fragmented World.* Novato, CA: New World Library, 2008.

———. *Soulcraft: Crossing into Mysteries of Nature and Psyche.* Novato, CA: New World Library, 2003.

Poetry Foundation. *Emily Dickinson.* No pages. Online: http://www.poetryfoundation.org/poets/ emily-dickinson.

Rainey, Lawrence. *The Annotated Waste Land with Eliot's Contemporary Prose.* New Haven, CT: Yale University Press, 2005.

Reagan, Charles E., and David Stewart. *The Philosophy of Paul Ricoeur: An Anthology of His Work.* Boston: Beacon, 1978.

Rohr, Richard. *Falling Upward: A Spirituality for the Two Halves of Life.* San Francisco: Jossey-Bass, 2011.

———. *Immortal Diamond: The Search for Our True Self.* San Francisco: Jossey-Bass, 2013.

———. *The Naked Now: Learning to See as the Mystics See.* New York: Crossroad, 2009.

———. *Quest for the Grail.* New York: Crossroad, 1994.

———. *The Universal Christ.* New York: Convergent, 2019.

———. *What the Mystics Know.* New York: Crossroad, 2015.

Sayers, Dorothy L. *Dante Alighieri, The Divine Comedy: Hell.* London: Penguin, 1949.

Schulweis, Harold M. *For Those Who Can't Believe.* New York: HarperPerennial, 1994.

Shapiro, Nat, and Nat Hentoff. *Hear Me Talkin' To Ya.* New York: Dover, 1966.

Streng, Fred, et al. *Ways of Being Religious.* Englewood Cliffs, NJ: Prentice-Hall, 1973.

Vande Kappelle, Robert P. *Beyond Belief: Faith, Science, and the Value of Unknowing.* Eugene: OR: Wipf & Stock, 2012.

———. *Blue Notes: Profiles of Jazz Personalities.* Eugene, OR: Resource, 2011.

———. *In the Potter's Workshop: Experiencing the Divine Presence in Everyday Life.* OR: Wipf & Stock, 2019.

———. *Iron Sharpens Iron.* Eugene: OR: Wipf & Stock, 2013.

———. *Refined by Fire: Essential Teachings in Scripture.* Eugene, OR: Wipf & Stock, 2018.

———. *Securing Life: The Enduring Message of the Bible.* Eugene, OR: Wipf & Stock, 2016.

———. *Walking on Water: Living into a New Way of Thinking.* Eugene, OR: Wipf & Stock, 2020.

Ward, Geoffrey C., and Ken Burns. *Jazz: A History of America's Music.* New York: Knopf, 2000.

Witherington III, Ben. *John's Wisdom: A Commentary on the Fourth Gospel.* Louisville: Westminster John Knox, 1995.

Index